ENJOY FAIR ISLE KNITTING

Enjoy Fair Isle Knitting

First published 2017.
ISBN 978 1 910997 14 7

Translator: Tomoko Nishimura and cooperator: Gaia Operations

Photographs: Susan Timmins with Chihiro.

A CIP catalogue record for this book is available from the British Library.

Printed and published by The Shetland Times Ltd, Gremista, Lerwick, Shetland, ZE1 0PX.

Enjoy Fair Isle Knitting

Chihiro Sato

The Shetland Times Ltd.
Lerwick
2017

CONTENTS

Granny Ume (right)

PREFACE

The beginning of my love of knitting goes back 56 years. I was sitting next to my grandmother, Ume, on the sunny veranda, coiling the wool around the knitting needle. I thought I was knitting!

It is strange that I still remember it vividly: one long piece of yarn changed into a warm jumper by my grandmother's hands. It was so pleasant to be with her, knitting joyfully, and this comfortable feeling has stayed through my life.

There is always knitting beside me. When I am sad, low-spirited, angry and, of course, when I am pleased. Yes. Knitting is my life's work. Fair Isle knitting, especially, is sheer bliss for me.

I'd like to express my genuine gratitude to the people of Shetland. I am so happy that I can publish a knitting book in Shetland. It will be a great pleasure to share this happiness with all of you who come across this book.

Chihiro Sato

> The reason why I keep coming back to Shetland is not only that I love knitting but also that the nature and the people enchant me.

CHAPTER 1

FAIR ISLE KNITTING & ME

The Shetland Islands are a subarctic archipelago of Scotland, lying northeast of the UK. There are more than 100 islands, of which Fair Isle is the most southern. Fifteen of the islands are inhabited; the total population is approximately 23,000. To get to Shetland is a 50-minute flight or a 13-hour trip by ferry from Aberdeen.

In 1989, I stayed one night in Shetland during my first trip there and my trophy was the Shade Card.

Now there are 216 colours, but at that time there were 107. I was enchanted by the beautiful colours and brought wool home. I was so excited, wondering which colour of wool I should knit first and what would I knit with mixed colours of wool?

At first I imported wool just for myself, but gradually the amount increased as attendances at my workshop grew, and also for my friends who visited Shetland with me. Eventually, I thought it would be best to stock all colours and start a shop, and the Shaela shop, which specialises in Shetland wool, was opened without me thinking too much about it.

In the early days I remember making shade cards (9-card sets) by hand, with my sister, who is not interested in wool or my workshop. Sitting on the floor, we would cut cardboard and stick it together to make it thicker, then make slits for the yarn and paste colour numbers and names that had been printed out by word processor (it was before the days of personal computers). On this mount we placed the yarn in numerical order with a crochet hook. It sounds like an endless task but even this was enjoyable to me. This is the process still used, but now I contract out this work.

I did the import, inspection, shipment inventory control and accounting all by myself as well as answering the phone calls. At the beginning everything was easy going; I could memorise all the names of customers and still had time to create.

After I took the Traditional Fair Isle Knitting course, I was even more attracted to Shetland. That made me want to teach and tell more about it (because of the trend, many knitting wool shops and handicraft shops were closing down and the internet became popular, but I now have three staff in my shop.) I feel that Fair Isle knitting is still popular among knitting lovers because it has a long tradition and still in its quiet boom.

The people I meet at my wool shop and classes relate to knitting both through the shop and my link with Shetland. These people and the people and nature of Shetland put energy into my enthusiasm for creating and make me enjoy this work. I am ever so happy.

The reason why I keep coming back to Shetland is not only that I love knitting but also that the nature and the people enchant me.

My first memory of Shetland when I visited in 1989 was the unpaved road, as if leading to the skies. Amazing stillness, clear air and beautiful blue sky... these were just incredible things for me from Tokyo.

The town of Lerwick is the centre, the houses have century-old stone chimneys and I remember that I was fascinated by the beauty of the flowers and stone-paved alleys. There were old stone houses, cute shops and beautiful knit shops on Commercial Street – the main street. Also there was a bookshop across from the post office at the end of this street. Everything I saw was fresh and sweet to me and I felt that I was lost in a picture book.

I ran up and down this stone lane to find a 'knitting belt'. More than thirty people (on the tour) looking for knitting gadgets made me ridiculously selfish. It was embarrassing, but still one of my memories. The extremely short stay made me want to visit again.

My knitting belt

After seven years, in April and September 1996, I got my wish. My memories of a beautiful place could have been distorted during the seven years, and I was horrified to see the new supermarket. I felt as if the picture book was trampled. But Shetland too cannot avoid the trend. I know it is important that things should be convenient for the islanders, so it is an egotism of the traveller to wish that the good old things should be kept as they were.

Whenever I see a beautiful
scene I mumble the colour
shade numbers spontaneously.
This must be an occupational
disease of a woolmonger

Tradition handed down – Whalsay's knitting club

But during this stay, the nature, people and everything fascinated me even more, and many things were the same as seven years ago. The bookshop and the post office were still at the end of Commercial Street. I was so happy and relieved to see them. These two places are still the same after twenty years and I regularly go there.

The 'Fair Isle Traditional Hand Knitting Course' in September 1996 widened my appreciation of colours and the joy of knitting again. And I met many people who were engaged in traditional knitting.

"You can hold the yarn and cast on the way you are used to." These words pulled me strongly into the Fair Isle knitting world. They never said "you should..." and never judged right or wrong. Since then, I believe that knitting is something 'to enjoy' although it started from people making garments to earn a living.

Now I stay in Shetland for longer periods than before. I always knit garments and try to use a new tip or method from the Shetland people; and also knit samples for the knitting class in Tokyo.

I joined a knitting night at three places – Scalloway Museum, Shetland Designer's shop and at the 'pink hall' at Hamnavoe in Burra Isle. Anyone can attend these knitting nights which are also demonstrations for tourists in summer. Knitters are aging, so we need to encourage the young generation and this effort is getting bigger every year. Since they stopped teaching knitting in schools, everyone is worried about the tradition disappearing. But many young people attended the knitting night at Shetland Designer's shop and that makes us hopeful about the future.

When I visited the island of Whalsay several years ago, children had started knitting as an extra-curricular activity group. Now they work hard so that they can exhibit their works at the local summer show. These small activities should build up a firm foundation for the next generations.

I have visited Shetland now for 22 years and I have learned from the patient locals how to live happily in a small community; to accept everything including good or bad, never interfere too much in others' matters and to mind my mouth.

In this book I introduce traditional Fair Isle knitting. It is how I learned but, of course, it is not the only way.

I really enjoy using a traditional Fair Isle knitting method (cut up); it is an efficient way to knit a pattern and add my own ideas and colourways. I've mostly kept to my teacher's method, however I do one thing differently: "Don't use close colours in expressing a pattern," she said, and when I showed my work to her, she said to me, "Your colours are very complicated."

People who aren't keen about grafting and sewing use 'break and knot'. They knit each row from the right side and cut the yarn at each end. After repeating this they tuck all the ends into the floating. This seems to take ages to finish but for them it is their usual way and is not a pain at all.

There are several ways of finishing and it varies according to whom you learnt from and also from community to community.

These days, the word 'steek' is one you see in every Fair Isle knitting book. But my teacher once said that she never taught that.

'Extra stitches' and 'steek' are different from each other. I wondered why steek is used everywhere and asked many people. Most of them said: "Steek is a name of openwork stitch when you knit lace, and the bridge of stitches that will later be cut open are called extra stitches... But that is okay, if they understand the word steek better then we will use it."

This is the Shetland style. But I always feel it is a shame and waste to distort the tradition. So I say so and write so in books, and I believe that we should respect the traditions and should not forget that the knitters have kept and passed them down.

When I asked "What is Fair Isle knitting?" – unexpectedly, many thoughts and answers were given:

"Using a knitting belt and knitting in the round using three knitting needles. Each row has one or two coloured patterns."

"It is a tough question. Not everyone uses a knitting belt, hard to identify Fair Isle patterns, Scandinavian influences, using many foreign patterns, but surely by knitting in the round using single or two colour wool (yarn)."

"Yes, you can identify Fair Isle patterns."

Fair Isle was on the route of ships and the islanders began to produce knitted goods to barter with the passing seafarers. In the beginning they were small things like gloves (mittens), caps and scarves. From the early 19th century merchants required slipovers and jumpers as well.

The main pattern was a hexagonal OX pattern. Small patterns in between and colours for rib (called basque) were not used then. In those days the people of the Shetland Mainland were knitting many repeated, small, simple patterns which were less complicated and different from Fair Isle patterns. Since knitted goods sold well, the merchants asked the Mainland people to produce as well.

There were lots of hand-knitted garments until knitting machines started being used in 1950. They then started knitting multi-coloured and decorative ribs. So were the small insertions which were easy to knit. These could be for a variation, but it seems to be borne from the idea to finish knitted items as quickly as possible. As these become very popular, they inserted solid stripes in between patterns to save time. This type of jumper became the main product and along with natural coloured goods, which saved dyeing, started to appear on the market.

Up until then, whether they liked it or not, knitting was a source of income for many families. In old photographs we can see people knitting in their spare time during herring fishing, and on their way to cut peat-turf and still knitting on their way back with a full kishie on their backs. Almost everyone knitted until about the 1970s.

I don't quite get it that there are many ideas and views for Fair Isle patterns. There are many stories to encourage the sales of knitting as merchandise and some plausible episodes were strung together and jumbled at the same time. But I do not say that everything should be exposed. There are many ways of understanding, so I think it is important to enjoy the wonderful knitting and pass it down.

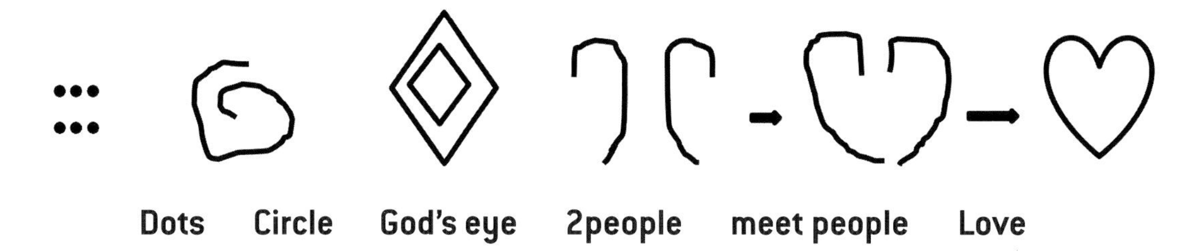

I've learned that these diagrams are the basis of ancient patterns and they made it clear that my impression of Fair Isle knitting patterns was different. They put these small patterns together to make a larger pattern and even circle it with a hexagon. Stitches of a pattern can be altered in many ways (e.g. inserting patterns in between) so they taught me that it is easy to put Fair Isle patterns together by grouping several rows of patterns.

Every summer I learn new things in Shetland which make me extremely pleased. I am not a Shetlander and cannot understand the language in full. Neither can I knit fast like them, nor can I use the knitting belt well. But to be among them, I can feel that my knitting has an air of this place.

When I work on my colourway, I always remember the sea, sky, peat, flowers, migratory birds, sheep (which, they say, exceeds the human population), cattle, Shetland ponies and the beautiful stone walls (dykes) of Shetland.

Whenever I see a beautiful scene I mumble the colour shade numbers spontaneously. This must be an occupational disease of a woolmonger.

But the islanders chuckle and say: "You're just like old folks."

In old days they used to talk about colourway in shade numbers. These words made me really happy, and I feel I have been accepted among the Shetlanders.

Cunningsburgh Primary School knitting club

Peerie knitter's hands

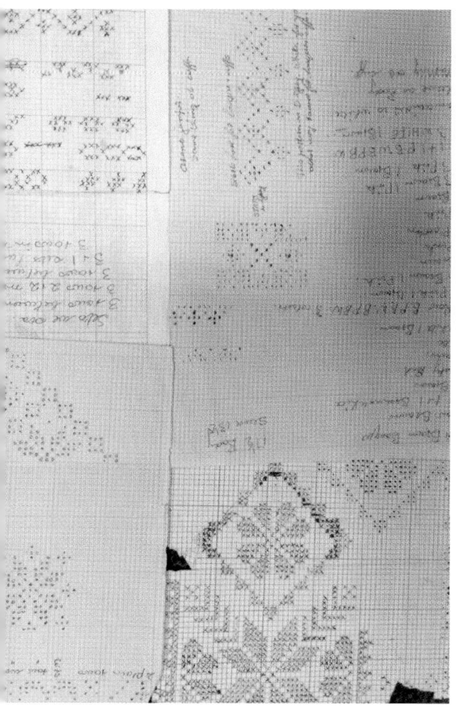

I believe that we should respect the traditions and should not forget that the knitters have kept and passed them down

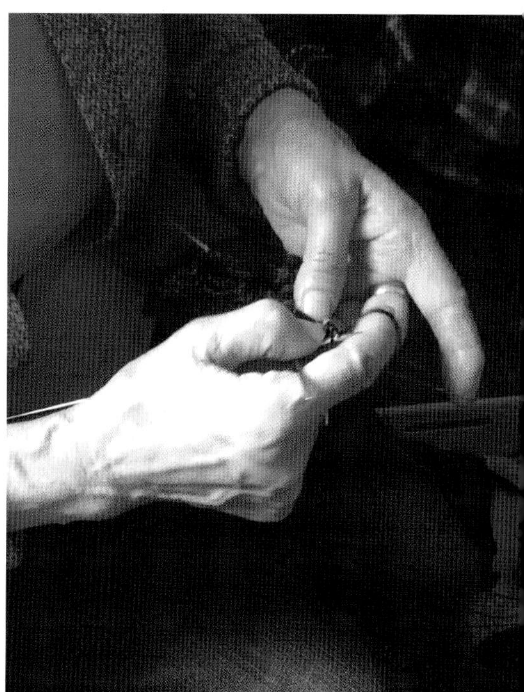

More experienced hands

CHAPTER 2

TRADITIONAL FAIR ISLE KNITTING

In this chapter, I would like to talk about "traditional style Fair Isle knitting" based on learnings from my experience. There are specific features, such as:

1. The body is knitted in the round from the bottom up to the shoulder. Knitting in the round means that you will always be knitting on the right side, which allows you to work Fair Isle patterns quicker. Also, most parts are knit stitches; purl is only required when ribbing.
2. The basic rule is to use only two colours in one row/round.
3. Extra stitches (a bridge of stitches which will later be cut open) are worked for openings, such as sleeves, neckband, front bands, which makes it possible to knit in the round up to the shoulders. Extra stitches are comprised of 12 stitches, regardless of whether the garment is for men, women, adult or children.
4. Extra stitches are cut open after working the body. After cutting them open, stitches for sleeves, neckband and front bands are picked up and worked individually.

It's not as complicated as you may think, so why not give it a try!

The steps illustrated on the next page are the steps for making slipovers, jumpers or cardigans. Those for slipovers and jumpers are quite similar, but additional steps are involved for cardigans. It would be better to acquaint yourself with these steps before starting a project.

By the way, vests are referred to as "slipovers" and sweaters "jumpers" in Shetland.

And I am following knitting words of my teacher in Shetland:

- Bind off → Cast off   STEEK → Extra stitches.

STEPS FOR FAIR ISLE KNITTING

STEP	Slipovers (Vests)	Jumpers (Sweaters)	Cardigans
1	Ribbing for the hem		
			Additional step: Making extra stitches for front bands
2	Work body to underarm		
3	Making extra stitches for armhole and sleeves		Making extra stitches for sleeves
			Additional step: Treatment for extra stitches for front bands
4	Making extra stitches for neck opening		Making extra stitches for neck opening
5	Preparation and joining of shoulders		
6	Neckband (worked in the round: Round neck, Square neck, V-neck)		Neckband (worked flat)
			Additional step: Making front bands
7	Ribbing for armhole	Making sleeves and tips	
8	Treatment for extra stitches		
9	Weaving in ends and washing		
			Additional step: Making button holes

KNITTING TRADITIONAL STYLE

The traditional styles of knitting are explained in this section. Basic steps are mostly the same for slipovers (vests), jumpers (sweaters) and cardigans, but please be sure to note there are some differences in the procedures. An overall flow for cardigans is described at the end in *'Steps for knitting cardigans'* *(see p.29)*

1 RIBBING FOR THE HEM

To begin, cast on stitches using one needle (or circular needle). (See illustration below.) Ribbing for the hem is worked in the round. There are quite a number of stitches so make sure that the stitches are not twisted. Beginning of round (BOR) and colour changes will be done at the left side of body for slipovers and jumpers.

LONG TAIL CAST ON

1 Put yarn over thumb and index finger

2 Place needle underneath the strand between the two fingers and hold yarn with right index finger

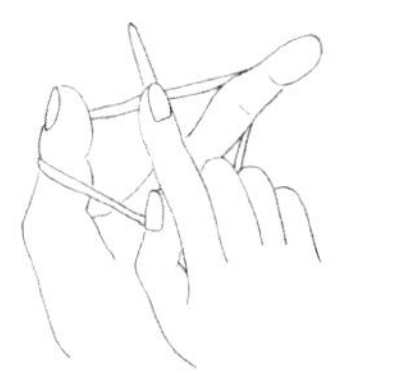

3 Holding yarn down, bring yarn and needle down forward to the left side

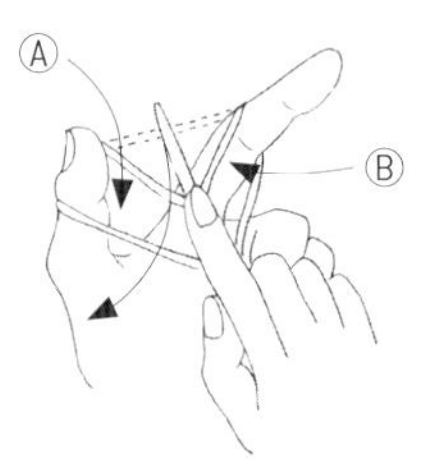

4 Insert tip of needle from underneath loop A and then into loop B

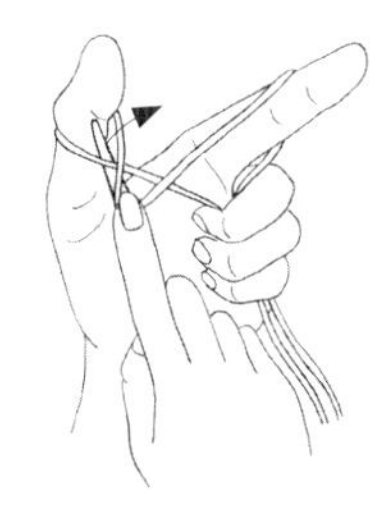

5 Into B from the front to back, picking up strand extending out from the index finger, and...

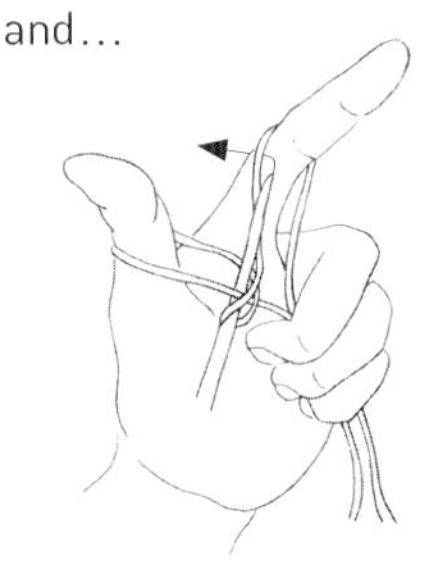

6 Carry yarn back into loop A, going downward

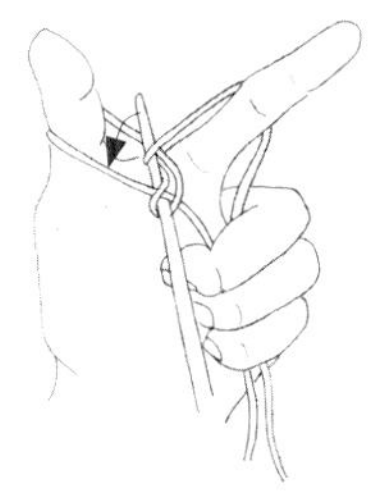

7 Drop loop A from thumb, and pick up and pull the strand extending out from the loop using thumb in order to tighten the loop

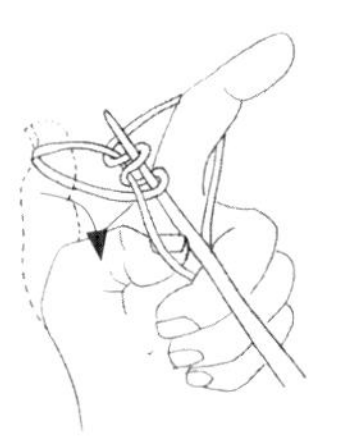

8 Continue pulling using thumb to tighten

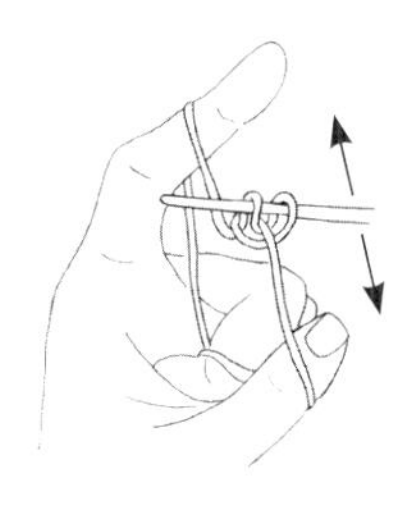

9 Repeat these steps to cast on the required number of stitches

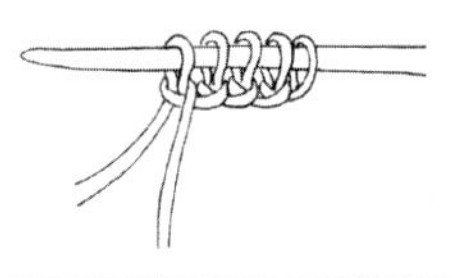

Note: These steps are those that I normally use and can be substituted with any other preferred method.

2 WORK BODY TO UNDERARM

Based on knitting chart and colour assignment, work front and back body to underarm. Then break yarn leaving an end of 3 to 5 cms.

When changing colours:

- Tie pattern colour yarn to pattern colour yarn and background colour yarn to background colour yarn.
- When working the row following a row only of background colours, tie pattern colour yarn on the background colour yarn.
- Do not continue using the same colour yarn on after the next round without cutting (not draw up yarn.)

3 MAKING EXTRA STITCHES FOR SLEEVES • ARMHOLE

1. Slip stitches for underarms onto waste yarn or stitch holder
2. Cast on 6 stitches on right needle using the yarn for the next row (1st row from underarm) (Figure 3-1 A)
3. Continue on working stitches on left needle to work front
4. Cast on 12 stitches over stitches on hold for right underarm (Figure 3-2)
5. Continue working back
6. Cast on 6 stitches at the end of round (Figure 3-1 B)

   Extra stitches for sleeve is now complete.
7. Tie yarn to the end of the last 6 stitches cast on to work the new row (2nd row from underarm). Note that this step only occurs when (1st row from underarm) is worked in one colour
8. Continue working based on chart and colour assignment until neck opening

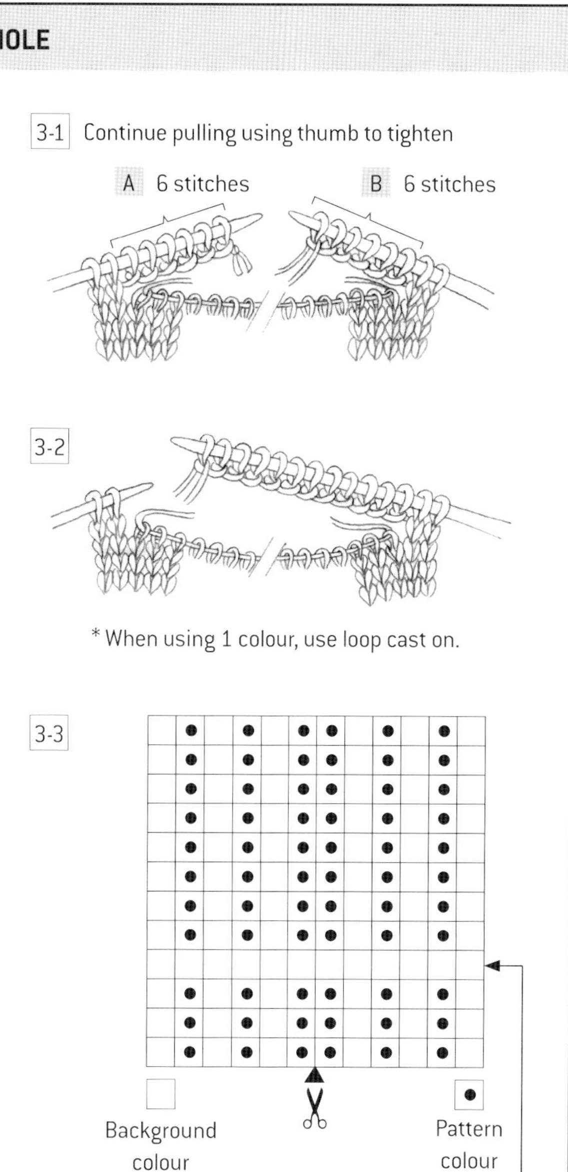

Note: For jumpers, armhole decreases will be done at both sides of the body stitches. There will be no increases or decreases within the extra stitches. Extra stitches will be worked in stripes (as in Figure 3-3), and the BOR and colour changes will be at the middle of extra stitches for left side of body.

4 MAKING EXTRA STITCHES FOR NECK OPENING

1. Slip stitches for neck opening onto waste yarn or stitch holder .
2. Begin from BOR at the left underarm, with the 6 extra stitches.
3. Work left front (when there is a decrease for the neckline starting on the 1st round, decreasing every round, X times, the 1st decrease is to be done at the end of the round at the left front).
4. Cast on 12 stitches over the neck stitches that are on hold (p.19, figure 3-2).
5. Work right front (when there is a decrease for the neckline starting on the 1st round, decreasing every round, X times, the 1st decrease is to be done at the beginning of this round at the right front).
6. Work 12 extra stitches for right side.
7. Work back.
8. Work the remaining 6 extra stitches for left side.

The round for making extra stitches for the neck opening is now complete.
Work up to shoulders following these steps.

Note: Decreases for the neckline are to be made at the end of the body on both sides of the neckline. There will be no decreases within the extra stitches.

5 PREPERATION AND JONING OF SHOULDERS

Prepare for joining shoulders

1. Be sure to work up to shoulders and cut yarn leaving an end of 3 to 5 cms.
2. Prepare to join shoulders.
3. Slip stitches onto right needle, until the first 6 extra stitches for right side are slipped onto the right needle.
4. Prepare pattern colour yarn and background colour yarn to work 1 row for BACK.
5. Make a knot leaving a long tail for background colour yarn approx. 3 times the length of shoulder, and 3 to 5 cms for pattern colour yarn. (Figure 5-1)

5-1 Making a knot with both yarns for back

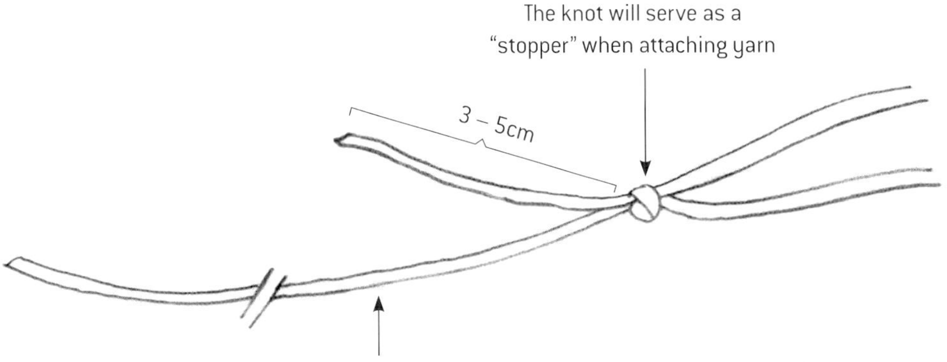

6. Using the pattern colour yarn, begin working from the 7th extra stitch of the right side seam, making sure that the stitches are worked tightly so that the knot is at the base of the stitch.
7. Work the remaining extra stitches in stripes, and continue to work a row for the back and 6 extra stitches on the other side.
8. Cut only pattern colour yarn leaving an end of 3 to 5cms. Now all the preparation is complete for joining shoulders. Leave background colour yarn as is, as it will be used for joining shoulders later on.

Steps for joining shoulders

1. Turn work inside out. Both shoulders will be joined from the shoulder towards the neck.
2. With the background colour yarn attached, join left shoulders together using three needle cast off with crochet hook. (Figure 5-2)
3. Continue using background colour yarn to cast off the extra stitches for front opening.
4. Join right shoulders following these same steps using the background colour yarn still attached.
5. After joining both shoulders, unravel the single row which was worked for back neck opening.
6. Cut unravelled yarn at the middle, and tie a knot at each side of the neck opening so that they won't loosen.

Note: These steps are somewhat customised based on my experience.

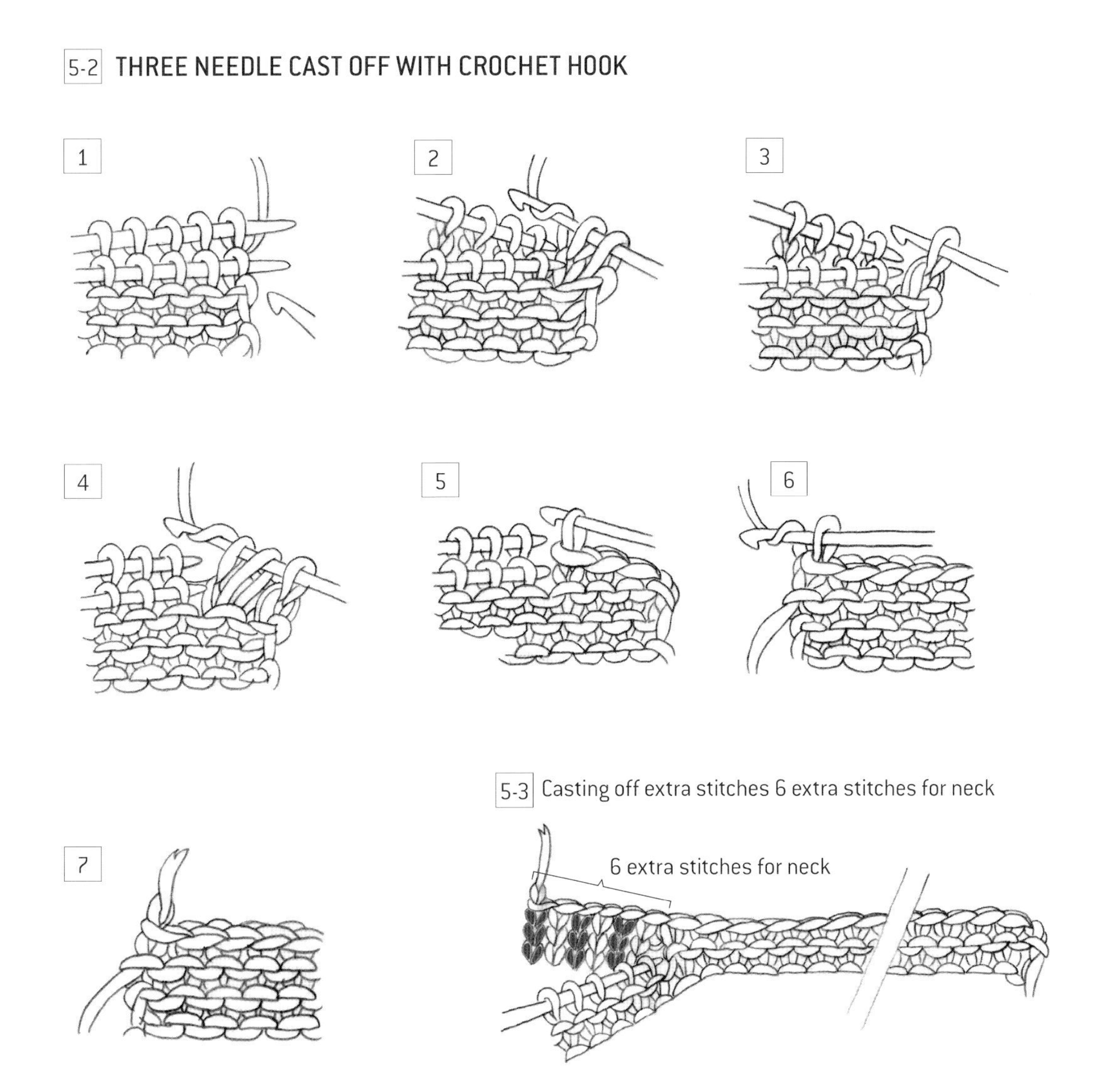

5-2 THREE NEEDLE CAST OFF WITH CROCHET HOOK

5-3 Casting off extra stitches 6 extra stitches for neck

6 NECKBAND (WORKED IN THE ROUND: ROUND NECK, SQUARE NECK, V-NECK)

ROUND NECK

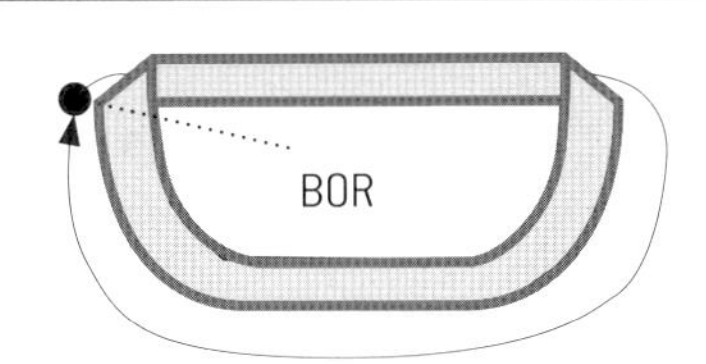

Pick up stitches so that the total number of stitches is a multiple of 4.

Start off picking up stitches from BOR.

1

Cut open at the centre of the 12 extra stitches for centre front

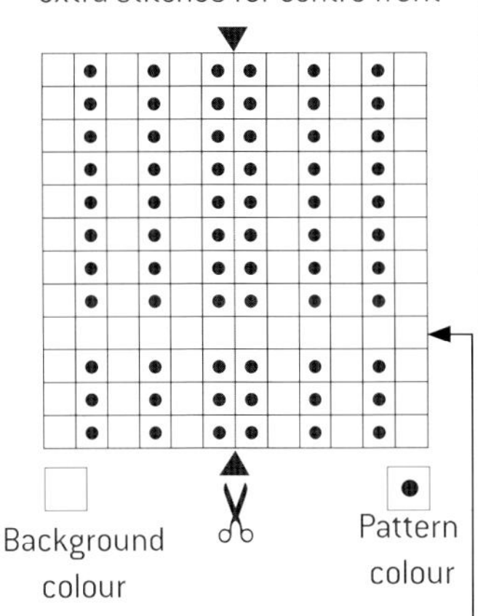

Base on the colour assignment for the row being worked, row with only one colour will be worked using only one colour.

2

Pick up stitches using the colour specified and pick up stitches from every stitch and from every row clockwise beginning from right shoulder

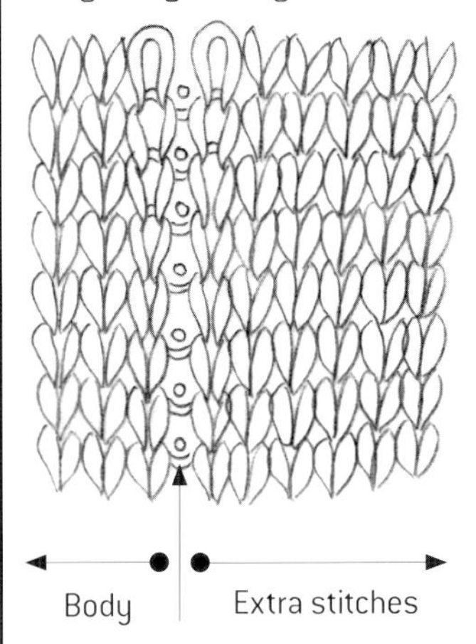

Picking up stitches between the body and the extra stitches.

SQUARE NECK

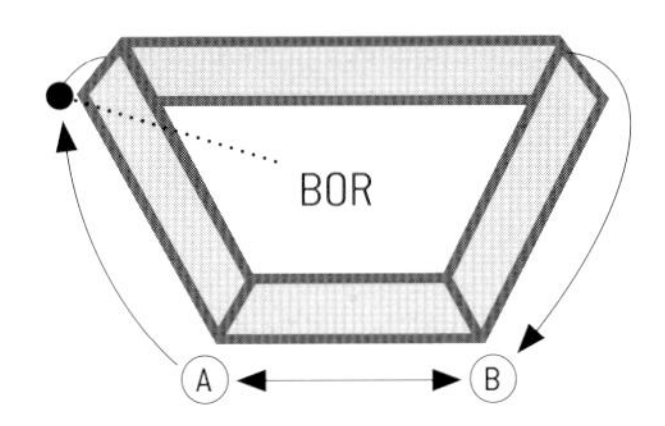

After picking up stitches from every stitch and from every row, place a marker on the 2 sts at each of the corners A and B. Decreases in the following rounds should be done so that these 2 sts will be centred; for both A and B, the first decrease will be a right-leaning decrease between the 1st of the 2 sts and the stitch before it, and a left-leaning decrease between the 2nd of the 2 sts and the following stitch.

Stitch count from the starting point to B should be a multiple of 4, and the sum [between A and B] and [from the stitch following A to end of round] should be a multiple of 4 plus 2 sts. Make sure not to include the 2sts at each of the corners A and B when making adjustments to the stitch count.

Note: This is my original design.

V-NECK

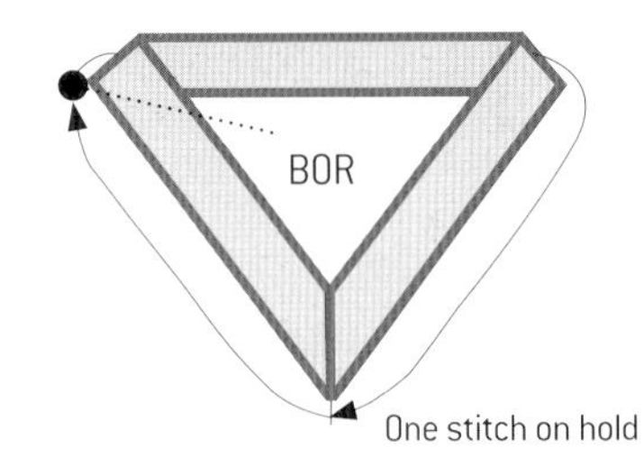

Adjust stitch count so that the number of stitches from BOR to the stitch before the held stitch is a multiple of 4. Stitch count from the one after the held stitch to end should be a multiple of 4 plus 2.

The held stitch at the centre of neckband should not be included when making adjustment for stitch count.

Make sure that the centre of neckband (the stitch on hold) becomes a KNIT stitch and decreases on every following round are made as a centred-double decrease.

3b

Adjust stitch count on the 2nd round while working 2x2 ribbing. Work a centred-double decrease (as shown below) at the centre front on every round. There will always be a knit stitch at the centre.

Centred-double decrease → Symbol

1

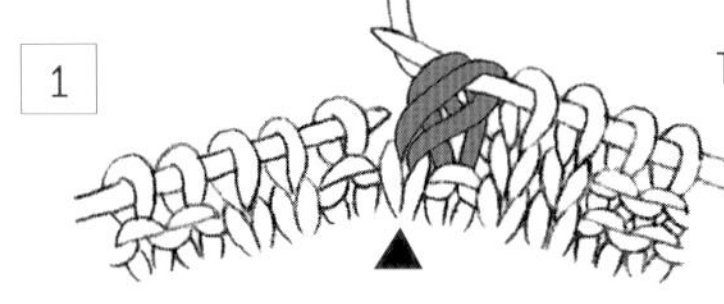

The held stitch from the front neck.

Slip 2 stitches together knitwise onto right needle.

2

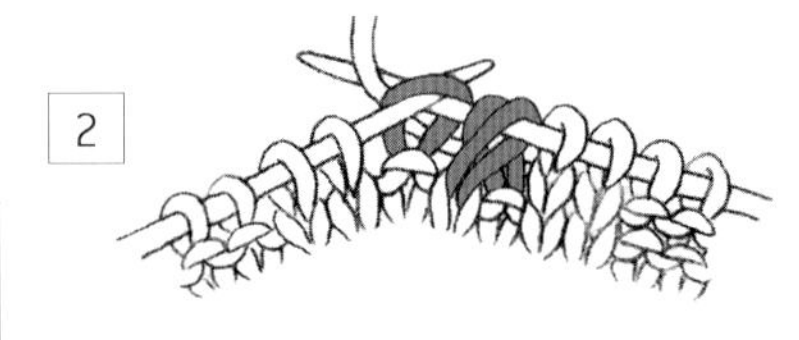

Knit the next stitch.

3

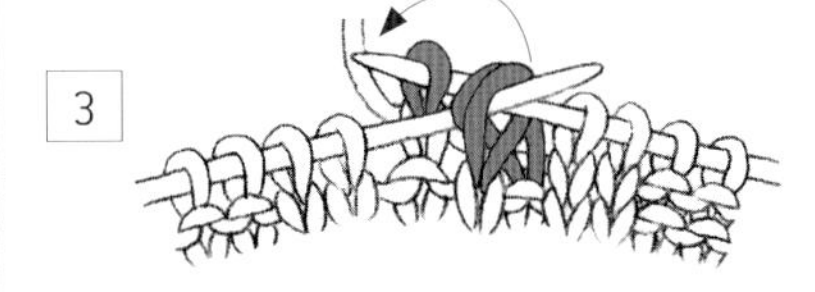

Pass the 2 slipped stitches in [1] over the stitch knit in [2]

4

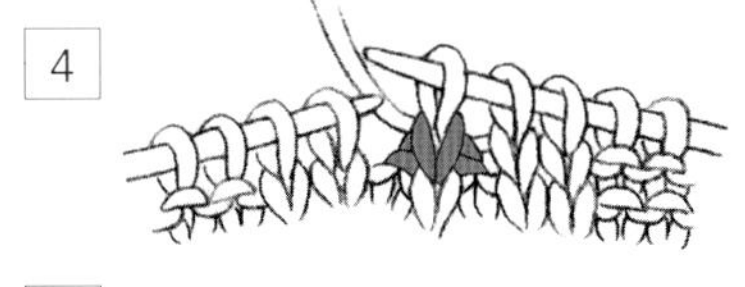

A centred-double decrease is done.

5

Repeat this every round.

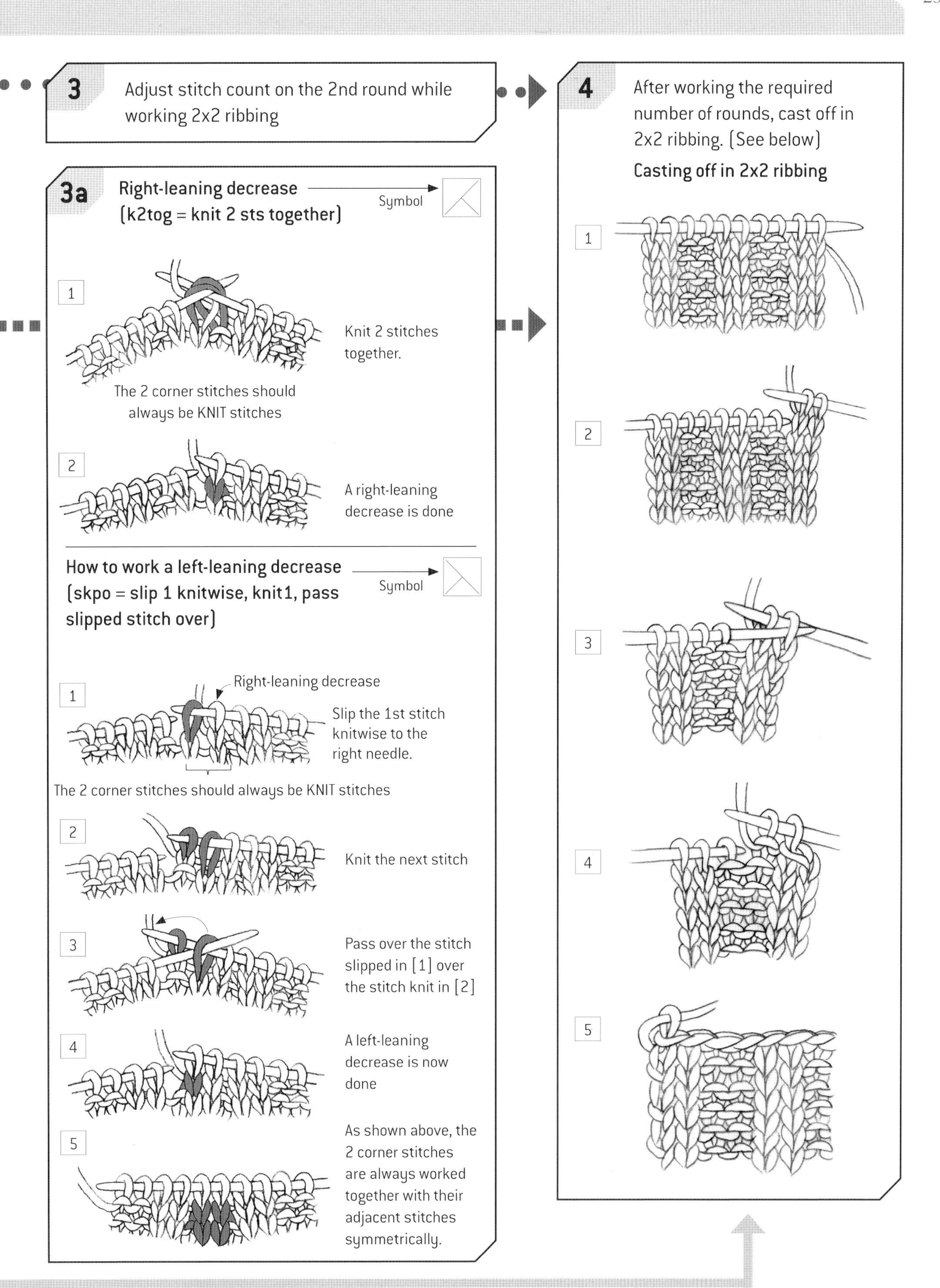
3
Adjust stitch count on the 2nd round while working 2x2 ribbing
3a
Right-leaning decrease
(k2tog = knit 2 sts together)
Symbol
1
Knit 2 stitches together.
The 2 corner stitches should always be KNIT stitches
2
A right-leaning decrease is done
How to work a left-leaning decrease
(skpo = slip 1 knitwise, knit1, pass slipped stitch over)
Symbol
1
Right-leaning decrease
Slip the 1st stitch knitwise to the right needle.
The 2 corner stitches should always be KNIT stitches
2
Knit the next stitch
3
Pass over the stitch slipped in [1] over the stitch knit in [2]
4
A left-leaning decrease is now done
5
As shown above, the 2 corner stitches are always worked together with their adjacent stitches symmetrically.
4
After working the required number of rounds, cast off in 2x2 ribbing. (See below)
Casting off in 2x2 ribbing
1
2
3
4
5

MAKING BORDER OF ARMHOLE FOR SLIPOVER

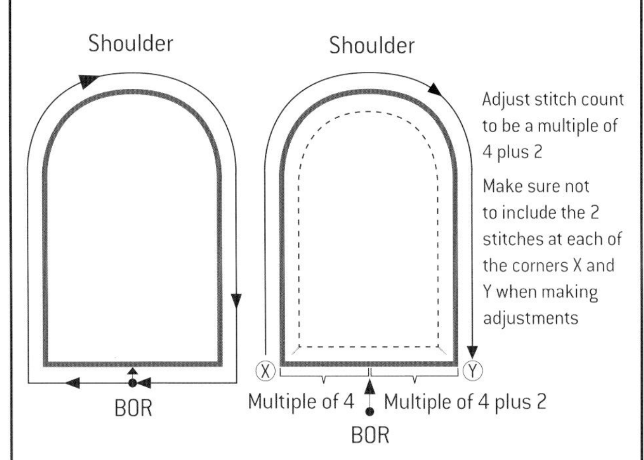

Mark the 2 knit stitches at both corners (Ⓧ&Ⓨ)

1. Cut open at the centre of the 12 extra stitches for armhole. (See p.22 [1])
2. Pick up stitches using the yarn specified. Start from the middle of stitches on hold for underarm and proceed clockwise, picking up every stitch and from every row.
3. After picking up all stitches, place a marker on the 2 stitches at each of the corners (X and Y).
4. Work in 2x2 ribbing on the 2nd round while making adjustments so that the 2 stitches at both corners X and Y are KNIT stitches.
5. Decreases for the armhole ribbing at the corners X and Y should be done as follows:

   The first decrease will be a right-leaning decrease between the 1st of the 2 stitches and the stitch before it (p23 [3a])

   The second decrease will be a left-leaning decrease between the 2nd of the 2 stitches and the following stitch. (p23 [3a])
6. After working the required number of rounds, cast off in 2x2 ribbing while continuing decreases at both corners. (p.25D)

   Note: The steps for this square armhole are an original method.

MAKING SLEEVES FOR JUMPERS AND CARDIGANS

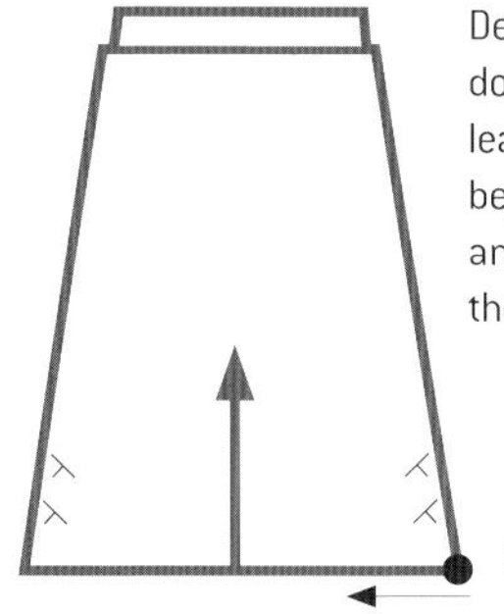

Decreases for sleeves are done by working a right-leaning decrease at the beginning of round (p.25B) and a left-leaning decrease at the end of round. (p.25C)

BOR (middle of stitches on hold)

Pick up all stitches
Adjust stitch count on the 2nd round (decreasing)
Decrease evenly

1. Cut open the centre of the 12 extra stitches for armhole.
2. Pick up stitches using the yarn specified. Start from the middle of stitches on hold for underarms and proceed clockwise, picking up every stitch and from every row.

   Work held stitches in knit stitches, and pick up stitches from rows based on [2] on page 22.
3. Adjust stitch count on the 2nd round. (When making adjustments, mark the stitches to be decreased beforehand to make the job easier)

   You may need to focus carefully when working the 2nd round, where you will need to decrease as evenly as possible while working the pattern. It will be easier to work the following rounds when this round is worked correctly.

   When stitch count is adjusted, continue working sleeves to the <<Cuffs>> based on the chart.
4. Decreases for sleeves are done at the centre of underarm. On the decrease row:

   Work a right-leaning decrease at the beginning of round. (See [B] on next page)

   Work a left-leaning decrease at the end of round. (See [C] on the next page)

   Both decreases will be in line at a centre of underarm. (See Tip (1) on page 26)

   Another way is to do a right-leaning double decrease along the centre of underarm. (Explanation in each instruction).

   There are instances when the pattern is worked in reverse order from the body depending on the pattern or colour combinations. This is due to the fact that the sleeves and body are worked in the opposite direction.
5. Work 2x2 ribbing for <<Cuffs>> and cast off in 2x2 ribbing. (See p25D)

   Note: In this step, some original steps are added based on learnings from my experiences.

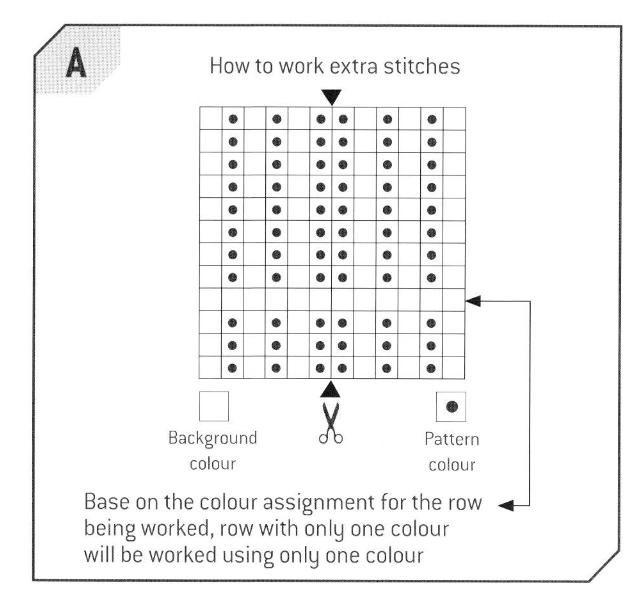
A
How to work extra stitches
Background colour
Pattern colour
Base on the colour assignment for the row being worked, row with only one colour will be worked using only one colour

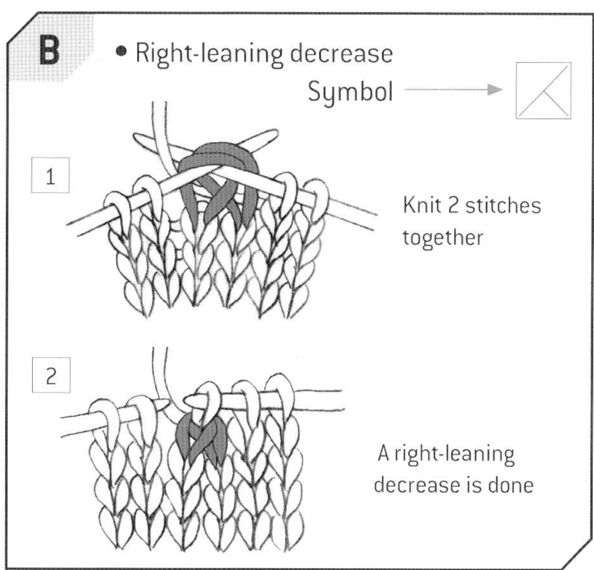
B
• Right-leaning decrease
Symbol
1
Knit 2 stitches together
2
A right-leaning decrease is done

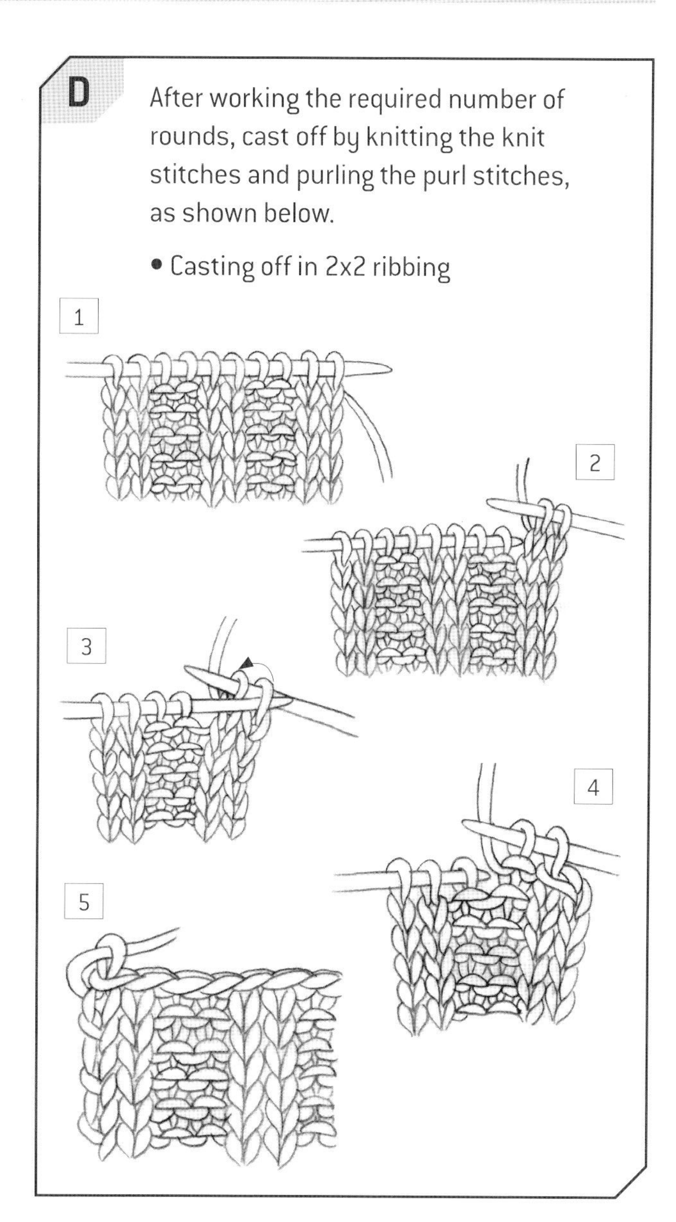
D
After working the required number of rounds, cast off by knitting the knit stitches and purling the purl stitches, as shown below.
• Casting off in 2x2 ribbing
1
2
3
4
5

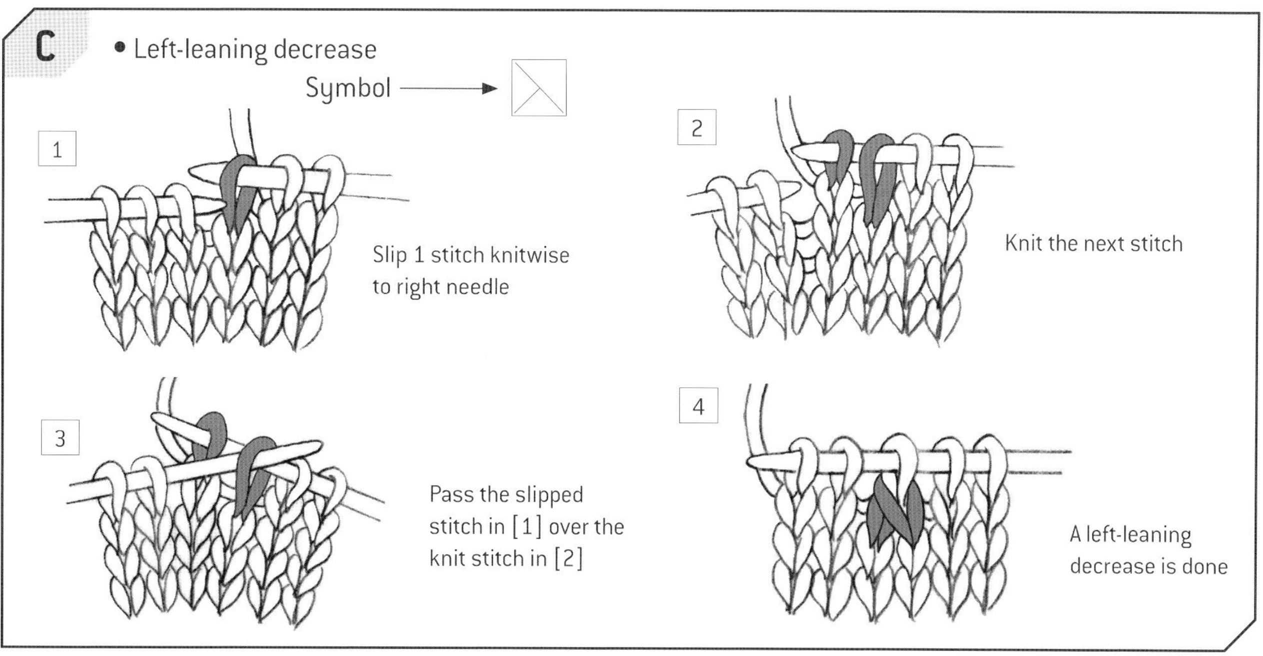
C
• Left-leaning decrease
Symbol
1
Slip 1 stitch knitwise to right needle
2
Knit the next stitch
3
Pass the slipped stitch in [1] over the knit stitch in [2]
4
A left-leaning decrease is done

TIP FOR WORKING SLEEVES (JUMPERS & CARDIGANS)

TIP 1 When work gets closer to the cuff and becomes difficult to work with 40cm circular needles, try working with the methods shown in Figures 7-1 and 7-2. Figure 7-1 shows how to work with two circular needles and Figure 7-2 with one longer circular needle.

TIP 2 For those whose ribbing tend to get loose, I highly recommend switching to needles that are 1 or 2 sizes smaller.

Figure 7-1 Working with two circular needles

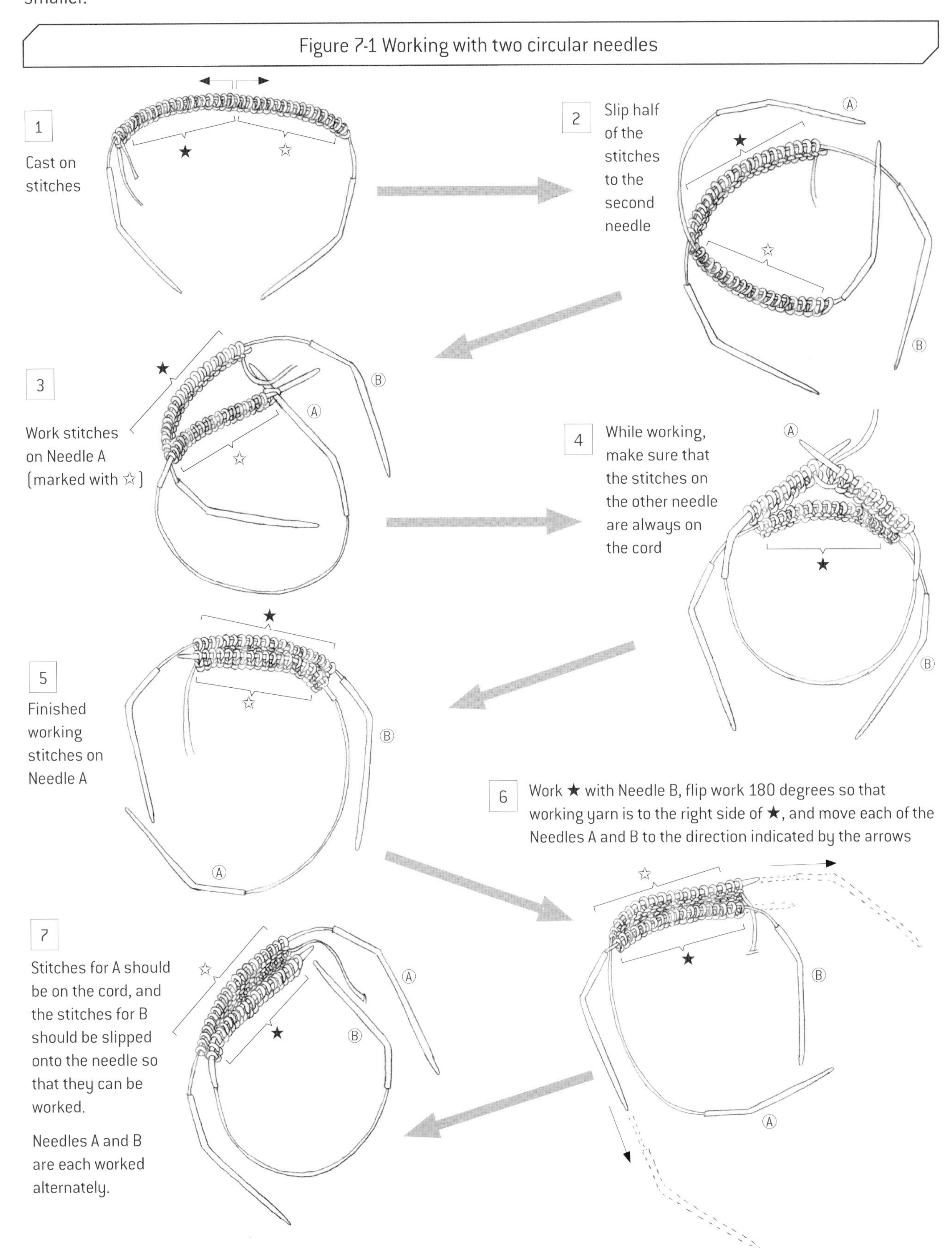

TIP 3 The following is a convenient way to reduce weaving in ends. When it's time to change colour, work the last 7 stitches on the previous round by weaving in the new colour yarn, just like when working Cowichan sweaters. The yarn being changed will not be cut but instead will be worked together by weaving them in the first 7 stitches of the next round. When the garment is finished, stretch out the fabric around the woven-in ends to even out the work.

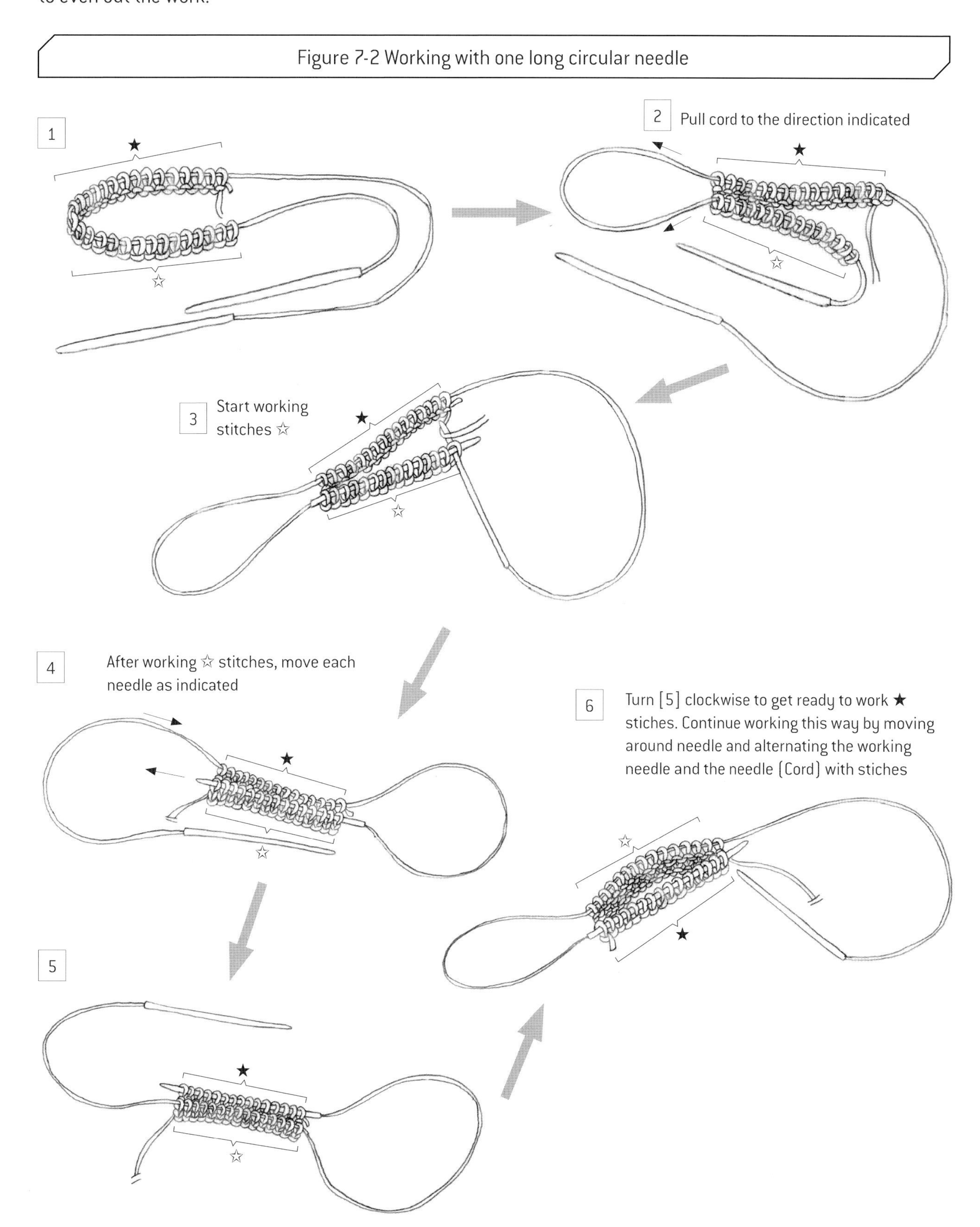

Figure 7-2 Working with one long circular needle

8 TREATMENT FOR EXTRA STITCHES

1. After cutting open the extra stitches, trim them to be 4.5 stitches wide remain from the body side.
2. Fold the remaining stitches twice – fold 2.5 stitches over to the back in 3-fold, so that 2 stitches will appear. Stitch this in place with similar colour yarn row by row. (See illustration to right)
3. Do not pin down the extra stitches but press them down firmly to the wrong side of garment with your left hand thumb. Insert needle and draw through toward the upper right-hand side to make a neat firm stitch.
4. The direction for this treatment of extra stitches for neck and front bands will be different; you will be working down-up for right front band, and from top-down for the left.
5. Extra stitches for armholes will be upside down and work in the round. (The front and the back side will not be worked separately)

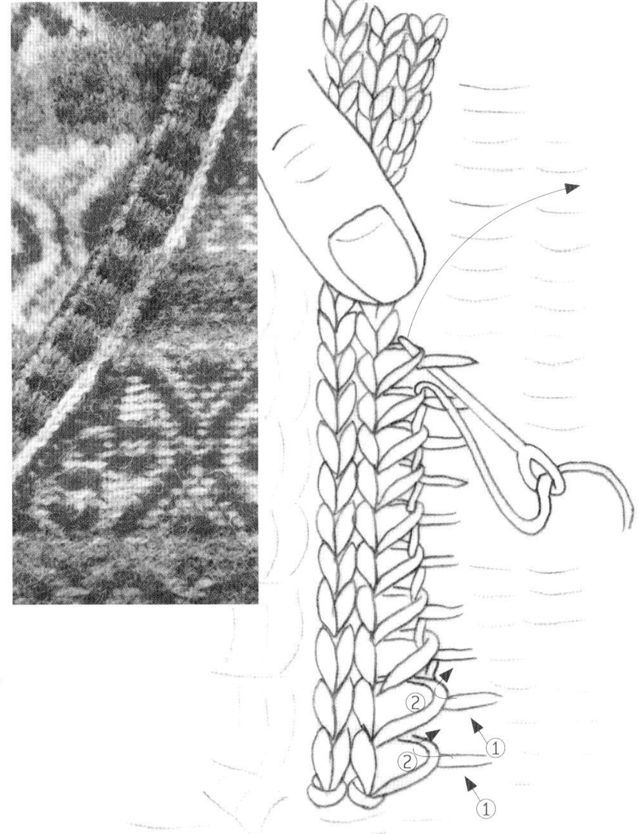

Knot and breaks (without cut up)

4 sts extra stitches using two together as lock (without sewing)

A cross sewing.

9 WEAVING IN ENDS AND WASHING

1. Slipovers, jumpers and cardigans are to be turned inside out; untie any ends that were loosely tied when changing yarns, tighten them securely and weave them into the floats.
2. Weave any other remaining ends into floats.
3. Loose ends are to be woven in by inserting the tip of a tapestry needle into the float and then threading the end into needle. This will allow for any length of loose ends to be woven in.
4. Once all ends are woven in, turn the garment over so that the right side is facing. (Tip 3: Reduce weaving in ends, p.27)
5. Hand wash using wool wash, without agitating but by gently pressing the garment. Washing will bring out the best features of the yarn. (I personally prefer using warm water when washing to allow the garment to felt lightly.)
6. Once dried, trim off all ends. Make sure that scissors are used parallel to the fabric.

OVERALL STEPS FOR KNITTING CARDIGANS

In this section, we will go over the overall steps for working a cardigan, as cardigans have several steps in addition to those for slipovers (vests) and jumpers (sweaters). Those points that are different from slipovers or jumpers are highlighted in bold letters.

1 RIBBING FOR THE HEM — SEE STEP 1

Cast on stitches referring to STEP 1 (on page 18). Cardigans are **worked flat with 3 stiches on both ends worked as KNIT stitches when facing the right side**. Working flat means once the stitches from right side are worked, the work is turned so that the next row is worked facing the wrong side. Continue working by turning between right side and wrong side.

2 MAKING EXTRA STITCHES FOR FRONT BAND — ADDITIONAL STEP

1. With yarn used for Row 1 of the body, cast on 6 stitches on to the right hand needle. (See page 18, Long tail cast on)
2. Continue working from left needle, in the order of right front, back and left front. (1 stitch is added for the back in order to adjust the pattern at the centre front)
3. Cast 6 stitches at the end of row. (Using backward loop cast on)

All extra stitches for the front bands are now done, and from here on the work will be in the round.

Beginning of round (BOR) and changing yarns will be **at the middle of the extra stitches for front bands.**

The pattern colour to be used for the new round (Round 2 for body) will be tied to the yarn after making the last 6 extra stitches.

See page 25 for how to work the extra stitches.

3 WORK BODY UP TO UNDERARM — SEE STEP 2

See procedures for changing yarns in STEP 2 (page 19).

Work up to underarms, **with extra stitches for front bands in between both fronts**, following the garment diagram and colour assignment.

4 HOW TO MAKE EXTRA STITCHES FOR SLEEVES — SEE STEP 2

1. Slip stitches for underarms onto stitch holder or waste yarn.
2. Begin working from the middle of the front band extra stitches and proceed to right front.
3. Cast on 12 stitches over stitches held for right underarm. (See page 19, Figure 3-2)
4. Continue working back.
5. Cast on 12 stitches over stitches held for left underarm. (See page 19, Figure 3-2)
6. Continue working left front.
7. Work 6 remaining extra stitches.

Extra stitches for armhole are now complete. Decreases for the sleeves are to be made on both sides of the body. No decreases or increases are made within the extra stitches.

Work until **1 row before neckline** following the garment diagram and colour assignment.

Beginning of round and colour changes will be **at the middle of the front band extra stitches.**

OVERALL STEPS FOR KNITTING CARDIGANS CONTINUED

5 TREATMENT FOR EXTRA STITCHES ALONG FRONT BANDS — ADDITIONAL STEP

Treatment for front band extra stitches will be done 1 row before making the extra stitches for neck opening.

1. Cast off the first 6 extra stitches using yarn (or yarns) to be used for the following row.
2. Work right front and the 12 extra stitches at the right side.
3. Work back and 12 extra stitches at the left side.
4. Work left front, cast off the remaining 6 extra stitches at the end of the round and break yarn.

6 MAKING EXTRA STITCHES FOR NECK OPENING — SEE STEP 4

The difference between cardigans and jumpers or slipover is that **the beginning of round is at the centre front**.

1. Slip stitches for neck opening onto waste yarn or stitch holder.
2. **Cast on 6 stitches onto right needle** using the yarn for the following row. (See p.19, Figure 3-1)
3. Work right front which is on the left needle (when there is a decrease starting on the 1st round, decreasing every round, X times, the 1st decrease is to be done at the beginning of the right front).
4. Continue working the 12 extra stitches for the right side and back, and 12 extra stitches for the left side.
5. After working left front (when there is a decrease starting on the 1st round, decreasing every round, X times, the 1st decrease is to be done at the end of the left front). **Cast on 6 stitches at the end of round**. (See p.25, Figure 3-1)

Extra stitches for the neck are now complete.

Beginning of round and colour changes will be **at the middle of the front band extra stitches**.

Decreases for the neckline are to be made at each end of the body. No decreases or increases are made within the extra stitches.

7 PREPARATION AND JOINING OF SHOULDERS — SEE STEP 5

8 NECKBAND (WORKED FLAT) — SEE STEP 6

1. Cut open at the middle of 12 extra stitches for neck opening. (See p.25A)
2. Pick up stitches using the colour specified, beginning from **the held stitches on hold at right front**, and pick up stitches from every stitch and from every row.

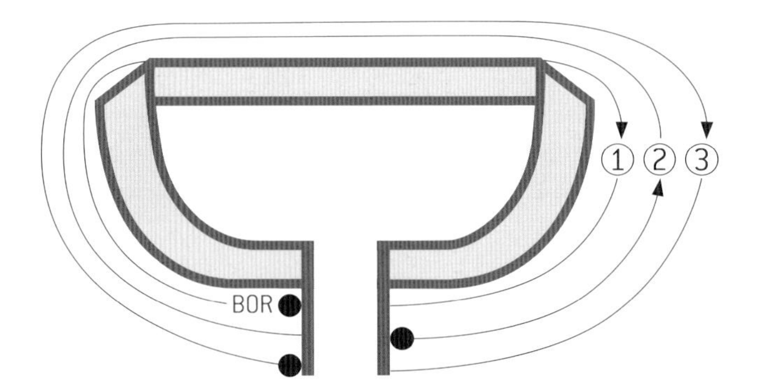

3. Adjust stitch count on the 2nd row, so that the 3 sts on each end will be KNIT stitches when facing the right side, and work in 2x2 ribbing for the rest of the stitches. (Decreases shall be made evenly so that the total stitch count is a multiple of 4)

4. After working the required number of rows, cast off by knitting knit stitches and purling purl stitches. [See p.23, step 4]

[When the garment has a collar, pick up stitches and work the collar after working fronts bands as in STEP 9]

9 MAKING FRONT BANDS — ADDITIONAL STEP

1. Cut open at the centre of the 12 extra stitches for centre front. [See p.25A]
2. Pick up stitches using the yarn specified from both right and left front bands, picking up from every row.
   - Stitches will be picked up from hem to neckline for the right front band, and from neckline to hem for left.
   - When picking up stitches for ribbing at the hem and neckline, start from the 2nd stitch from the edge. Pick up stitches for extra stitches based on p.16 [2] of STEP 6. There will be a gap of one row between ribbing and the extra stitches, but begin picking up stitches from half a stitch from the edge to minimize the gap.
3. After working the required number of rows according to the colour assignment, cast off by knitting the knit stitches and purling the purl stitches.

10 MAKING SLEEVES & TIPS — SEE STEP 7

11 TREATMENT FOR EXTRA STITCHES — SEE STEP 8

12 WEAVING IN ENDS AND WASHING — SEE STEP 9

13 MAKING BUTTON HOLES — ADDITIONAL STEP

1. After washing the cardigan, place a pin to mark where you would like to attach buttons along the 2 purl stitches on the right button band for women [and left button band for men].
2. Attach buttons using yarn or thread along left front band opposite the marking pins. I have settled to using a 2mm suede cord to attach buttons, by threading it through the button and tying it onto the left front band, making a knot. This is simple and is long-lasting.
3. Make button holes where you marked with pins. Using tapestry needle or crochet hook, pull the strand between purl stitches and open up the stitch vertically as well to open the hole.

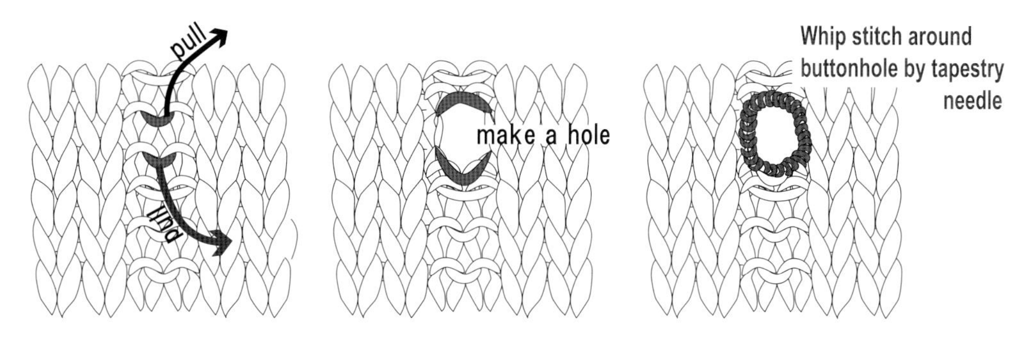

4. Whip stitch around these buttonholes using a tapestry needle.

HOW TO READ GARMENT DIAGRAMS

Lastly, I would like to simply explain how to read garment diagrams. Garment diagrams are illustrations of 3-dimentional garments worked in the round which are spread out into 2 dimensional form.

Dotted lines indicate sections that are connected. There may be garment diagrams where the balance of the neck opening is different from actual. This is done in order to standardise the spread charts, making it simpler and easier to read.

I believe knitting is all about balance.

Trying to get everything right all at once would be quite impossible. If you set your focus on certain points or parts, and achieve them one by one, you will be able to build on your achievements to be able to knit beautifully.

Do not give up, and always enjoy knitting by imagining yourself wearing the garment you are working on.

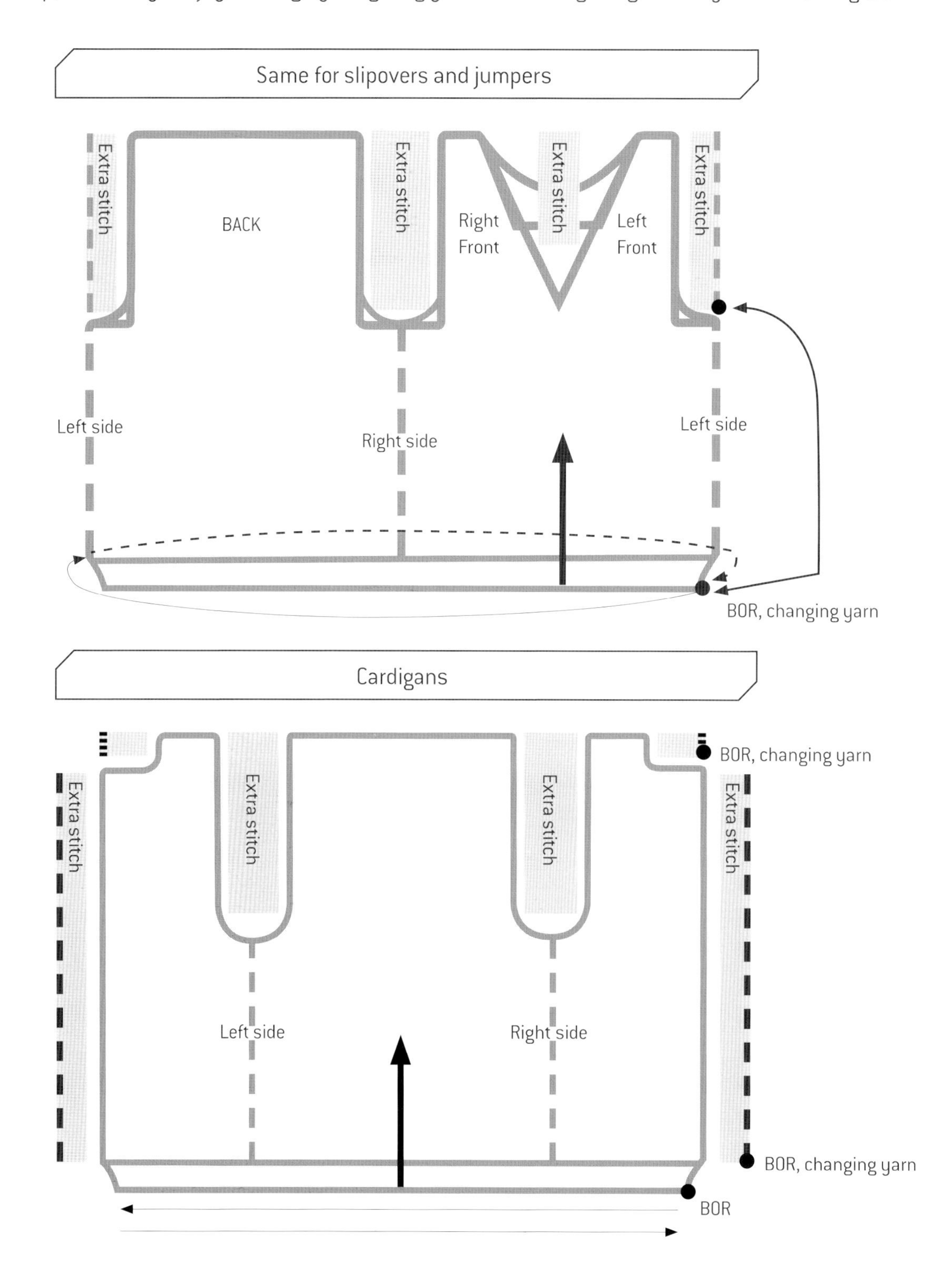

LONG TAIL CAST ON WITH TWO COLOURS

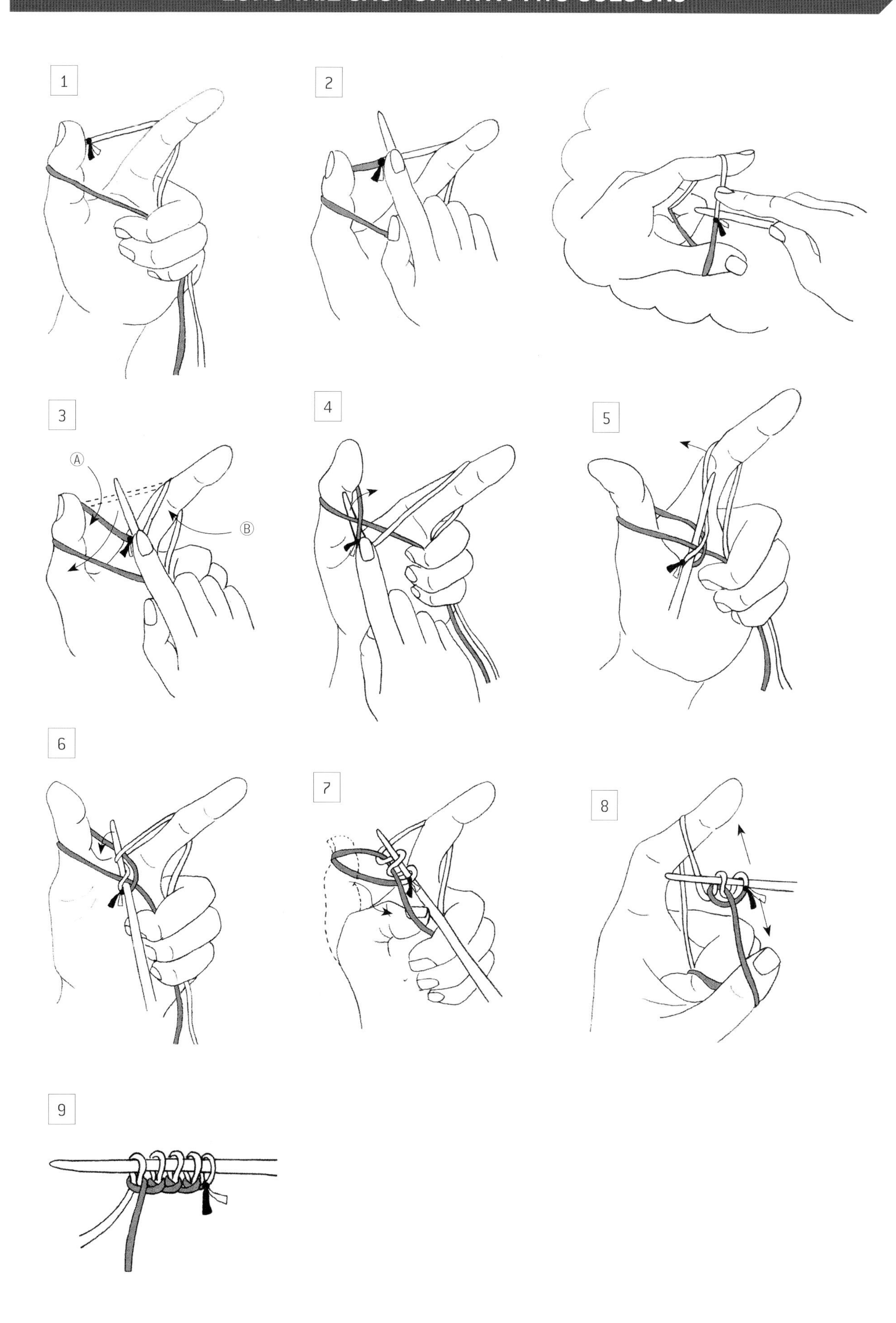

RESIZING (ALTERING SIZE)

If I were to start writing all the details of altering sizes in Fair Isle knitting I could write another book. So I will tell you the basic outline of it based on what Shetland knitters and designers have taught me.

You should first remember that everybody has a different hand. The easiest way to alter the size is to change the needle size. If you want to alter more you should note the following methods used in Fair Isle knitting – the traditional way.

Width

1. Width is based on the pattern, so you should use an even number of patterns in one round. If you use an odd number of patterns you will have a different pattern on the left and right sides. (Note: shawls, caps, ponchos etc. are excepted.)
2. Each pattern contains a number of stitches so, for example, a pattern with 12 stitches means you would need to reduce stitch count by 24 stitches to make a smaller size, or you have to add 24 stitches to make a bigger size. However, I use a pattern with 42 stitches in this book – meaning reducing by 84 stitches or adding 84 stitches for alteration – so sometimes this method makes it too small or much too big.
3. When skilled knitters in Shetland alter the size they reduce the number of stitches between patterns or they make a few modifications to the original patterns. These alterations will affect the whole combination of patterns in the garment, so you need experience and a wide knowledge to work this way.

Length

1. Length is easier to change than width. However, when you use a pattern which has a large number of rows you might find it difficult to alter.
2. You need to have the same pattern at the beginning of the body and at the end of the sleeves, and also need to make sure that the pattern matches at the shoulders.

In my experience of instructing Fair Isle knitting, if you want to knit well you need to knit a few garments and learn the methods of constructing patterns and also get to know your hand and consistency of tension. That is the quickest way to become a good knitter.

My friend is a skilled spinner and knitter and she told me a really nice story. A beginner asked her, "Do you have a tip for knitting?" as she struggled to knit with three needles and knitting belt.

My friend answered her, "Oh, I have a good tip!"

"Please teach me."

"The tip is practice."

And she said to me, "Chihiro, no magic in it, only practice."

Now I am sure that you will first find and feel enjoyment in knitting and then you will build up your skill and challenge yourself by knitting more and more.

ABBREVIATIONS		SYMBOLS
BGF	background colour (main colour)	
BOR	beginning of round	
CDD	centred-double decrease (2 sts decreased)	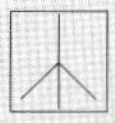 ⅄
cm	centimetre	
cn	cable needle	
dec(s)	decrease(s) / decreasing	
EOR	end of round	
g	gram(s)	
inc	increase(s) / increasing	
k	knit	 |
k2tog	knit next 2 stitches together (1 st decreased)	 ⟋
kfb	knit into front and back of the same stitch (1 st increased)	
LH	left-hand	
m1	Make 1. Bring the tip of the left-hand needle under the strand between stitches, from front to back, knit through the back of this loop (1 st increased)	
p	purl	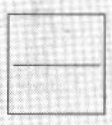 —
PC	pattern colour (contrast colour)	
rev ST st	reverse stocking stitch (stockinette stitch) purl on RS, knit on WS	
RH	right-hand	
rnd(s)	round(s)	
RS	right side	
skpo	slip 1 stitch, knit 1 stitch, pass slipped stitch over (1 st decreased)	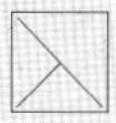 ⟍
sl 1	slip 1 stitch, purlwise	
st(s)	stitch(es)	
WS	wrong side	
yo	yarn over needle (1 st increased)	
{}	repeat directions inside brackets as many times as indicated	

THE PATTERNS

"When I work on my colourway, I always remember the sea, sky, peat, flowers, migratory birds, sheep, cattle, Shetland ponies and the beautiful stone walls (dykes) of Shetland."

The colours I use have changed
over the years and I feel
something new is beginning.

1 THE BEGINNING
Shawl

After publishing my second book, I felt a strong connection with Shetland.
The colours I use have changed over the years and I feel something new is beginning.
The colour of Shetland's sea and beautiful dawn gave me this colourway.
The edges represent the waves.

Yarn

Total 6 colours – 17 balls

Total weight of stole – 341g

 150 (Atlantic) 5 balls

 162 (Neptune) 4 balls

 185 (Sunglow) 2 balls

 271 (Flame) 2 balls

 462 (Ginger) 2 balls

 600 (Violet) 2 balls

Tools & Notions

Circular needles: 2.75mm (40cm
and 3mm (40cm)

Crochet hook: 2.3mm crochet hook

Tapestry needle: Small and medium

Stitch markers

Cable needle (cn)

Tension

1 pattern stitch

(Large) Three waves: 14 sts x 17 rows = 4 cm x 4.5 cm

(Medium) Anchor: 18 sts x 11 rows = 5 cm x 2.8 cm (including single color rows underneath and on top)

Finished measurement

Length: 129 cm

Width: 50 cm

INSTRUCTIONS

This stole is worked in the round with *extra stitches* in between, which are cut open afterwards.

Border at the bottom and top:

Variation of cables –

Total of 134 rows including cast on, worked flat.

Row 1: Using 2.75mm (40cm) circular needle and #150 yarn, cast on 15 sts.

Row 2 (WS): Purl.

Row 3 (RS): K7, 4/4 Right Cross (slip 4 sts onto cn and hold in back, K4, K4 from cn).

Rows 4 to 8: Continue working in purl for even-numbered WS rows and knit for odd-numbered RS rows twice more, and work WS row once more.

Row 9: K1, 3/3 Right Cross (slip 3 sts onto cn and hold in back, K3, K3 from cn), K8.

Continue working as established, working Row 3 and Row 9 each on every 12th row, up to Row 134.

After working Row 134, cast off so that the width for the beginning and end of work are mostly the same.

Cut yarn leaving a 3cm tail. Make one more for top.

When working the body of stole, pick up stitches along the side edge closer to 3/3 Right Cross.

TIP: The sizes of the two pieces can be kept consistent by working them consecutively.

Body of stole – Knit in the round throughout

Round 1: Change to 3mm needle. Cast on 6 sts with #150 using loop cast-on and pick up and knit 181 sts along the side (closer to 3/3 Right Cross) of one of the border cables already made. (Refer to illustration on p.42.). Then cast on 6 sts at the end. Join cast-on stitches on both ends to work in the round.

Rounds 2 to 454: Tie #162 and #462 onto #150, and break #150. Continue working according to colour assignment, while working *extra stitches* in stripes with the two colours used for working the round, or in one colour if the round uses only one.

Work until 1 round before the last.

NOTE: *The Three Waves pattern uses the same colour combination but is worked differently.*

Round 455: When working the last round with #150, cast off 6 *extra stitches* at BOR, work body and cast off the remaining 6 *extra stitches* at EOR.

Attach border

Once the body of the stole is finished, sew on the other border with tapestry needle. Make adjustments when joining as body has more stitches and needs to be decreased evenly, so that the finished width matches the border on the other side.

Finishing *extra stitches* and weaving in ends (see p.28)

- Cut open at the centre of the *extra stitches*. Trim the *extra stitches* to be 4.5 stitches wide.
- Using #150 yarn and crochet hook, insert hook into the last st of the stole body from RS and into the WS of the adjacent *extra stitch*, put YO hook and draw through so that the *extra stitches* fold over to the WS. Do this for both sides. This makes it easier when stitching down the *extra stitches*.

Fold 2.5 stitches over to the back in 3-fold, so that 2 knit stitches will appear.

Stitch this in place with similar colour yarn row by row, as shown on p.28.

Washing

- After weaving in all ends, be sure to hand wash. Wash as normal wool wash. Washing will bring out the best features of the yarn.
- Once dried, trim off all ends. Make sure that scissors are used parallel to the fabric.

KNITTING CHART

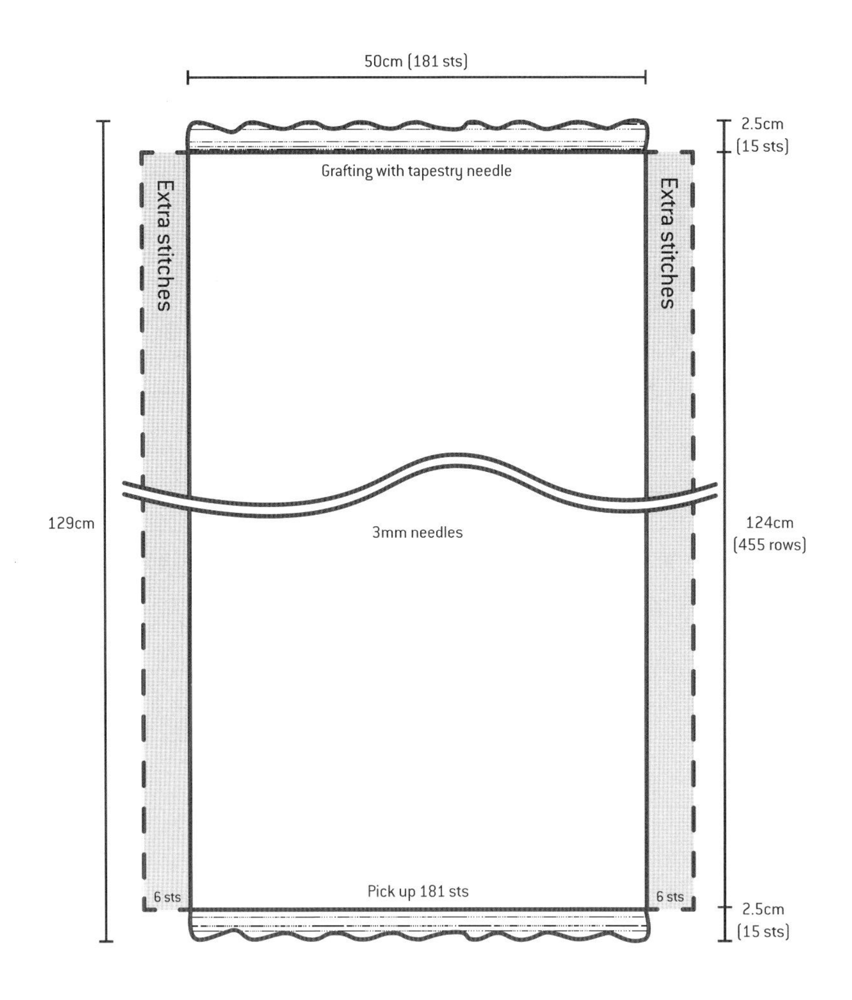

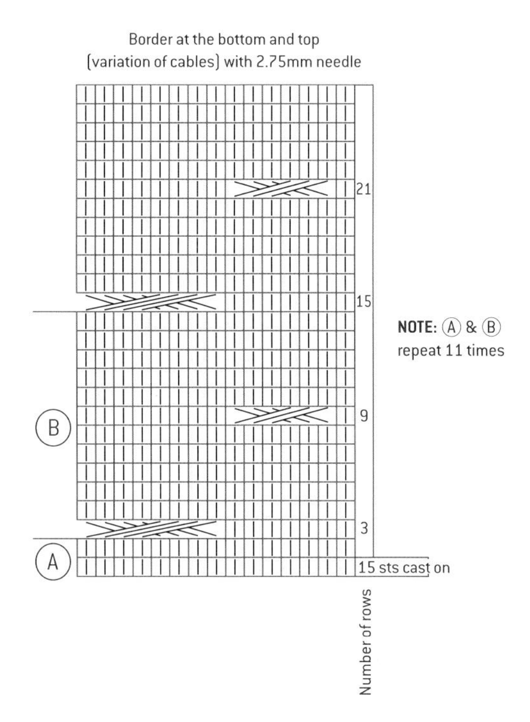

NOTE: Variation of cable's chart is based on how it will appear on RS

Detail of border at the bottom and top

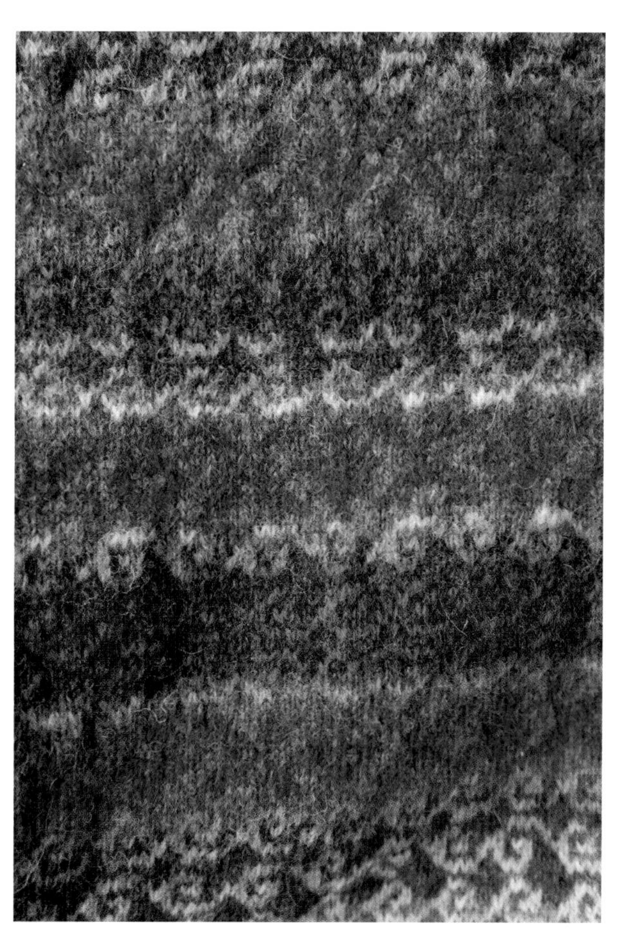

Detail of pattern

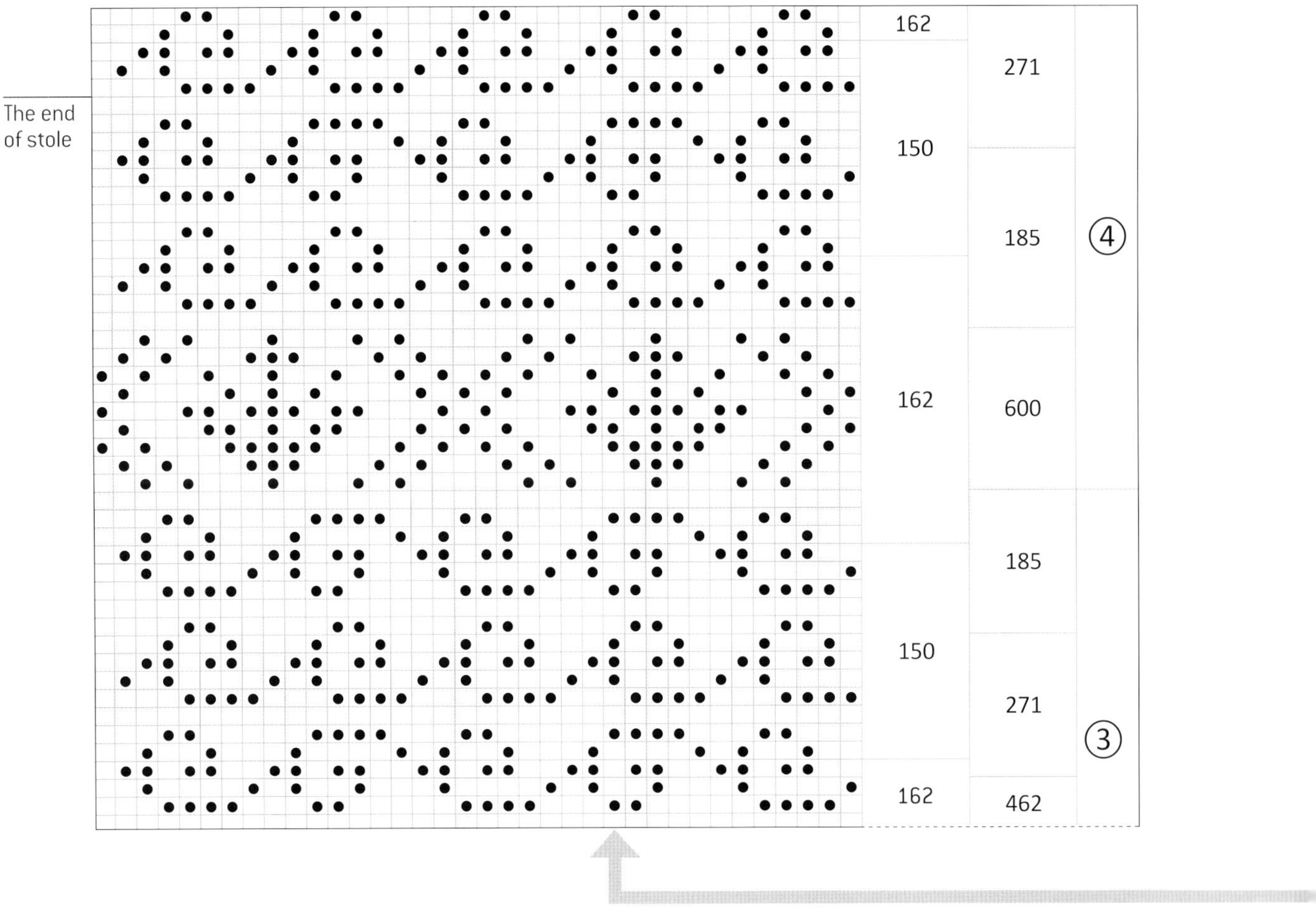

The end of stole

162

271

150

185

④

162

600

185

150

271

③

162

462

BGC	PC	
162	600	③
150	462	②
	271	
162	185	
	600	
	185	①
150	271	
	462	
162	271	
	600	
	185	A
150	271	
162	462	
150		
BGC	PC	

Begin to follow from A, and then repeat

Repeat 3 times [① - ④] and knit until another edge of stole.

”

The atmosphere in winter
was totally different from
summertime.

“

2 WINTER MEMORY
Women's cardigan

White and black are always difficult colours for me. Once I had a chance to stay in snowy Shetland. The atmosphere in winter was totally different from summertime. Very quiet. And only Shetlanders on the island. This wonderful experience encouraged me to use natural white and optical white. Strangely, this collaboration matches the view from my window in Tokyo.

Yarn

Total 5 colours – 22 balls

Total weight of cardigan – 495g

103 (Sholmit) 2 balls

104 (Nat. White) 9 balls

122 (Granite) 3 balls

274 (Green Mist) 5 balls

768 (Egg Shell) 3 balls

Tools & Notions

Circular needles: 2.5mm (40cm, 60cm and 80cm or longer), 2.75mm (40cm)

Crochet hook: 2.3mm

Tapestry needle: Small and medium

Waste yarn (to hold stitches)

Stitch markers

Buttons (desired number)

Tension

1 pattern stitch

(Medium) Ivy pattern: 20 sts x 12 rows = 5.8cm x 3.2cm

(Narrow) Two types of pattern:
4 sts x 4 rows / 4 sts x 5 rows = 1.2cm x 1.3cm / 1.2cm x 1.5cm

(Narrow) Chain pattern:
10 sts x 5 rows = 3.2cm x 1.5cm

Finished measurement

Bust circumference: 102cm

Back neck to sleeve edge: 78.5cm

Length: 62.5cm

INSTRUCTIONS

Worked in the round up to shoulders, apart from hem, by working *extra stitches* in between for front opening, armholes and neckline.

Ribbing for hem

Worked flat for 18 rows, including cast on.

Row 1: With 2.5mm 60cm circular needle and with colour #103 yarn, cast on 320 sts.

Row 2: Tie #768 onto #103. Begin on the WS row by P3 with #768 and continue working in corrugated 2x2 ribbing by repeating [K2 with #103, P2 with #768], and end P3 with #768.

Row 3: Switch #103 to #274 and #768 to #122. Work in corrugated 2x2 ribbing by purling K stitches and knitting P stitches. (See chart on p. 52.)

Rows 4 & 5: Work as established in Row 3. 3 purl stitches should appear at the beginning and end of row on RS.

Rows 6 to 18: Work as for Row 2, changing K stitches from #122 to #768 and P stitches from #274 to #104. After working Row 18, break both yarns leaving a 3cm tail.

Body

<<Work to underarm>>

Round 1: Change to 3mm needle. Cast on 6 sts on RH needle using #274, which is assigned for Round 1 based on colour assignment chart, K160, YO to increase 1, and continue to K160.

At the end of the round, cast on 6 sts using backward loop cast-on.

This together with the first 6 cast-on sts makes the set of *extra stitches* for front band. Proceed to work in the round.

NOTE: *Refer to Page 25 for working with extra stitches.*

Rounds 2 to 133: Work according to the colour assignment and work *extra stitches* in between. Make sure to knit the YO through the back loop.

<<To make *extra stitches* for armhole>>

1. Using tapestry needle, thread waste yarn through underarm stitches on each side, by identifying the centre of the underarm stitches.
2. The centre stitch of the right underarm will be 81st stitch from BOR, and the centre of the left underarm will be 81st stitch from EOR.

NOTE: ***Identifying the centre stitch following the Ivy pattern will not be simple, as the top and***

bottom sections of this Ivy pattern are not symmetrical. It would be easier to use another pattern that is symmetrical and follow the stitch all the way up to the current row.)

After working Round 133: Thread waste yarn through the 'centre stitch' together with 10 sts on each side (21 sts all together). These stitches will still be on the cord of the circular needle.

Do this for both underarms.

Round 134: Switch from #122 to #103 and work to the stitches held for right underarm.

Remove the 21 sts with waste yarn from needle. Cast on 12 sts. (See p. 33.)

Proceed working along the back body up to the stitches held for left underarm. Remove held stitches from needle in the same way as for right underarm, cast on 12 sts and work to EOR. *Extra stitches* for both armholes are now made.

Be sure to decrease at both sides of armholes every 2nd rnd 5 times.

Round 188: (Round 55 from underarm) Cast off 6 *extra stitches* using 2 colours before proceeding to right front. Work 12 *extra stitches*, then back body, 12 *extra stitches*, then left front, and lastly cast off 6 *extra stitches* at EOR. Break yarn.

<<To make *extra stitches* for neck opening>>

After working Round 188: Thread 15 sts at the beginning and end of round waste yarn.

Round 189: Cast on 6 sts using #104 and #274 (See p.33), decrease at the beginning and end of body and cast on 6 sts once more.

These 12 sts will become the *extra stitches* for neck opening, and the centre of these *extra stitches* will become the BOR. All subsequent colour changes will be done here.

Decreases will be worked on both sides of the *extra stitches* as follows.

(Note that no increases or decreases will be made within the 12 *extra stitches*.)

Rounds 190 to 210: Decrease 1 st every rnd 8 more times, then 1 st every 2nd rnd 6 times, and work 1 rnd even to shoulder. Break yarn leaving a 3cm tail.

Join shoulders

1. Prepare for shoulder seam by working 1 additional row for back by slipping stitches onto RH needle, up to the centre of *extra stitches* for right sleeve.
2. Tie a knot using #104 and #274 yarn, which will be used for working the additional row. Leave a 3cm tail for #104, and about three times the shoulder length for #274. The knot will be used as a 'stopper', and will be worked from the centre of the *extra stitches* for right sleeve, across back body following colour assignment chart, to the centre of *extra stitches* on the other side.

   Leave the BGC #274 as is and cut PC #104 leaving a 3cm tail.
3. Turn the work inside out.

   Using the remaining #274 yarn and crochet hook, work (three needles cast off) starting from the shoulder edge. Cast off the 6 *extra stitches* for the neckband separately using slip stitch cast-off. (Make sure that the *extra stitches* are not joined together with back neckband.) (See p.21)
4. Join the other shoulder as well using three needle cast off with crochet hook with #274 yarn which was kept longer, and cast off *extra stitches* using slip stitch cast-off.
5. Unravel back neck stitches. Cut the unravelled yarn at the middle and tie at the base of both shoulders.

Sleeves

1. Cut open *extra stitches* and pick up and knit into all stitches and rows beginning at the centre of the held stitches using #274 yarn. Pick up and knit stitches from between *extra stitches* and body. (See page 28[2]) Adjust stitch count to 160 sts on the second round.

NOTE: *This cardigan has a pattern which cannot be worked symmetrically, therefore be sure to work sleeve in reverse order of the colour assignment chart.*

2. Decrease at inside sleeve every 2nd rnd 12 times, every 4th rnd 18 times, and then every 6th rnd 10 times. Decrease by knitting to the last st of the previous round (the round before the decrease), slip the last st onto RH needle unworked, and then work a double decrease (SK2PO = Sl1, K2 tog, pass slipped st over knit st) between the last st of the previous round and the first 2 stitches of the decrease round. This way, the decrease for inside sleeves will not be missed. Then work 35 rnds even.

   <<Cuff>>
3. **Round 1:** After working 191 rnds, change to 2.5mm circular needle and work in corrugated 2x2 ribbing (K2 with #768, P2 with #104).

   Rounds 2 to 10: Work as established in Round 1.

   Rounds 11 to 13: Switch #768 to #122 and #104 to #274, and reverse knit stitches and purl stitches.

   Round 14: Switch #274 to #103 and #122 to #768, work in corrugated 2x2 ribbing as Round 10. (See p.52)

Cast off with #103 using tapestry needle. (See sewn cast off on page 123.)

4. Work other sleeve in the same way and cast off using tapestry needle.

Front bands

Worked flat, by cutting open at the centre of *extra stitches*.

Row 1: With 2.5mm (60cm) circular needle and #104 yarn, pick up all rows. Pick up 206 sts.

NOTE: *Begin picking up stitches from the bottom of hem ribbing for right front and the neck edge for left front. Be sure to leave a selvedge stitch when picking up stitches from the ribbing section of hem and neckline, and between body (see p.22[2]) and extra stitches for body. There will be a need to shift by one-half of a stitch when picking up stitches between ribbing section to body section with extra stitches, and be sure to pick up stitches tightly to avoid any gaps.*

Rows 2 to 10: Tie #768 onto #104 and work in corrugated 2x2 ribbing.

First and last 2 sts should appear as knit stitches from RS. Continue working 8 more rows using the same colours.

Rows 11 to 13: Change #768 to #122 and #104 to #274 and work corrugated 2x2 ribbing, but reversing K sts and P sts for 3 rows.

Rows 14 & 15: Change #274 to #103 and #122 to #768 and work corrugated 2x2 ribbing as in Row 10.

Then cast off with #103, knitting K sts and purling P sts. Be sure cast off is not too loose.

Work the same for the other front band.

Neckband & Turndown

Worked flat.

<<Neckband>>

Row 1: Using 2.5mm circular needle (40cm long) and #104, pick up and knit 135 sts in total, beginning with the 8th stitch of the right front band, along the right front neck, then to back neck and along left front neck, and ending on left front band before the 8th stitch from the centre.

Rows 2 to 11: Tie #274 onto #104, and work in corrugated 2x2 ribbing (P2 with #274, K2 with #104), beginning and ending with purl stitches (so that they will appear as knit stitches on RS), and decreasing 1 st at the centre back. Total 134 sts. Break #104.

Row 12: Work in knit with #274 to EOR.

<<Turndown>>

Row 1: Switch to 2.75mm circular needle and tie #768 and #103 onto #274. Work flat in corrugated 2x2 ribbing (K2 with #103, P2with #768). Last 2 sts will be K2.

Row 2 (WS): Continue in corrugated 2x2 ribbing, repeating (P2 with #103, K2 with #768) until EOR.

Rows 3 to 12: Change #103 to #104. Continue in corrugated 2x2 ribbing, repeating (K2 with #104, P2 with #768) on odd number rows, and (P2 with #104, K2 with#768) on even number rows.

Continue working in corrugated 2x2 ribbing in this manner for 10 rows, reversing knit and purl sts between RS and WS.

Rows 13 & 14: Change #104 to #103 and work 1 row in 2x2 ribbing, repeating (K2 with #103, P2 with #768), and reversing knit and purl sts on Row 14. And break #768 and #103.

Rows 15 to 20: Tie #274 and work in reverse stockinette stitch for 6 rows. Cast off in purl.

Treatment for extra stitches, see p.28.

Weaving in ends and washing, see p.28.

Make button holes, see p.31.

Make button holes in between stitches and work whip stitch around the hole.

Neckband construction

Collar detail

KNITTING CHART

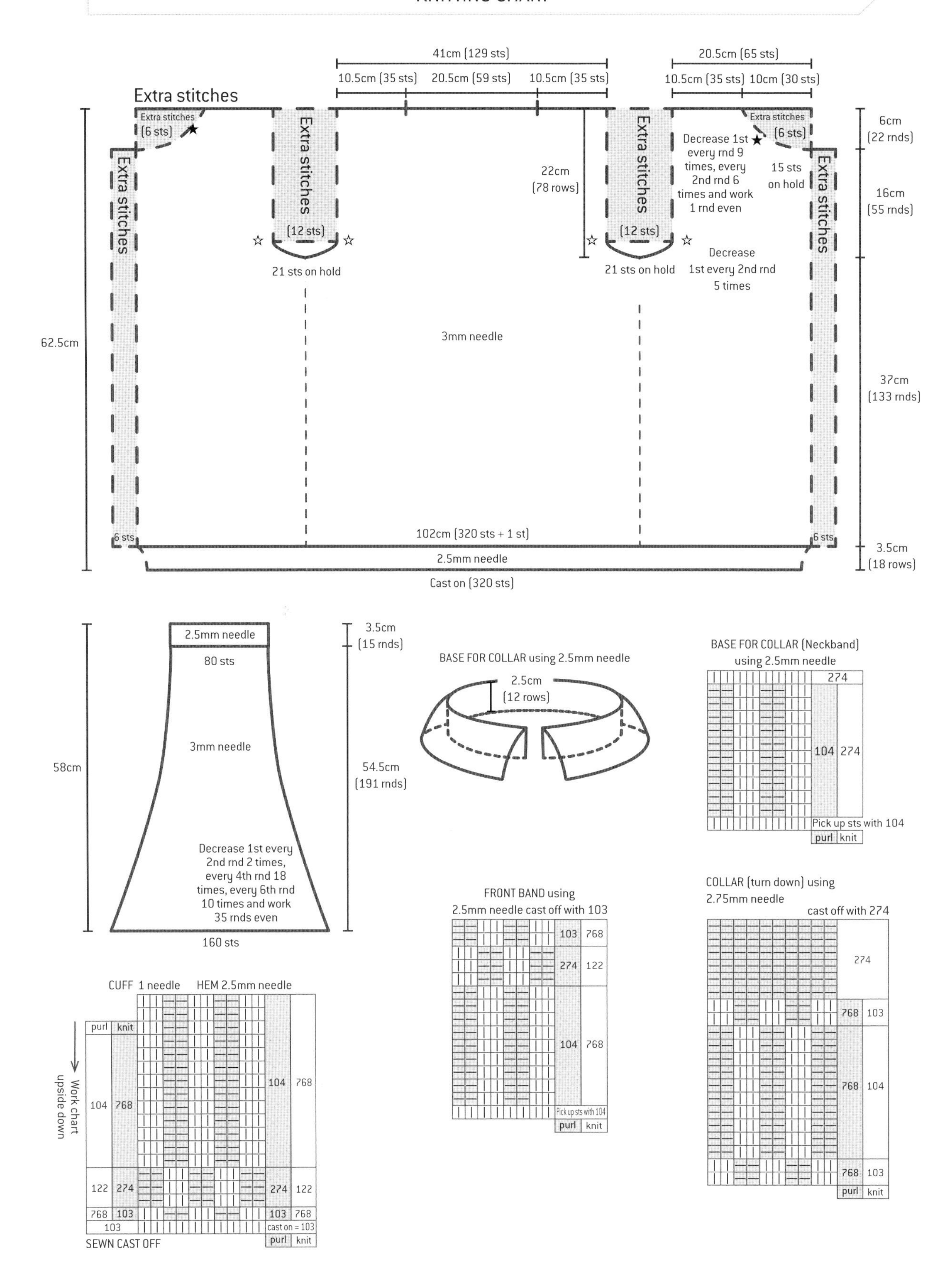

NOTE: Colour assignment for ribbing is based on how it will appear on RS

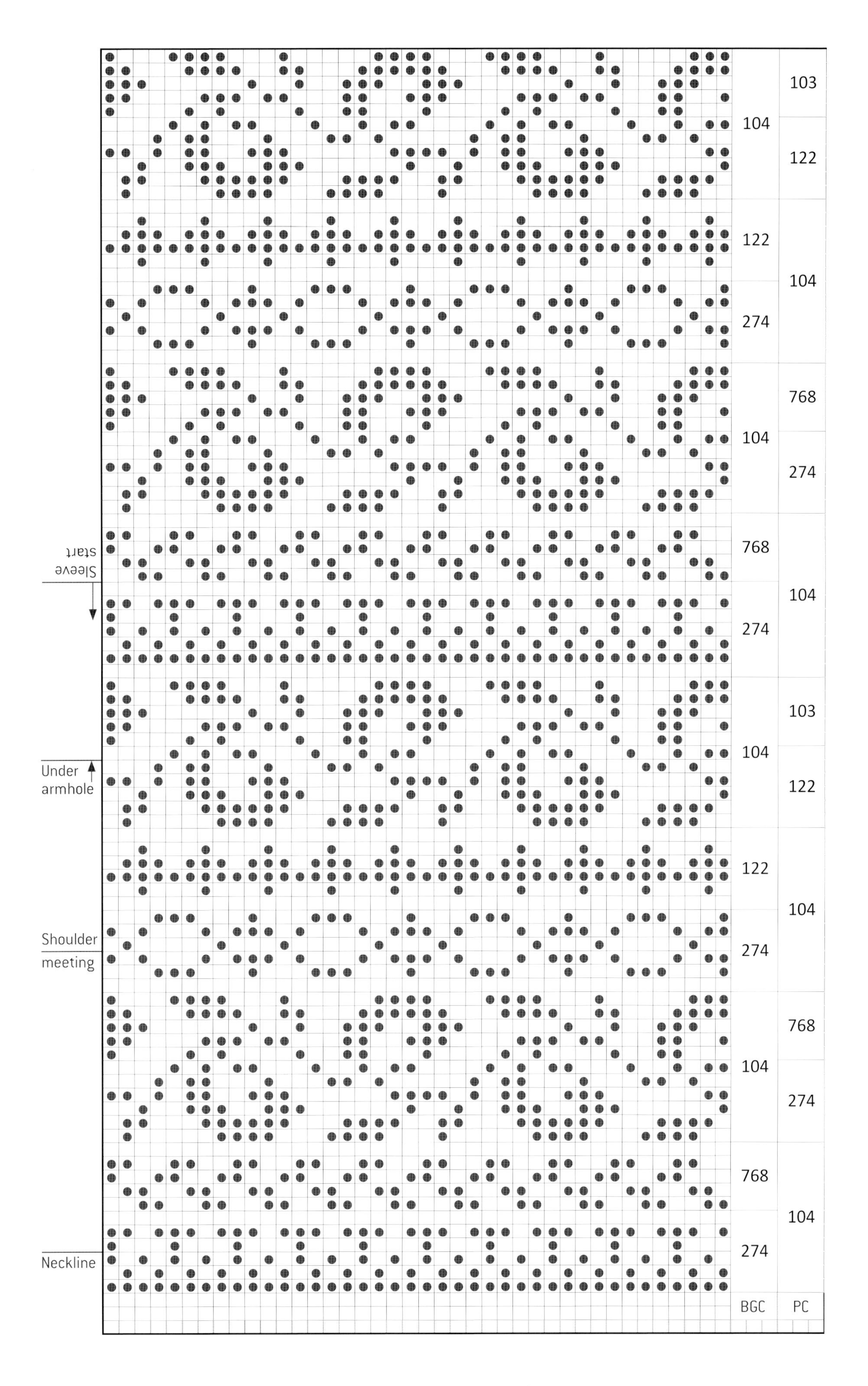

104
122
274
104
768
274
104
122
274
104
768
274
BGC
103
122
104
768
274
104
103
122
104
768
274
104
PC
Sleeve start
Under armhole
Shoulder meeting
Neckline

”

One particular picture
struck me. It was an old
water mill's wooden door.
It is still there near the sea.

3 WATER MILL
Women's long cardigan

This work was completed in March 2008. One particular picture struck me.
It was an old water mill's wooden door. It is still there near the sea.
I gathered many colours which the picture shows and knitted a colour sample in one sitting. But I felt I needed more subtle colours which I didn't have at that time.
Now I have 216 colours and I was really pleased to knit it all over again.

Yarn

Total 18 colours – 33 balls
Total weight – 750g

 122 (Granite) 3 balls

 125 (Slate) 2 balls

 127 (Pebble) 2 balls

 140 (Rye) 3 balls

 153 (Wild Violet) 1 ball

 180 (Mist) 2 balls

 183 (Sand) 1 ball

 238 (Osprey) 1 ball

 272 (Fog) 4 balls

 274 (Green Mist) 2 balls

 319 (Artichoke) 1 ball

 335 (Asparagus) 1 ball

 768 (Egg Shell) 2 balls

 789 (Marjoram) 1 ball

 791 (Pistachio) 2 balls

 1130 (Lichen) 2 balls

 1270 (Purple Haze) 1 ball

 1390 (Highland Mist) 2 balls

Tools & Notions

Circular needles: 2.5mm (40cm, 80cm or longer)
2.75mm (60cm)
3mm (40cm, 80cm or longer)

Crochet hook: 2.3mm

Tapestry needle: Small and medium

Waste yarn (to hold stitches)

Marker, desired number of buttons

Tension

1 pattern repeat

(Wide) Octagon: 30 sts x 19 rows = 9.8cm x 5.5cm

(Medium) Flower pattern: 30 sts x 17 rows = 9.8cm x 5cm

(Small) Heart pattern: 10 sts x 7 rows = 3.2cm x 2.1cm

Finished measurement

Chest circumference: 130cm

Back neck to sleeve: 73cm

Length: 92.5cm

INSTRUCTIONS

Worked in the round up to shoulders, apart from hem, by working *extra stitches* in between front opening, armholes and neckline.

Ribbing for hem

Worked flat for 38 rows, including cast on.

Row 1: With 2.75mm (60cm) circular needle and colour #1130 yarn, cast on 420 sts.

Row 2: Tie #238 onto #1130. Begin on the WS row by P3 with #1130 and continue working in corrugated 2x2 ribbing by repeating (K2 with #238, PS with #1130) and end P3 with #1130.

Row 3: Begin on the RS row by K3 with #1130 and continue working in corrugated 2X2 ribbing by repeating (P2 with #238, K2 with #1130) and end K3 with #1130.

Row 4: Cut #238 and switch to #1390 and continue to work in K2, P2 ribbing.

Row 5: Switch #1390 to #335 and continue.

Rows 6 & 7: Switch #335 to #272 and continue.

Row 8: Switch #272 to #789 and continue.

Row 9: Switch #789 to #791 and continue.

Row 10: Switch #791 to #1270 and continue working in ribbing.

Row 11: This time switch from #1130 to #140 for knit stitches and work purl stitches with #1270.

Rows 12 to 15: Work as established in Row 11.

Rows 16 to 30: Switch #140 to #122 and work in K2, P2 ribbing for 15 rows.

Row 31: Switch #1270 to #153 for purl stitches and continue.

Rows 32 & 33: Switch #153 to #272 and continue.

Rows 34 & 35: Switch #272 to #238 and continue.

Rows 36 to 38: Switch #238 to #125 and continue up to Row 38. Break yarn leaving a 3cm tail.

Body

<<Work to underarm>>

<<To make *extra stitch*es for front band>>

Round 1: Switch to 3mm circular needle and cast on 6 sts on RH needle with #125 and begin working based on colour assignment chart. Work 210 sts, YO (to make 1), continue working 210 sts, then cast on 6 sts using backward loop cast-on. The last 6 sts together with the first 6 stitches make up the *extra stitch*es for front band, and from here on will be worked in the round.

NOTE: *The BOR will be at the centre of the extra stitches, and yarns will be switched at this point. Extra stitches are to be worked in stripes, alternating both colours used for the round. Work as shown on p.25. Make sure to knit the YO (made on the previous round) through the back loop.*

Rounds 2 to 216: Work based on colour assignment chart up to Round 216.

<<To make *extra stitch*es for armhole>>

1. After working Round 216, there will be 14 large Octagon patterns, 7 for each front and back. Since the front body will be cut open, there will be 3.5 pattern repeats each on left and right sides separated by the *extra stitch*es in the middle.
2. Looking at the 7 pattern repeats on the back body, identify the stitch located at the centre of both sides. The centre stitch on the right side will 106th stitch from BOR, and for the left side it will be 106th stitch from EOR. Mark these 2 sts.
3. Thread waste yarn through tapestry needle and thread 21 side sts (10 sts on each side of the marked st plus the marked st). These 21 side sts will be kept on hold for both left and right sides.

Round 217: Work to the held stitches. *Remove needle from the 21 sts and cast on 12 sts using #180 and #272.* Continue working back and repeat from * to* and continue working to EOR.

*Extra stitch*es for both armholes are now made.

Round 218 to 260: Work for 43 rnds based on colour assignment chart.

Round 261: At the beginning cast off 6 *extra stitch*es in each colour yarn, and then continue working body. At the end of the round, cast off the remaining 6 *extra stitch*es in the same way and cut yarn.

<<To make *extra stitch*es for neck opening>>

After working Round 261, slide 15 sts each for neckline on waste tapestry using yarn needle and keep them on hold.

Round 262: At the beginning of this round, cast on 6 sts with the two colours that will be used in this round, and decrease at the beginning and end of the round. Then cast on 6 sts at the end of the round.

NOTE: *These 12 newly cast-on sts will be the extra stitches for neck opening, and the centre of these 12 sts will be the new BOR and the point where colours will be switched.*

Rounds 263 to 288: Decrease 1st every round for the next 3 rounds at the beginning and end of body (no increases or decreases will be made within the *extra stitch*es), then decrease 1st every 2nd rnd 11 times and work 1 rnd even.

This will be the shoulder. Cut yarn leaving a 3cm tail.

Join shoulders

1. Prepare for shoulder seam by working 1 additional row for back by slipping stitches onto RH needle, up to the centre of *extra stitches* for right sleeve.
2. Tie a knot using #122 and #183 yarn, which will be used for working the additional row. Leave a 3cm tail for #122, and about three times the shoulder length for #183. The knot will be used as a 'stopper' and will be worked from the centre of the *extra stitches* for right sleeve, across back body following colour assignment chart, to the centre of *extra stitches* on the other side.
3. Turn work inside out.

   Using the remaining #183 yarn and crochet hook, work three needles cast off starting from the shoulder edge. Cast off the 6 *extra stitches* for the neckband separately using slip stitch cast off. (Make sure that the *extra stitches* are not joined together with back neckband.) (See p.21)
4. Join the other shoulder as well, using three needles cast-off with crochet hook with #183 yarn which was kept longer, cast-off *extra stitches* using slip stitch cast-off.
5. Unravel back neck stitches. Cut the unravelled yarn at the middle and tie at the base of both shoulders.

Sleeves

1. Cut open *extra stitches* and pick up and knit into all stitches and rows beginning at the centre of the held stitches using #1390 yarn.

   Pick up and knit stitches from between *extra stitches* and body. (See page 22.)

   Adjust stitch count to 160 sts on round 2.

NOTE: *This cardigan has a pattern which cannot be worked symmetrically, therefore be sure to work sleeve in reverse order of the colour assignment chart.*

2. Decrease at inside sleeves every 2nd rnd 18 times, every 4th rnd 22 times: Decrease by knitting to the last stitch of the previous round (the round before decrease), slip the last stitch onto RH needle unworked, and then work a double decrease (SK2PO = SL1, K2 tog, pass slipped sts over knit sts) between the last stitch of the previous round and the first 2 sts of the decrease round. This way the decrease for inside sleeves will not be missed. Then work 13 rnds even.

   <<Cuff>>

3. **Rounds 1 & 2:** After working 137 rnds, change to 2.5mm circular needle and work in K2, P2 ribbing, knitting with #127, purling with #274.

   Rounds 3 & 4: Switch #274 to #1390 and work 2 rnds.

   Rounds 5 to 9: Switch #127 to #140 and work 5 rnds.

   Round 10: Switch from #1390 to #1270 and work 1 rnd.

   Rounds 11 & 12: Switch from #140 to #1130 and work 2 rnds. Cut #1270 leaving 3cm tail.

   Round 13: Work 1 round in reverse stockinette stitch with #1130 only.

   Cast off using tapestry needle. (See sewn cast off on p. 123.)

4. Work the other sleeve in the same way.

Neckband and fronts bands

<<Neckband>>

Worked flat by cutting open at the centre of *extra stitches*.

Work neck band using 2.5mm circular needle (40cm) and pick up and knit into all stitches and rows. Make sure to adjust stitch count to be a multiple of 4 on the next row (WS row). When working this row, make sure that the first and last 3 sts will be knit sts on RS and the remaining worked in K2, P2 ribbing. Work a total of 18 rows.

Row 1: Pick up and knit into all stitches and rows (total of 121 stitches) using #789.

Row 2: Tie #122 onto #789 on the following row and work the first 3 sts with purl sts with #122, followed by K2, P2 ribbing (K2 with #789, P2 with #122), decrease 1 st at the centre back to make a total of 120 sts, and end by purling the last 3 sts with #122.

Row 3 & 4: Using #122 and #789. Work Row 3 the first and the last 3 sts will be K sts. Work Row 4 will be P sts.

Rows 5 & 6: Switch #789 to #272 and continue working in K2, P2 ribbing.

Row 7: Switch #272 to #335 and continue working in K2, P2 ribbing.

Row 8: Switch #335 to #319 and continue working in K2, P2 ribbing.

Rows 9 & 10: Switch #319 to #153 and continue working in K2, P2 ribbing.

Row 11: Switch #153 to #183 and continue working in K2, P2 ribbing.

Rows 12 & 13: Switch #183 to #180 and continue working in K2, P2 ribbing.

Row 14 & 15: Switch #122 to #768 and continue working in K2, P2 ribbing.

Row 16: Switch #768 to #127 and continue working in K2, P2 ribbing.

Row 17: Work as established in Row 16.

Row 18: Break off #180 and purl to end using #127.

Cast off with tapestry needle using sewn cast-off. (See page 123.) This finishes the neckband.

<<Front bands>>

Work front band using 2.5mm circular needle (80cm), by picking up and knitting into all rows.

Make sure to adjust stitch count the next row (WS row). When working this row, the first and last 2 sts will be P sts and the remaining will be worked in K2, P2 ribbing.

Row 1: Using #272, pick up and knit a total of 291 sts for each left and right front band.

With RS facing, start from the edge of ribbing at hem for left front and from edge of neck band ribbing for right front.

NOTE: *When picking up and knitting stitches, begin from 1 stitch inside from the edge of the neckband or hem, and pick up and knit from in between the extra stitches and body (see p.22) When moving onto or working from a ribbing section, there will be a gap of half-a-stitch. Work over this gap tightly to make the gap less obvious.*

Row 2 (WS): After picking up and knitting 291 sts, tie #122 onto #272 and work in K2, P2 ribbing (P2 with #122, K2 with #272) beginning and ending with P2 sts. Decrease 1 st, either at the middle of row or where the gap may seem obvious.

Rows 3 to 6: Work as established in Row 2.

Work on RS, begging and ending with K2 sts.

Rows 7 to 14: Switch #122 to #140 and continue working in K2, P2 ribbing.

Rows 15 & 16: Switch #140 to #1130 and continue working in K2, P2 ribbing.

Row 17: Break off #140 and cast off using #1130 by knitting the K sts and purling the P sts. Be sure that the cast off does not loosen.

Work the other front band in the same way.

Treatment for extra stitches, see p.28.

Weaving in ends and washing, see p.28.

Make button holes, see p.31.

Make button holes in between stitches and work whip stitch around the hole.

The colouration

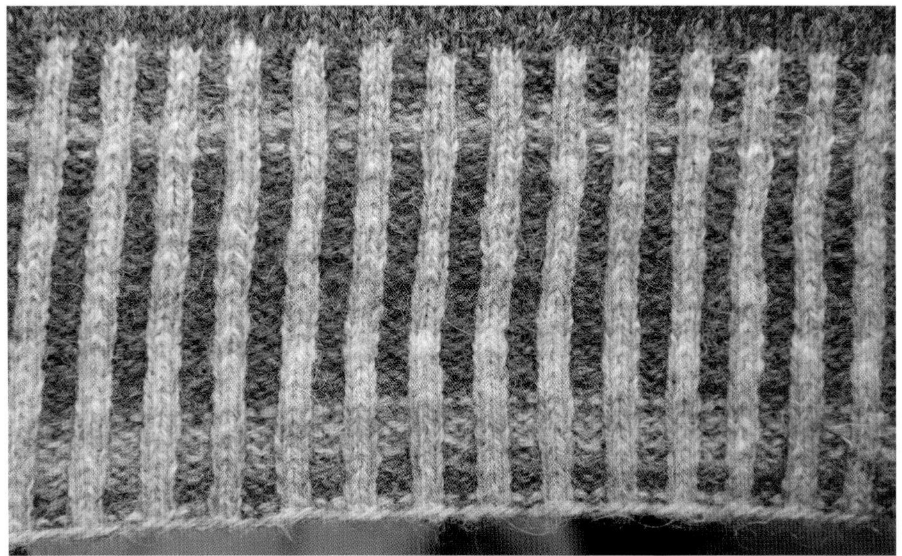

Rib detail

KNITTING CHART

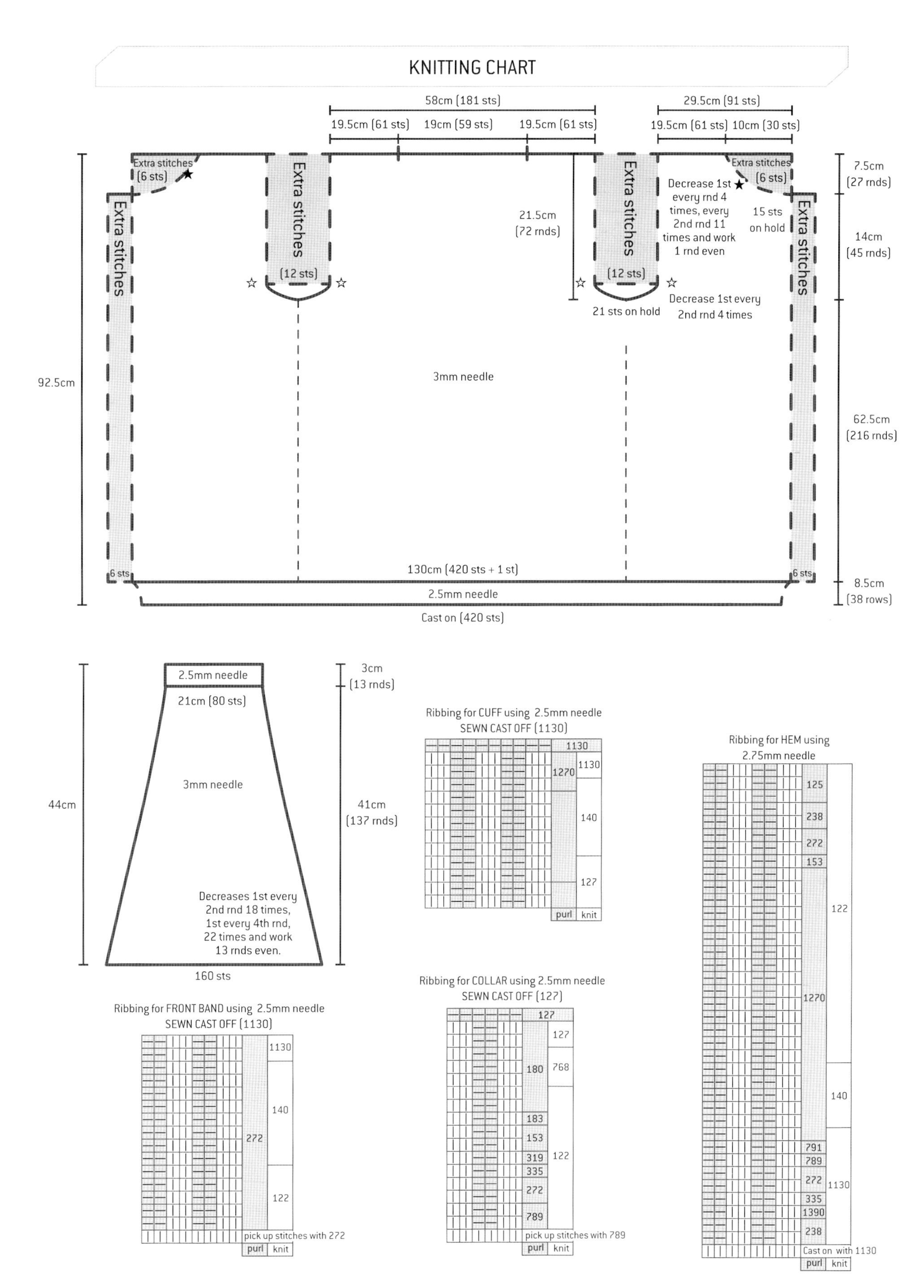

NOTE: Colour assignment for ribbing is based on how it will appear on RS

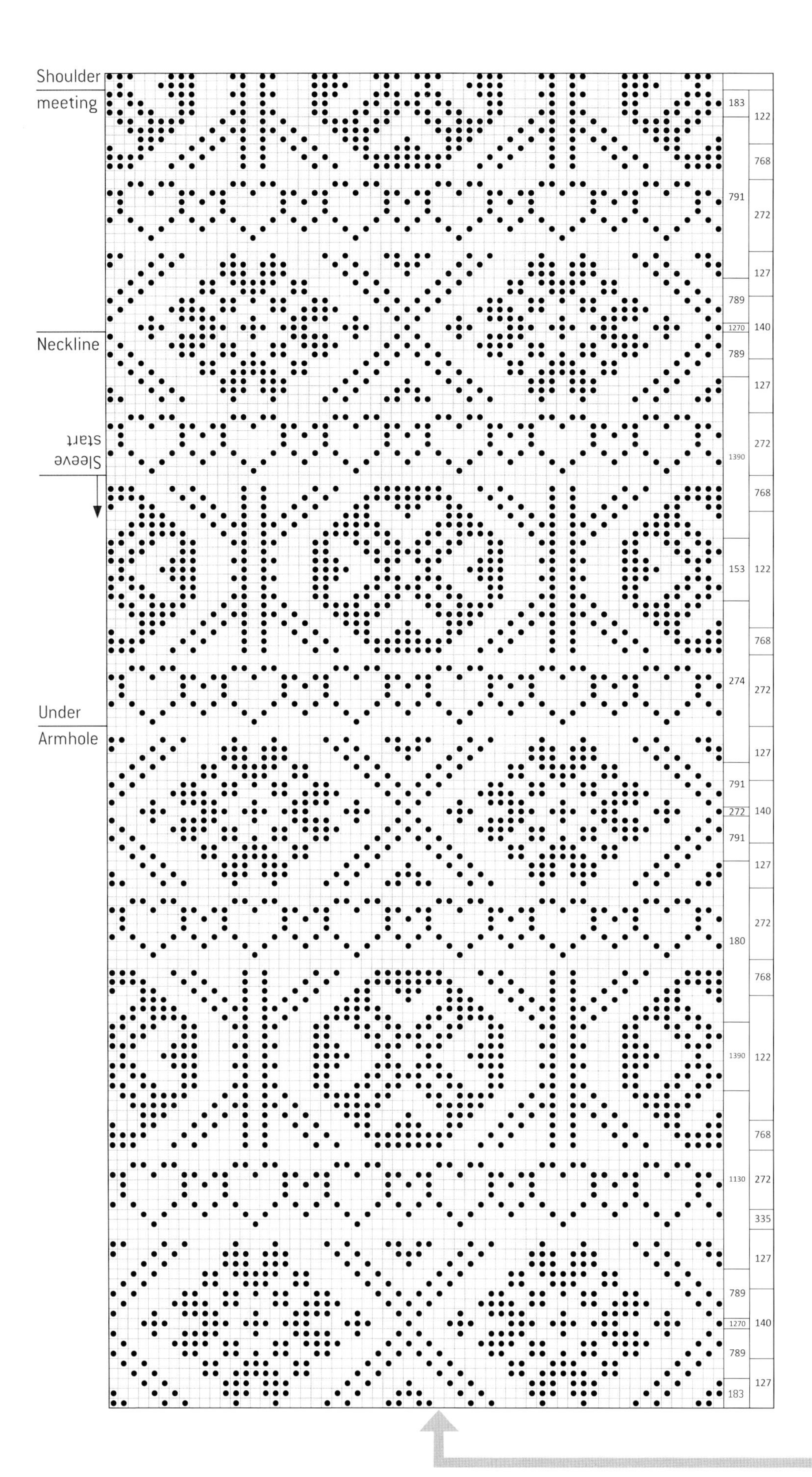
Shoulder meeting
Neckline
Sleeve start
Under Armhole
183
122
768
791
272
127
789
1270
140
789
127
272
1390
768
153
122
768
274
272
127
791
272
140
791
127
272
180
768
1390
122
768
1130
272
335
127
789
1270
140
789
127
183

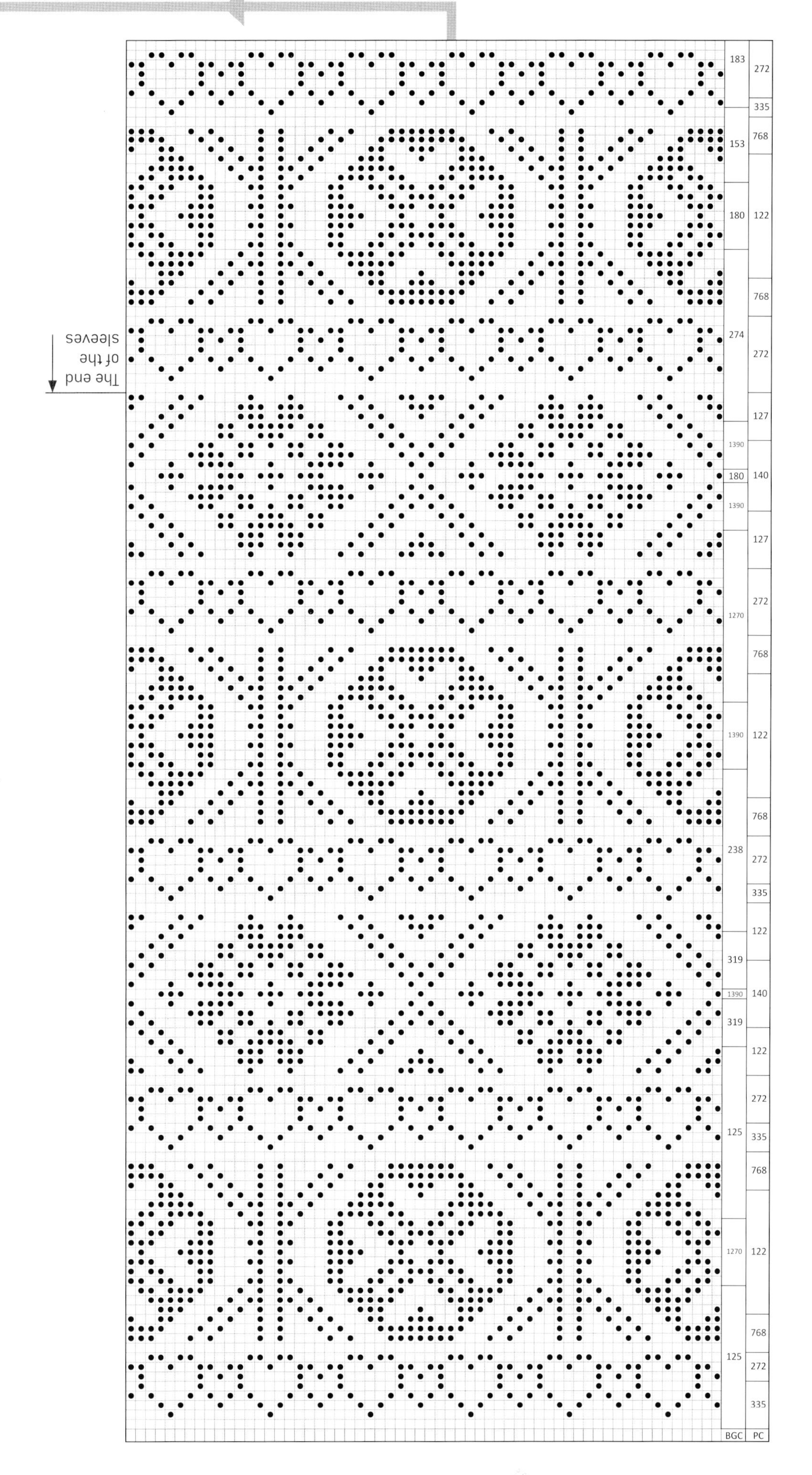
The end of the sleeves
183
272
335
153
768
180
122
768
274
272
127
1390
180
140
1390
127
272
1270
768
1390
122
768
238
272
335
122
319
1390
140
319
122
272
125
335
768
1270
122
768
125
272
335
BGC
PC

Water
Mill

”

This colouration overlaps with
the very old cherry blossom
tree facing my house.

“

4 SAKURA
Women's jumper

For this I used an old pattern 'Zig Zag' and simple colouration.
Both shaela (102) and rye (140) are my favourite colours
and that is why I named my yarn store 'Shaela'.
This colouration overlaps with the very old cherry blossom tree facing my house.

Yarn

Total 6 colours – 20 balls

102 (Shaela) 5 balls

103 (Sholmit) 4 balls

127 (Pebble) 4 balls

140 (Rye) 3 balls

343 (Ivory) 2 balls

550 (Rose) 2 balls

Total weight of jumper – 445g

Tools & Notions

Circular needles: 2.5mm (40 and 60cm), 3mm (60cm and 80cm or longer)

Crochet hook: 2.3mm

Tapestry needle: Small and medium

Waste yarn (to hold stitches)

Stitch markers

Tension

1 pattern stitch

(Medium) Flowers 12 sts x 11 rows = 3.7cm x 3cm

(Medium + Zigzag) Wave and Cross pattern

12 sts x 23 rows = 3.7cm x 6.5cm

Finished measurement

Bust circumference: 104cm (96cm, 111cm)

Back neck to sleeve edge: 74.5cm (72.5cm, 78cm)

Length: 59.5cm (59.5cm, 69cm)

INSTRUCTIONS

Worked in the round up to shoulders by working *extra stitches* in between for armholes and neck opening.

Ribbing for hem

Round 1: With 2.5mm 60cm circular needle and with colour #102 yarn, cast on 336 (312, 360) sts. Cast on is counted as 1 round.

Round 2: Tie #103 onto #102. Corrugated 2x2 ribbing is worked slightly differently – K1 with #102, K1 and P1 with #103, and P1 with #102. 1 knit st and 1 purl st are worked in the same colour.

Work 28 rnds in this variation of corrugated 2x2 ribbing and break yarn leaving a 3cm tail.

Body

<<Work to underarm>>

Round 1: Change to 3mm needle. Work 1 round with #140 by tying it onto either one of the remaining tail ends from the hem.

Rounds 2 to 115 (115, 145): Tie #127 onto #140 and work up to Round 115 (115, 145), by changing colours according to colour assignment. Then break yarn leaving a 3cm tail.

<<To make extra stitches for armholes and neck opening>>

1. After working Round 115 (115, 145)

   Thread yarn needle through first 10 (10, 11) sts, from BOR and 9 (9, 10) sts from EOR. So that 19 (19, 21) sts are on waste yarn to keep on hold for underarm.

   Make sure that the stitch at the centre of the held stitches always matches the centre of the pattern.

2. Identify which stitches are to be held for the opposite underarm. This is easier by looking at larger patterns as a guide. In this case, this will be the Rhombus (Flower) pattern right below the current pattern. The stitch between the 14th and 15th (13th and 14th, 15th and 16th) Rhombus (Flower) pattern repeat will be the 'centre stitch' for the opposite underarm. That will be 169th (157th, 181st) stitch from BOR. Follow this stitch together with 9 (9, 10) sts on each side all the way up to the current row, and they shall be kept on hold by threading waste through using tapestry needle, while they are still on cord of the circular needle. Be careful not to sew waste yarn into these stitches.

3. Stitch for neckline are also identified by the 'centre stitch', which is located between the 7th and 8th Rhombus (Flower) pattern

repeat. The 'centre stitch' of S-size is located at the centre of 7th pattern from BOR. The 'centre stitch' of L-size is located at the centre of 8th pattern from BOR. Follow this stitch to the current round and mark this stitch with waste yarn. (These centre stitches will be 85th, 79th, 91st stitch from BOR.)

Round 116 (116, 146): Remove the 19 (19, 21) sts for left underarm from needle. Cast on 6 sts on RH needle using #103 and #140 (#103 and #140, #127 and #140) yarn, and proceed working along the front body. Work based on colour assignment, but disregard those stitches which have been removed.

Work up to the stitch marked for neck opening. Remove the marked stitch from needle.

Cast on 12 sts on RH needle using #103 and #140 (#103 and #140, #127 and #140) yarn. (See p.33)

Continue working along the remaining front up to the held stitches for the right underarm. Remove held stitches from needle and cast on 12 sts. Continue working, disregarding the stitches removed from needle. Cast on 6 sts at EOR.

Extra stitches are now made for both armholes and neck opening.

NOTE: *From here on, no increases or decreases will be made within these extra stitches, and the extra stitches will be worked in stripes with the two colours used for working the round or in one colour if the round uses only one. (Refer to p.25 for working with extra stitches.)*

From the next round, work decreases for neckline, and 1st dec every 2nd rnd 3 times (all sizes are the same) for both armholes, while working three extra stitch sections during the round.

The first 6 extra stitches will be the BOR and all subsequent colour changes will be made here.

Round 117 (117, 147): Begin by working 6 *extra stitches* in stripes (see p.25) and knit the first 2 left front sts together, then work according to colour assignment until the 2 sts before neck opening, then SKPO (Sl1, K1, pass slipped st over knit st) using #103 (#140, #127). Work 12 *extra stitches* for neck opening, followed by K2tog the first 2 body sts using #103 (#140, #127).

Work until the 2 sts before the *extra stitches* for the other armhole, SKPO these 2 sts, then work *extra stitches* in stripes as before.

Continue working the back until the 2 sts before the remaining 6 *extra stitches*, SKPO these 2 sts and then work *extra stitches* in stripes. Round to 193 (193, 227).

Round 118 (118, 148) onward:

Work body and *extra stitches* according to colour assignment, and at the same time work decreases (as done in Round 117 on both sides of the neck opening) 1st every 2nd round 9 (9, 13) times, then 1st every 4th rnd 14 (14, 13) times and then work 2 rnds even (all sizes are the same). Break yarn leaving a 3cm tail.

Join shoulders

1. Prepare for shoulder seam by working 1 additional row for back by slipping stitches onto RH needle, up to the centre of *extra stitches* for right sleeve.
2. Tie a knot using #343 and #102 (all sizes are the same) yarn which will be used for working the additional row. Leave a 3cm tail for #343 and about three times the shoulder length for #102. The knot will be used as a 'stopper', and will be worked from the centre of the *extra stitches* for right sleeve, across back body, to the centre of *extra stitches* on the other side.

   Leave the BGC as is and cut PC leaving a 3cm tail.
3. Turn the work inside out.

   Using the remaining #102 yarn and crochet hook, work three needles cast-off starting from the shoulder edge.

   Cast off the 6 *extra stitches* for the neckband separately using slip stitch cast-off. (Make sure that the *extra stitches* are not joined together with back neckband.) (See p.21)
4. Join the other shoulder as well, using three needles cast-off with #102 yarn which was kept longer, and cast off *extra stitches* using slip stitch cast-off.
5. Unravel backneck stitches. Cut the unravelled yarn at the middle and tie at the base of both shoulders.

Sleeves

1. Cut open at the centre of *extra stitches* and pick up and knit into all underarm stitches and rows beginning at the centre of the held stitches using #127 (#127, #140) yarn. Pick up and knit stitches from between *extra stitches* and body. (See page 22.) Adjust stitch count to 160 (160, 168) sts on the second round.
2. Decrease at inside sleeve every 2nd rnd 12 times (all sizes are the same), every 4th rnd 18 (18, 16) times, every 6th rnd 10 times (10, 14) and then work 18 (18, 12) rnds even.

Decrease by knitting to the last st of the previous round (the round before the decrease), slip the last st onto RH needle unworked, and then work a double decrease (SK2PO = Sl1, K2tog, pass slipped st over knit st) between the last st of the previous round and the first 2 sts of the decrease round. This way, the decrease for inside sleeves will not be missed.

<<Cuff>>

3. After working 174 (174, 184) rnds for sleeve, change to 2.5mm circular needle and work in the variation of corrugated 2x2 ribbing, using #102 and #103 yarn as described for hem (1 knit st and 1 purl st worked in the same colour) for 14 rounds. Finish by casting off using tapestry needle with #102. (See sewn cast off on p. 123.)
4. Work other sleeve in the same way.

Neckband

Work in round, by cutting open at the centre of *extra stitch*.

Round 1: Using 2.75mm circular needle and #102 yarn, pick up all stitches and rows beginning at the right back neck. Pick up row is counted as 1 rnd.

Round 2: Tie #103 yarn, and work the variation of corrugated 2x2 ribbing, (1 knit st and 1 purl st worked in the same colour). Decrease 1 st (1 st, 3 sts) for back neck. To work left-front neckline. And then work a Centered Double Decrease (CDD or S2KPO = slip 2 stitches tog knitwise, knit next st and pass slipped stitches over) at the bottom of the 'V' for every rnd. During this round, work until the 2 sts before the marked stitch, purl 1, work CDD, purl 1, and then knit 2 and so on. Make sure that the marked stitch is always the centre stitch of CDD.

Round 3: Continue working 10 more rnds, while decreasing at the bottom of 'V'.

Finish by casting off with #102 yarn and using tapestry needle and by making CDD. (See sewn cast off on page 123.)

When decreasing every rnd at the bottom of 'V', the stitches on both sides of the CDD will keep changing from purl 1, or knit 2, but are always symmetrical.

TIP: As it may be confusing when working with the same colour for 1 knit st and 1 purl st for the 2x2 ribbing, try focusing on the 2x2 ribbing.

An alternative is to cast off with #102 by knitting K sts and purling P sts, being careful not to cast off too tightly. CDD should be worked at the bottom of the 'V' as well.

Treatment for extra stitches, see p.28.

Weaving in ends and washing, see p.28.

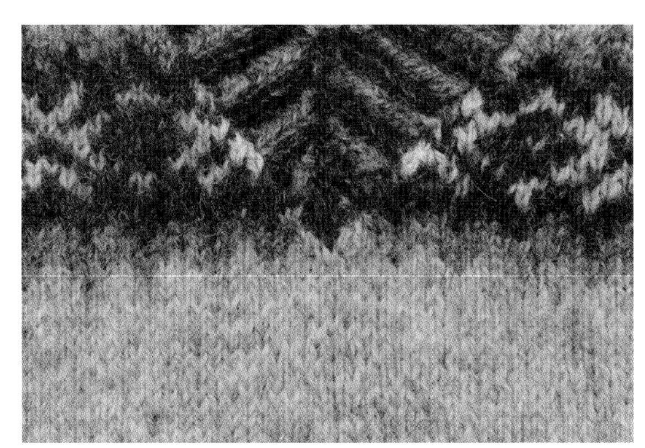

V-neck detail

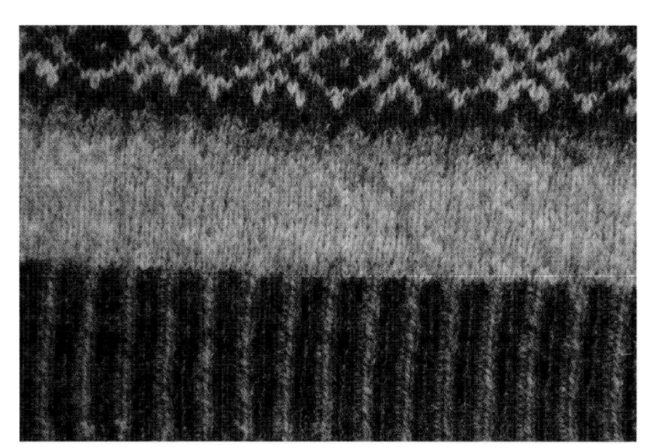

Rib detail

Pattern detail

KNITTING CHART

● = Large size

● = Medium size

● = Small size

44cm (143 sts) 40cm (131 sts) 47cm (153 sts)

15cm (49 sts) 17cm (55 sts) 15cm (49 sts)
12.5cm (41 sts) 15cm (49 sts) 12.5cm (41 sts)
14.5cm (47 sts) 15cm (49 sts) 14.5cm (47 sts)

Extra stitches

6 sts

Extra stitches

12 sts

Extra stitches

Extra stitches

6 sts

22cm (78 rnds)
22cm (78 rnds)
23cm (82 rnds)

Decrease 1st every 2nd rnd 10 times, 1st every 4th rnd 14 times and work 2 rnds even.

Decrease 1st every 2nd rnd 14 times, 1st every 4th rnd 13 times and work 2 rnds even.

Decrease 1st every 2nd rnd 3 times

1st on hold

59.5cm
59.5cm
69cm

(9 sts)
(10 sts)
On hold

(19 sts)
(21 sts)
On hold

(10 sts)
(11 sts)
On hold

22cm (78 rnds)
22cm (78 rnds)
23cm (82 rnds)

32cm (115 rnds)
32cm (115 rnds)
40.5cm (145 rnds)

3mm needle

104 (336 sts) 96cm (312 sts) 111cm (360 sts)

1 needle / 2.5mm

5.5cm
(28 rnds)

Cast on (336 sts) (312 sts) (360 sts)

1 needle / 2.5mm

3cm
(14 rnds)

24cm (80 sts)
24cm (80 sts)
26cm (84 sts)

3mm needle

52.5cm
52.5cm
55cm

49.5 (174 rnds)
49.5 (174 rnds)
52 (184 rnds)

Decrease 1st every 2nd rnd 12 times, 1st every 4th rnd 16 times, 1st every 6th rnd 4 times and work 12 rnds even.

Decrease 1st every 2nd rnd 12 times, 1st every 4th rnd 18 times, 1st every 6th rnd 10 times and work 18 rnds even.

Pick up stitches for neckband total stitch 203 sts (203 sts, 215 sts)

1st on hold

Ribbing for HEM using 2.5mm needle

··· 103

··· 102

Cast on with 102

Ribbing for CUFF using 2.5mm needle

102 SEWN CAST OFF

··· 103

··· 102

Ribbing for NECKBAND using 2.75mm needle

102 SEWN CAST OFF

··· 103

··· 102

Pick up stitches with 102

NOTE: Colour assignment for ribbing is based on how it will appear on RS

Variation of 2X2 ribbing: change colours after every (k1, p1) and (p1, k1)

BGC	PC
140	103
103	102
343	102
103	102
140	103
127	140
127	550
127	140
140	103
103	102
343	102
103	102
140	103
127	140
127	550
127	140

Some of the shells have extremely lovely gradation of colours which I tried to show in this work.

5 THE VOICES OF MUSSELS
Women's jumper

A beautiful and clear sea surrounds Shetland. Moreover, it's cold water produces good mussels. Some of their shells have extremely lovely gradation of colours which I tried to show in this work. I have changed the proportion of the background colour to express the 'surge in' (surge of the waves coming in).

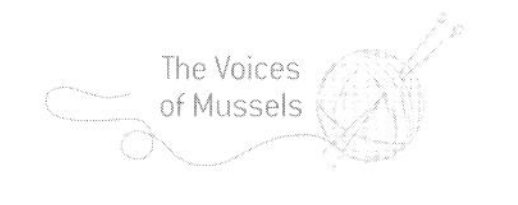

Yarn

Total 8 colours – 25 balls

 127 (Pebble) 3 balls

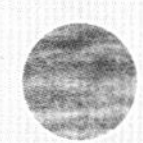 180 (Mist) 3 balls

 322 (Lomond) 6 balls

 547 (Orchid) 2 balls

 562 (Cyclamen) 2 balls

 603 (Pot-pourri) 1 ball

 630 (Dove) 4 balls

 768 (Egg Shell) 4 balls

Total weight of jumper – 468g

Tools & Notions

Circular needles: 2mm (40cm), 2.5mm (40cm, 60cm and 80cm or longer), 3mm (40cm, 60cm and 80cm or longer)

Crochet hook: 2.3mm

Tapestry needle: Small and medium

Waste yarn (to hold stitches)

Stitch markers

Tension

1 pattern stitch

(Medium) Zigzag pattern 6 sts x 13 rows = 1.2cm x 4cm

(Medium) The diamond + small heart 6 sts x 25 rows = 1.2cm x 7.2cm (Including single colour rows underneath and on top)

Finished measurement

Bust circumference: 106cm

Back neck to sleeve edge: 77cm

Length: 61cm

INSTRUCTIONS

Worked in the round up to shoulders by working *extra stitches* in between for armholes and neck opening.

Ribbing for hem

Round 1: With 2.5mm 60cm circular needle and with colour #322 yarn, cast on 360 sts. Cast on is counted as 1 round.

Rounds 2 & 3: Tie #180 onto #322 and work in corrugated 2x2 ribbing by repeating [K2 with #322, P2 with #180].

Rounds 4 to 6: Switch #322 to #630 and work in corrugated 2x2 ribbing by knitting P sts and purling K sts – [P2 with #180, K2 with #630].

Rounds 7 to 14: Switch #630 to #322 and work in corrugated 2x2 ribbing as in Row 2, by repeating [K2 with #322, P2 with #180].

Round 15: Switch #180 to #630, and work in corrugated 2x2 ribbing, by repeating [K2 with #322, P2 with #630].

Break 162 yarn leaving a 3cm tail, leaving #630 yarn.

Body

<<To work to underarm>>

Round 1: Change to 3mm needle. Work 1 round with #630 which is the remaining tail from the hem.

Rounds 2 to 113: Tie #127 onto #630, work according to colour assignment, changing BGC and PC, and continue working up to Round 113.

NOTE: *The Diamond shape surrounded by the small Heart pattern repeats the same colour combination, but the zigzag pattern repeats a different balance of three colour combinations.*

<<To make *extra stitches* for neck opening>>

After working Round 113: Thread waste yarn through the centre stitch for front body (91st stitch from BOR). This stitch will be kept on hold for neck opening.

Round 114: Work according to colour assignment and work until the 2 sts before neckline. SKPO these 2 sts.

Remove the held centre stitch from needle and cast on 12 sts on RH needle using #630. Then knit the next 2 body sts together (K2tog). This decreases 1 st on each side of the neckline.

Continue working decreases for neckline by working 2 sts together once every 2nd rnd 3 times, every 4th rnd 20 times, and work 1 rnd even before reaching shoulder.

NOTE: *The extra stitches will be worked in stripes. (Refer to p.25 for working with extra stitches.)*

Rounds 115 to 125: Work up to Round 125. Then break #322 and #768 both leaving a 3cm tail.

<<To make *extra stitches* for armhole>>

After working Round 125: To make *extra stitches* for armhole, thread waste yarn using yarn needle through 21 underarm sts on each side. For the first set of underarm sts this will be last 10 sts from EOR and the first 11 sts from BOR. The underarm sts for the other side can be identified by the centre stitch of Diamond shaped pattern which is the 30th st of the pattern (181st stitch from BOR). Thread waste yarn through this st together with 10 sts on each side, 21 sts all together. (These stitches will still be on the cord of the circular needle.)

NOTE: *As most Fair Isle patterns are symmetrical vertically and horizontally, it is quite easy to identify the centre stitch for underarm. But be sure to mark the centre underarm stitch and count the pattern repeats on the front and back of body to check that they are the same.*

Round 126: Remove the 21 stitches left underarm with waste yarn from needle. Cast on 6 sts on RH needle using #180 and #322. Proceed working along the front body according to colour assignment but disregard those stitches which have been removed. Work left front, the *extra stitches* for neck opening in stripes, then right front, up to the stitches held for the right underarm.

Remove underarm stitches from needle. Cast on 12 sts, and work until EOR, disregarding those stitches which have been removed. Cast on 6 sts at EOR.

Extra stitches for both underarms are now made. (Refer to p.25 for working with *extra stitches*.)

Round 127: Begin working decreases for armholes 1 st every 2nd rnd 5 times for both sides while.

Round 127 will be worked as follows:

Begin by working 6 *extra stitches,* K2tog, then work left front the neckline *extra stitches*, right front until the 2 sts before *extra stitches* for right armhole, then SKPO (Sl1, K1, pass slipped st over knit st).

Knit the *extra stitches* on the other side.
Followed by K2tog the first 2 back body sts. Then work back body until 2 sts remain, then SKPO (Sl1, K1, pass slipped st over knit st), and lastly work the remaining 6 *extra stitches*. This completes the round.

Rounds 128 to 201: Continue working according to colour assignment whole working both decreases for neckline and armholes.

Work up to shoulder, then break both #322 and #768 leaving a 3cm tail.

Join shoulders

1. Prepare for shoulder seam by working 1 additional row for back by slipping stitches onto RH needle, up to the centre of *extra stitches* for right sleeve.
2. Tie a knot using #180 and #322 yarn which will be used for working the additional row. Leave a 3cm tail for #180 and about three times the shoulder length for #322. The knot will be used as a 'stopper', and will be worked from the centre of the *extra stitches* for right sleeve, across back body based on colour assignment, to the centre of *extra stitches* on the other side.

   Leave #322 as is and cut #180 leaving a 3cm tail.
3. Turn the work inside out.

   Using the remaining #322 yarn and crochet hook, work three needle cast-off (See p.21) starting from the shoulder edge. Cast off the 6 *extra stitches* for the neckband separately using slip stitch cast-off.

   (Make sure that the *extra stitches* are not joined together with back neckband.)
4. Join the other shoulder as well, using three needle cast-off with #162 yarn which was kept longer, and cast off *extra stitches* using slip stitch cast-off.
5. Unravel back neck stitches. Cut the unravelled yarn at the middle and tie at the base of both shoulder.

Sleeves

1. Cut open at the centre of *extra stitches* and pick up and knit into all stitches and rows beginning at the centre of the held stitches using #630 yarn and 3mm needle (40cm). Pick up and knit stitches from between *extra stitches* and body. (See p.22) Adjust stitch count to 172 sts on the second round.
2. Decrease at inside sleeve every 2nd rnd 18 times, every 4th rnd 28 times, and then work 29 rnds even.

   Decrease by knitting to the last st of the previous round (the round before the decrease), slip the last st onto RH needle unworked, and then work a double decrease (SK2PO = Sl1, K2tog, pass slipped st over knit st) between the last st of the previous round and the first 2 stitches of the decrease round. This way, the decrease for inside sleeves will not be missed.

<<Cuff>>

3. **Round 1:** After working 177 rnds for sleeve, change to 2.5mm circular needle and work in corrugated 2x2 [K2 with #322, P2 with #630] for 1 round.

   Rounds 2 to 10: Switch from #630 to #180 and work in corrugated 2x2 [K2 with #322, P2 with #180] for 9 rnds.

   Rounds 11 & 12: Use same colour yarn #180 and #322 and work in corrugated 2x2 ribbing by knitting P sts and purling K sts [P2 with #180, K2 with #322].

   Round 13: Break #180 leaving a 3cm tail. Purl with #322 to EOR.

   Finish by casting off with #322 and tapestry needle. [See sewn cast off on p.121 or 113]

4. Work other sleeve in the same way.

Neckband

Using 2mm circular needle [40cm long], pick up and knit from every stitch and row. This jumper's band is knitted with stockinette stitches and made double

Round 1: Cut open at the centre of extra stitches using 2mm circular needle [40cm] and #562, pick up and knit all stitches and rows beginning at the right back neck.

Round 2: After picking up and knitting 226 sts, adjust stitch count to a total of 192 sts by decreasing 8 sts along back neck, and 13 stitches along each side of the front neckline.

Centred 4-st: Decrease will be worked every round by working until the 2 sts before the held stitches, then slip the next 3 sts together knitwise onto RH needle, knit the next 2 sts together and pass the slipped 3 sts over knit stitch.

Make sure that the centre stitch of the 4-st decrease is the centre stitch of the held stitches.

Round 3 to 11: Work 10 more rnds working the 4-st decrease on every round.

Round 12: P with #332 [change from #562.]

Rounds 13 to 22: Knit and at the same time, increase 1 st on both sides of the centre front stitch of the V neck by knitting into the front and back loop of the same stitch.

Using tapestry needle, fold the section worked with #322 to the WS of garment and sew down evenly to the base of the fabric worked with #562.

TIP: When folding the bottom point of front neckline be sure not to sew them down too tight.

NOTE: *The V neck will loosen if the knit stitches for the neckline border are worked loosely. If this is a concern, it is recommended that the gauge be checked in stockinette stitch in advance, and the stitch count be adjusted accordingly.*

Treatment for extra stitches, see p.28.

Weaving in ends and washing, see p.28.

KNITTING CHART

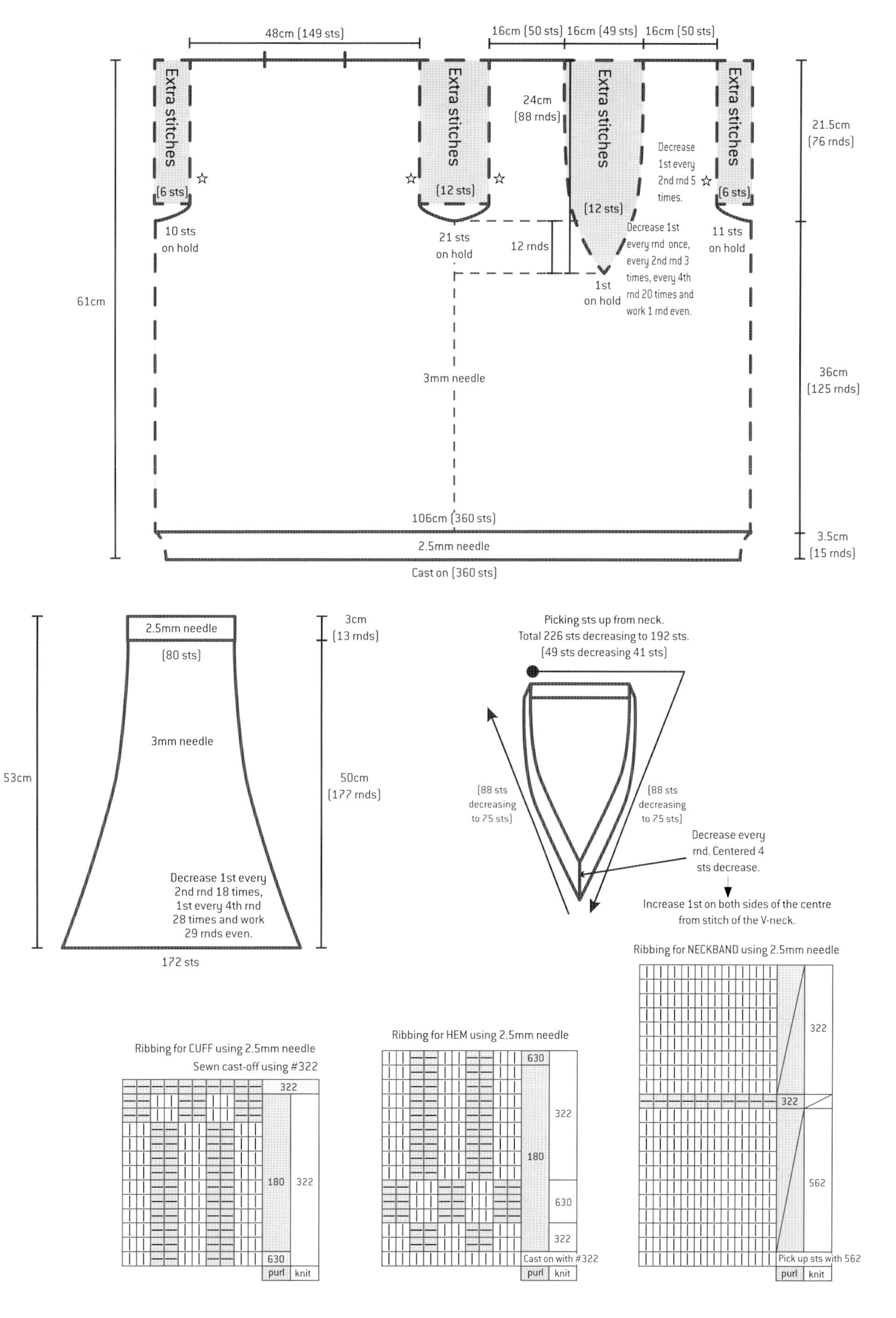

NOTE: Colour assignment for ribbing is based on how it will appear on RS

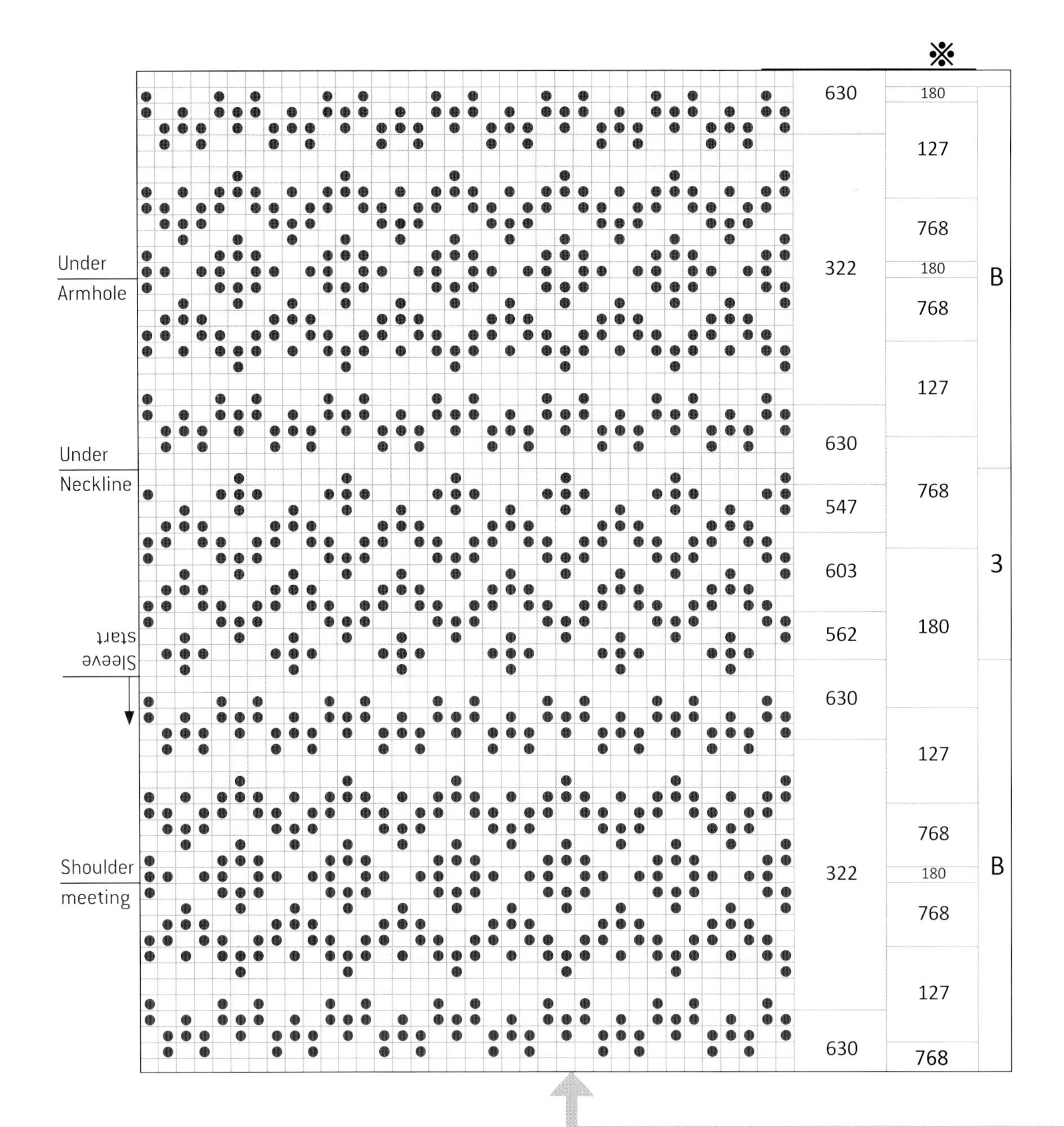

※
630
180
127
322
768
180
768
B
Under
Armhole
127
630
Under
Neckline
768
547
603
3
180
562
Sleeve
start
630
127
322
768
180
768
B
Shoulder
meeting
127
630
768

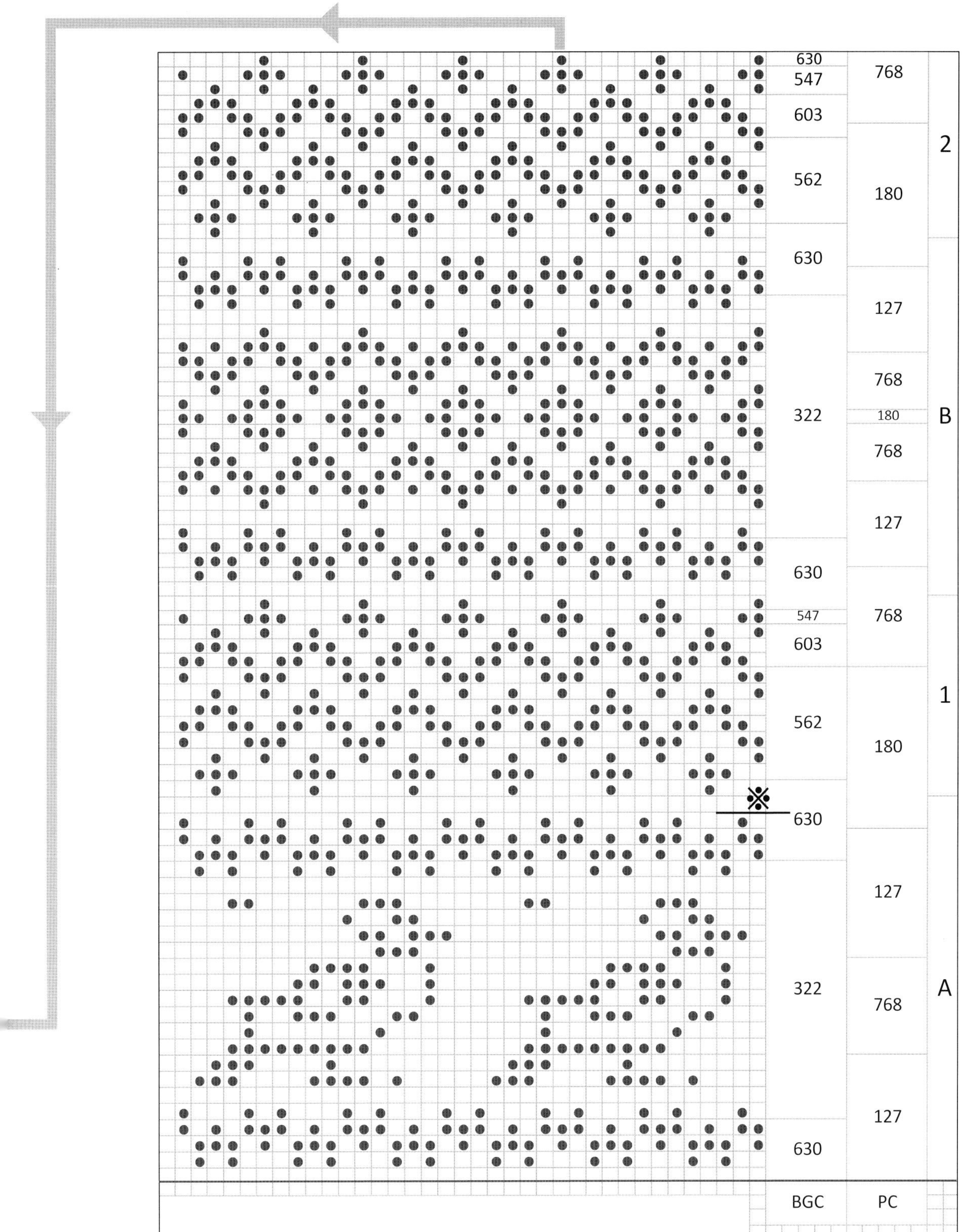

630
547
603
562
630
322
630
547
603
562
※
630
322
630

768
180
127
768
180
768
127
768
180
127
768
127

2
B
1
A

BGC PC

Begin to follow A (is only once at beginning)
and then repeat -1-B-2-B-3-B-4-B

Elegance intermingles with
charm, like herself.

6 COCKATIEL
Women's tailcoat

My dear friend left this very simple colouration as a keepsake.
Elegance intermingles with charm, like herself. I am proud of the flounce of the tail.
It is a complicated one but also an enjoyable one to knit.

Yarn

Total 4 colours – 25 balls

 140 (Rye) 7 balls

 268 (Dog Rose) 1 ball

 365 (Chartreuse) 13 balls

 547 (Orchid) 4 balls

Total weight of jacket – 588g

Tools & Notions

Circular needles: 2.5mm (40 and 80cm or longer)
2.75mm (40, 60 and 80cm or longer)
3mm (40, 60 and 80cm or longer)

Crochet hook: 2mm or 2.3mm

Tapestry needle: Small and medium

Crochet hook: 2mm and 2.3mm

Waste yarn (to hold stitches)

Stitch markers

Tension

1 pattern stitch

(Larger) 24 sts x 19 rows (including single colour rows underneath and on top) = 8cm x 5.7cm

(Medium) 24 sts x 13 rows = 8cm x 4cm

Finished measurement

Bust circumference:105cm

Back neck to sleeve: 76cm

Length: 99cm at back, 42cm at front

INSTRUCTIONS

* This jacket uses traditional Fair Isle knitting techniques and short rows for a swallow-tail like finish. Note that the stitch counts are not evenly divided between the front and the back of body. *Extra stitche*s for the upper body and lower body are made separately, which adds more work, but is rewarding in the end.

Lower body: After cast on, the stitches before and after *extra stitche*s are increased using KFB (knitting into the front and back of the same stitch) twice every 2nd rnd 23 times, and then once every 2nd rnd 48 times.

Round 1: With 3mm 60cm circular needle and colour #365 yarn, cast on 99 sts and break yarn leaving a 3cm tail.

Round 2: To work in the round with the knit side of the cast-on stitches facing, cast on 6 sts with #365 on RH needle. Knit first st on LH needle and KFB twice, K93, KFB twice and K last st. Continue casting on 6 sts. (*Extra stitches* for lower body are now made.)

Round 3: Tie #547 yarn onto #365 and slide the tied knot to the base of working yarn. Place a stitch marker on RH needle and (K1 in PC #547, K1 in BGC #365) 3 times. (Refer to p.25 for working with *extra stitche*s.)

Begin working according to colour assignment.

However, for this garment, 2 sts on both ends are always worked in the BGC #365. Therefore proceed working 2 sts with #365, 2 sts with #547, the next 3 sts with #365. The last 2 sts of the body are worked with #365, followed by the *extra stitche*s (K1 with #365, K1 with #547) 3 times. This completes Round 3.

Round 4: Switch #365 yarn to #140 and work *extra stitche*s after the marker. Work 2 sts with #140 and KFB twice with the colour as per colour assignment. Which means that the 2 sts for the first KFB will be worked with #140, but for the second KFB work the first st with #547 through the front loop and the second with #140 through the back loop. Follow the colour assignment accordingly, and the 4th stitch from last will be worked with #140 through the front loop and with #547 through the back loop. The following KFB will be worked with #140 as well as the last 2 sts.

Rounds 5 to 47: Work up to Round 47, working increases and subsequent rounds based on the colour changes resulting from these increases. But the first and last 2 sts will always be worked in the BGC. Increases will be made with the 3rd and 4th stitch from the

BOR and EOR on every 2nd rnd. This approach helps when working the border.

Round 48: Knit the first 2 sts and KFB (as done before) in the 3rd stitch with #365, and KFB into the 3rd stitch from last st and knit remaining 2 sts with #365.

Continue increasing in the same way every 2nd rnd 47 more times. (48 times in total.)

Round 143: Cast off 6 *extra stitch*es at the BOR, work evenly for body, then cast off 6 *extra stitch*es at EOR. (287 sts on needle.)

Upper body

Cast on stitches on both ends of the lower body (including *extra stitch*es) and work in the round. Decreases will be worked at the centre front, *extra stitch*es will be made for armholes and worked up to shoulders.

Making left and right front body

Round 1 (Round 144 from bttom): Work the first st with #365, and continue casting on 79 sts using the knitted cast-on.

Tie #547 onto #365. The first 6 sts will be the *extra stitch*es, so work (#547, #365) 3 times, then work according to colour assignment – with #365, K2tog (knitting 2 sts together) and work 4 sts, then #547, #365, #547, then 2 sts with #365, and continuing on to the EOR.

Leave #547 as is and with #365 cast on 79 sts using the backloop cast-on, then break #365 leaving a 3cm tail. (Total 313 sts on needle.)

Tie #365 onto #547 and work according to colour assignment. Work SKPO (slip, knit, pass slipped st over) with the 8th and 7th stitch from last, and the last 6 *extra stitch*es in (#365, #547) 3 times.

Extra stitches for upper body are now made.

This will be the basis for working the upper body in the round. Work according to colour assignment while decreasing at BOR and EOR every 2nd rnd 41 times, every 3rd rnd 12 times and then work 1 round even to shoulder.

<<To make *extra stitches* for armhole>>

After working Round 56: The 96th stitch from BOR, excluding *extra stitch*es, will be the first of 17 sts to be held on waste yarn for the underarm. Make sure the 17 sts matches the stitches marked in the colour chart (See p.89) In the same way, the 96th stitch from EOR, excluding extra stitches, will also be the first of 17 sts to be held on waste yarn for the underarm on the other side. For both sets of 17 sts, thread waste yarn using tapestry needle.

Round 57: The *extra stitch*es in stripes using #268 and #140. And then knit next 2 body sts following the *extra stitch*es together (K2 together) and continue to work 94 sts according to colour assignment. Remove held stitches from needle.

Cast on 12 sts using #140 and #268 (See p.33) and continue working.

When reaching the stitches held for the other underarm, remove the stitches threaded with waste yarn from needle, and then cast on 12 sts using #140 and #268 yarn. Work until the 2 sts before the *extra stitch*es, SKPO these 2 sts and work *extra stitch*es. This completes Round 57 and *extra stitch*es are made for both armholes.

Rounds 58, 60, 62: When working the *extra stitch*es for sleeve opening, SKPO the 2 sts before the *extra stitch*es, work *extra stitch*es and K2tog the 2 sts following the *extra stitch*es. These are decreasing for both sides of armholes.

Work **Rounds 59 and 61** even.

Continue decreasing at BOR and EOR, at the same time working the decreases for front bands.

Join shoulders

Round 121: Cast off the *extra stitch*es using #268 and #140 alternately. Continue working body stitches up to the *extra stitch*es at EOR and cast off these *extra stitch*es in the same way. Break yarn.

1. Prepare for shoulder seam by working 1 additional row for back by slipping stitches onto RH needle, up to the centre of *extra stitches* for right sleeve.
2. Tie a knot using #140 and #268 yarn which will be used for working the additional row. Leave a 3cm tail for #268 and about three times the shoulder length for #140.

   The knot will be used as a 'stopper', and will be worked from the centre of the *extra stitch*es for right sleeve, across back body to the centre of *extra stitch*es on the other side.

   Leave the BGC #140 as is and cut PC #268 leaving a 3cm tail. Move to below.
3. Turn the work inside out.

   Use the remaining #140 yarn and crochet hook to work three needle cast-off to join 38 sts for front and back shoulders, beginning at the left shoulder edge. Cut yarn. Join 38 sts for right shoulder in the same way using the #140 tail.

4. Join the other shoulder as well, using three needles cast-off with crochet hook with #183 yarn which was kept longer, cast-off *extra stitches* using slip stitch cast-off.
5. Unravel back neck stitches. Cut the unravelled yarn at the middle and tie at the base of both shoulders.

Collar

Row 1: Using 2.5mm 40cm needle and #365 yarn, pick up and knit all stitches from right front, back and to left front neckline.

Rows 2 to 43: On Row 2, adjust stitch count to 124 sts Begin on the WS row by P3 and continue working in 2x2 ribbing repeating with #365 yarn, end with P3.

All even numbered rows: Work as Row 2; and all odd numbered rows: Repeat [K2, P2], be sure to begin and end with K3.

Then cast off using tapestry needle. (Refer to sewn cast off on page 123.)

TIP: When decreasing to adjust stitch count, work 2 sts together at the transition between front and back collar to even out gaps.

Sleeves

Cut open at the centre of the *extra stitch*es. Work in round.

Round 1: Using 3mm needle 40cm and with #365 yarn, pick up and knit 148 sts.

Rounds 2 to 120: Work according to colour assignment, and decrease 1 st at inside sleeve every 2nd rnd 10 times, and then every 4th rnd, 20 times. Then work 20 rounds even.

Change to shorter circulars to accommodate for the fewer stitches. (Use shorter circulars or use techniques such as the magic loop.) See p.26-32.

TIP: For decreasing at inside sleeve: Decrease by knitting to the last st of the previous round, slip the last st onto RH needle unworked, and then work a double decrease (SK2PO = Sl1, K2tog, pass slipped st over knit st) between the last st of the previous round and the first 2 sts of the decrease round. This is a method I learned that will not interrupt the pattern by working the decreases. Also the decreases for inside sleeves will not be missed.

<<Cuff>>

Rounds 1 to 18: Change to 2.5mm circular needle and work in 2x2 ribbing for 18 rnds.

Round 19 (Increase round): Change to 2.75mm needle and increase by making 1 purl st in between the 2 purl sts of the 2x2 ribbing already established: Repeat [K2, P1, M1P (make 1 purl st by picking up the strand running between the next st and purling it through the back loop), P1] until EOR. (110 sts in total.)

Rounds 20 to 50: Work as established, repeating (K2, P3).

Cast off in the same way as for collar.

Work the same for other sleeve.

Front bands

Worked flat in reverse stockinette stitch and box stitch using two different size needles.

This border can be used for other items as well.

Row 1: Pick up stitches from every row for front band using 2.5mm needle and #365 yarn, from the bottom of hem ribbing for right front and from the neck edge for left front.

Row 2 (WS): Adjust stitch count to 36 sts while knitting both right and left collars and decrease the body section stitches from 121 to 118 sts. Total 154 sts in front band in knit.

Row 3 (RS): With 2.5mm needle and RS facing, work 1 more row in purl (reverse stockinette).

Row 4 (WS): Change to 3mm needle. Tie #140 to #365 and repeat (P2 with #365, K2 with #140) until 2 sts remain at EOR, and end in P2 with #365.

Row 5 (RS): Repeat (K2 with #365, P2 with #140) and end in K2 with #365.

Row 6 (WS): Change #140 to #268 and repeat (K2 with #268, P2 with #365) and end in K2 with #268.

Row 7 (RS): Repeat (P2 with #268, K2 with #365,) and end in P2 with #268.

The pattern stitch here alternates 2 knit sts and 2 purl sts every 2 rows.

Rows 8 & 9: Change #268 back to #140 and work as Row 4 and 5.

Row 10 (WS) to Row 14: Switch needle back to 2.5mm needle, and work in reverse stockinette stitch for 5 rows.

With the RS facing cast off in purl.

NOTE: *Here, it is better to cast off normally rather than using tapestry needles for the reverse stockinette stitch curl better.*

Work the other front band in the same way by picking up stitches with the RS facing.

Border for Hem

Worked by using three needle sizes (2.5mm, 2.75, and 3mm). 3 knit sts stay the same while the purl sts are increased to create the

elegant movement at the lower back body. #365 yarn is used and worked flat throughout.

*** Upper body (p.88 B-3)**

Row 1: With the RS of work facing, pick up and knit all stitches using 2.5mm needle, from the bottom of front band and along the 73 sts cast on for upper body.

Row 2 (WS): Repeat (P3, K2) while adjusting stitch count to be 78 sts, and end with P3.

Row 3 (RS): Repeat (K3, P2) and end with K3.

Rows 4 to 12: Repeat Rows 2 and 3. Then cast off using tapestry needle. (Refer to sewn cast off on page 123.)

Work the other side in the same way and cast off.

* **Lower body (p.88 B-4)**

Row 1 (RS): With collar facing towards you and using 2.5mm needle, pick up and knit all stitches starting from the stitches along the front bottom body to your right continuing along the bottom cast-on edge and then from all along the front edge of the opposite side of body.

Row 2 (WS): Repeat (P3, K2) while adjusting stitch count to 383 sts, and end the row with P3.

Row 3 (RS): Repeat (K3, P2) ending the row with K3.

Row 4 (WS): Change to 2.75mm needle, repeat (P3, K1, M1K, K1) ending the row with P3.

Row 5 (RS): Repeat (K3, P3) ending the row with K3.

Row 6 (WS): Repeat (P3, K3) ending the row with P3.

Rows 7 to 13: Repeat Rows 5 and 6 three more times and Row 5 once more.

* **Short Rows (p.88 B-5–10)**

Begin working short rows. Short rows are worked using the Japanese short rows method, where the row is worked to the turning point, turn work, and first st of the next row is slipped purlwise onto RH needle. A removable marker or safety pin is attached around the working yarn before working the row. The loop of yarn held by the marker will be used to close the gap when working subsequent rows.

Row 14 (WS): Begin working short rows; P3 and repeat (K3, P3) until 12 sts remain at the EOR, turn.

Row 15 (RS): Sl1, K2 and repeat (P3, K3), until 12 sts remain at the EOR, turn.

Row 16 (WS): Change to 3mm needle, Sl1, P2 and repeat (K3, P3) until 12 sts remain before last turn. (24 sts remaining in total.)

Row 17 (RS): Sl1, K2, and repeat (P3, K3), until 12 sts remain at the EOR, turn.

Rows 18 to 21: Repeat the last 2 rows 2 more times. (48 sts remain on each side.)

Row 22 (WS): Still using 3mm needle, Sl1, P2, K3, then repeat (P3, K1, M1, K1, M1, K1) until 9 sts remain before last turn. Turn.

Row 23 (RS): Sl1, P4 and repeat (K3, P5) until 9 sts remain before last turn. Turn.

Row 24 (WS): Sl1, P4 and repeat (K5, P3) until 13 sts remain before last turn. Turn.

Row 25 (RS): Sl1, K2, then repeat (P5, K3) until 13 sts remain before last turn. Turn.

Row 26 (WS): Sl1, P2, K5 until 11 sts remain before last turn. Turn.

Row 27 (RS): Sl1, P4, repeat (K3, P5) until 11 sts remain before last turn. Turn.

Row 28 (WS): Sl1, K4, P3 until 13 sts remain before last turn. Turn.

Row 29 (RS): Sl1, K2, repeat (P5, K3) until 13 sts remain before last turn. Turn.

Row 30 (WS): Sl1, P2, then repeat (P3, K5) until 11 sts remain before last turn. Turn.

Row 31 (RS): Sl1, P4, repeat (K3, P5) until 11 sts remain before last turn. Turn.

Rows 32 to 67: Even numbered rows (WS): Sl1, K4, repeat (P3, K5) until 8 sts remain before last turn. Turn.

Odd numbered rows (RS): Sl1, P4, repeat (K3, P5) until 8 sts remain before last turn. Turn.

Row 68 (WS): Work as established on previous row, at the same time, close the short row gap by working the loop of yarn held by marker together with the next stitch. Work to the EOR.

Cast off stitches using tapestry needle. (Refer to sewn cast off on page 123.)

TIP: Casting off sts for the hem border is a long process, therefore it would be better not to use a long tail to begin with.

With the RS facing and using tapestry needle, join the border worked for the upper body (by picking up sts from cast-on sts to the bottom edge of the front band) with the border worked for the bottom body. Join both left and right sides.

Treatment for extra stitches, see p.28.

Weaving in ends and washing, see p.28.

Collar and facing

Detail of back and movement of tail

Detail of cuff

Expression of garment

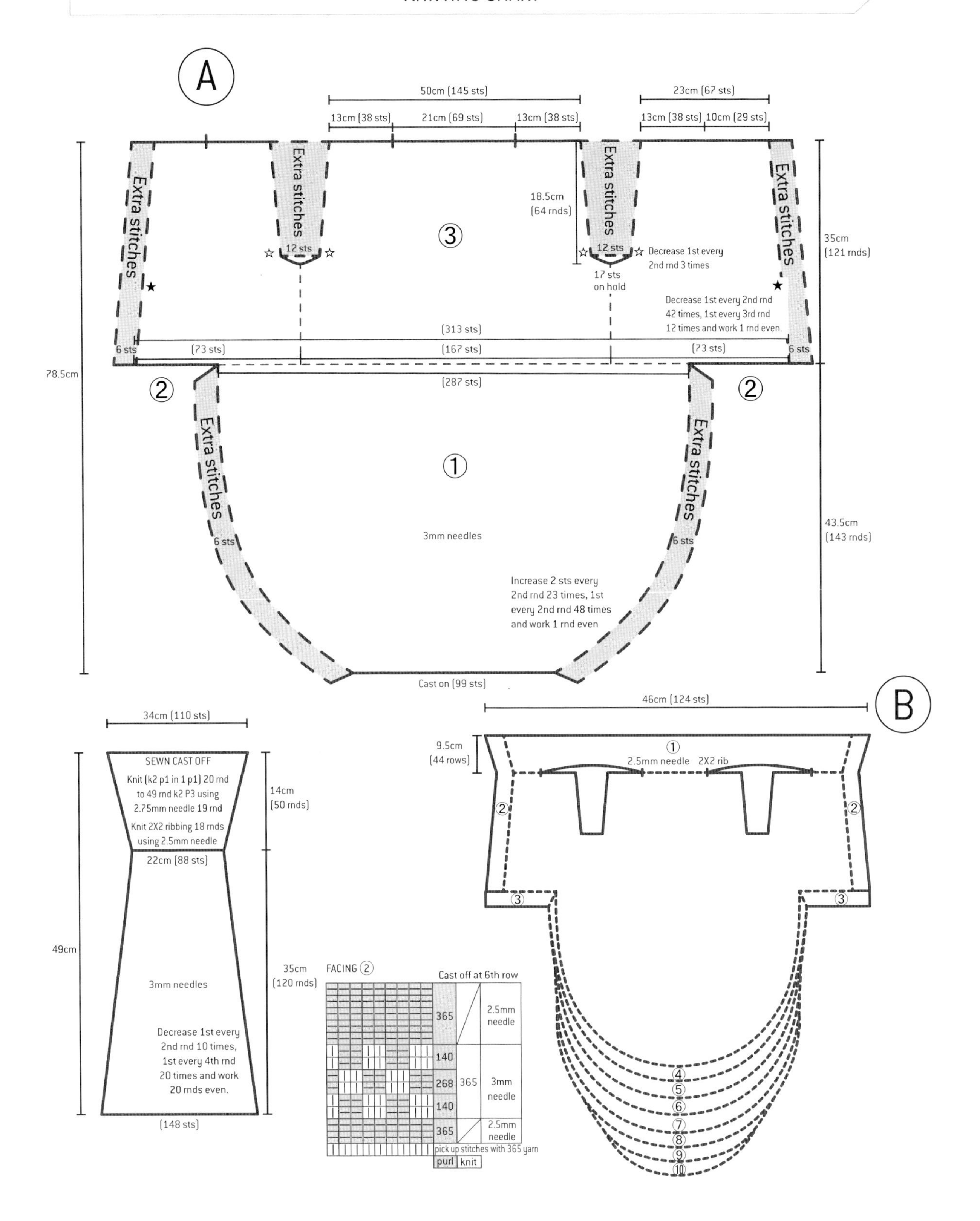
A
50cm (145 sts)
23cm (67 sts)
13cm (38 sts)
21cm (69 sts)
13cm (38 sts)
13cm (38 sts) 10cm (29 sts)
Extra stitches
Extra stitches
Extra stitches
Extra stitches
18.5cm
(64 rnds)
③
12 sts
12 sts
Decrease 1st every
2nd rnd 3 times
17 sts
on hold
35cm
(121 rnds)
Decrease 1st every 2nd rnd
42 times, 1st every 3rd rnd
12 times and work 1 rnd even.
(313 sts)
6 sts
(73 sts)
(167 sts)
(73 sts)
6 sts
78.5cm
②
(287 sts)
②
Extra stitches
Extra stitches
①
6 sts
3mm needles
6 sts
43.5cm
(143 rnds)
Increase 2 sts every
2nd rnd 23 times, 1st
every 2nd rnd 48 times
and work 1 rnd even
Cast on (99 sts)
34cm (110 sts)
SEWN CAST OFF
Knit (k2 p1 in 1 p1) 20 rnd
to 49 rnd k2 P3 using
2.75mm needle 19 rnd
Knit 2X2 ribbing 18 rnds
using 2.5mm needle
14cm
(50 rnds)
22cm (88 sts)
49cm
3mm needles
35cm
(120 rnds)
Decrease 1st every
2nd rnd 10 times,
1st every 4th rnd
20 times and work
20 rnds even.
(148 sts)
46cm (124 sts)
B
9.5cm
(44 rows)
①
2.5mm needle 2X2 rib
②
②
③
③
④
⑤
⑥
⑦
⑧
⑨
⑩
FACING ②
Cast off at 6th row
365
2.5mm
needle
140
268
365
3mm
needle
140
365
2.5mm
needle
pick up stitches with 365 yarn
purl
knit

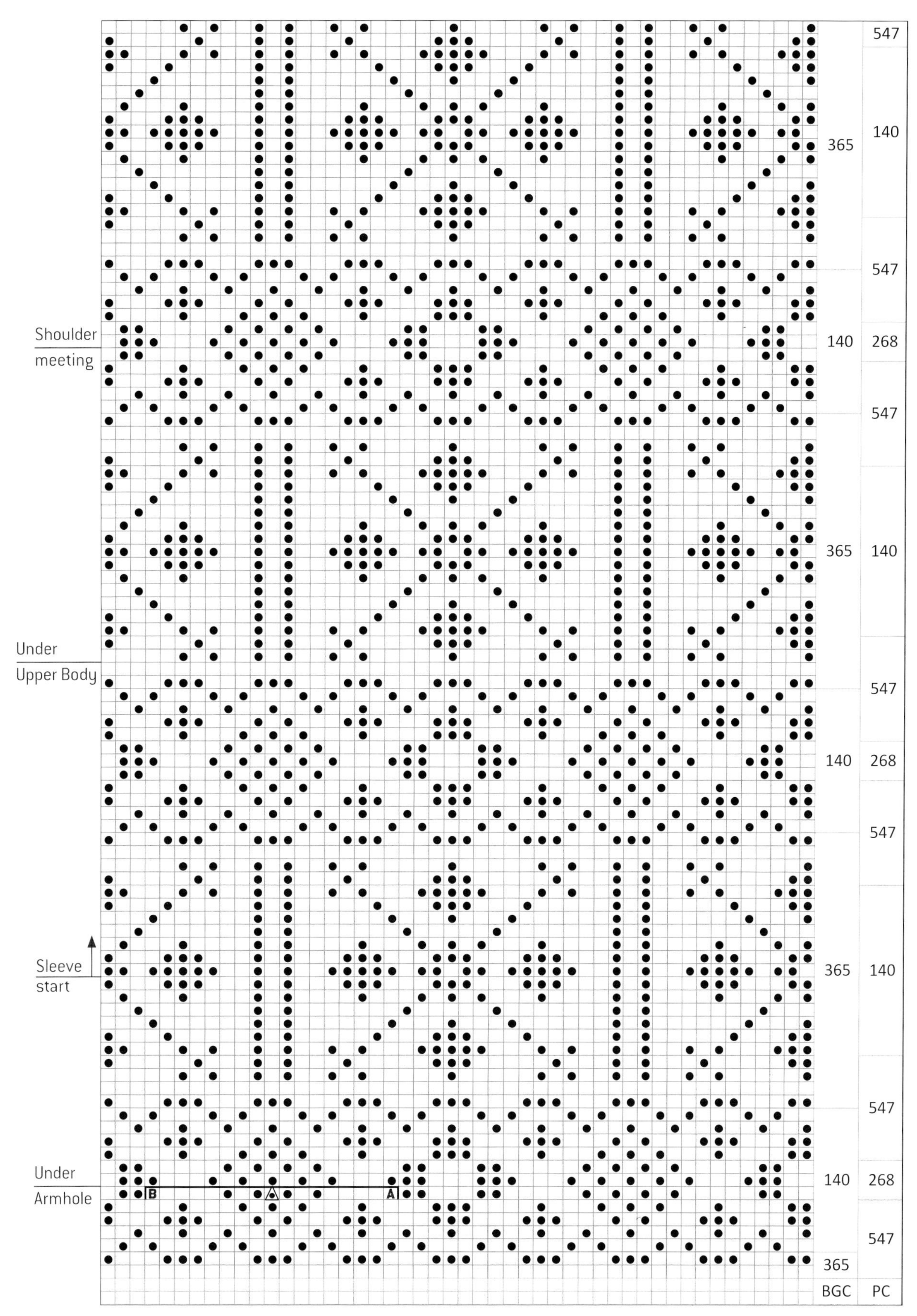

A is 96th stitch from BOR
B is 96th stitch from EOR
} A + B 17 sts on hold for under armhole

”

This must be a strange habit I got
as a Shetland yarn shopkeeper
for more than 20 years.

“

7 OCTOBER IN SHETLAND

Men's slipover

I am always thinking how I can show the wonderful scenes I see. I replace the colours with the numbers of closest colours on the shade card of the yarn. This must be a strange habit I got as a Shetland yarn shopkeeper for more than 20 years. This work portrays the blooming heath covered hills, but I cannot present you the aroma.

Yarn

Total 4 colours – 15 balls

198 (Peat) 4 balls

235 (Grouse) 5 balls

239 (Purple Heather) 3 balls

998 (Autumn) 3 balls

Total weight of slipover – 305 g

Tools & Notions

Circular needles: 2.75mm (40 and 60cm), 3mm (60cm)

Crochet hook: 2.3mm

Tapestry needle: Small and medium

Waste yarn (to hold stitches)

Stitch markers

Tension

1 pattern stitch

(Medium) Flower: 12 sts x 9 rows = 3.8cm x 3cm

(Medium) Cross: 12 sts x 9 rows = 3.8cm x 3cm

(Small) Hexagon: 12 sts x 5 rows = 3.8cm x 1.8cm

(Diamond): 6 sts x 7 rows = 1.9cm x 2.2cm

Finished measurement

Bust circumference: 112cm (106cm)

Cross Back: 42cm (40cm)

Length: 63cm (54cm)

INSTRUCTIONS

Worked in the round up to shoulders by working *extra stitches* in between for armholes and neck opening.

Ribbing for hem

Round 1: With 2.75mm 60cm circular needle and colour #235 yarn, cast on 360 (336) sts. Cast on is counted as 1 round.

Rounds 2 to 4: Tie #198 onto #235 and work in corrugated 2x2 ribbing by repeating [K2 with #235, P2 with #198].

Rounds 5 & 6: Switch #198 to #998 and work in corrugated 2x2 ribbing by knitting P sts and purling K sts – [P2 with #998, K2 with #235].

Round 7: Switch #998 to #198 and work in corrugated 2x2 ribbing as in Row 2, by repeating [K2 with #235, P2 with #198].

Rounds 8 to 18: Switch #198 to #239 and work in corrugated 2x2 ribbing by repeating [K2 with #235, P2 with #239].

Break yarn leaving a 3cm tail.

Body

<<To work to underarm>>

Round 1: Change to 3mm needle. Tie #198, as assigned for Round 1, onto tail end of #239 remaining from hem and knit 1 rnd.

Rounds 2 to 129 (99): Tie #998 onto #198 and work according to the colour assignment up to Round 129 (99).

Break yarn leaving a 3cm tail.

<<To make *extra stitches* for armhole and neck opening>>

1. **After working Round 129 (99)**, using yarn needle and with waste yarn, thread needle through first 30 (27) sts from BOR and 29 (26) sts from EOR so that 59 (53) sts are on waste yarn to keep on hold for underarm. Make sure that the stitch at the centre of the held stitches always matches the centre of the pattern.
2. Then identify which stitches are to be held for the opposite underarm. This is easier by looking at larger patterns as a guide. In this case, this will be **the cross pattern** right below the current pattern. The stitch between the 15th and 16th (14th and 15th) pattern repeat will be the 'centre stitch' for the opposite underarm. Follow this st together with 29 (26) sts on both sides all the way up to the current row, and they shall be kept on hold by threading through waste yarn using tapestry needle, while they are still on cord of the circular needle. Be careful not to sew waste yarn into these sts.

3. Stitches for neckline are also identified by the 'centre stitch', which is located at the centre of the 8th **Cross pattern** between 7th and 8th Cross pattern. Follow this st to the current round and mark this st with waste yarn.

Round 130 (100, 134):

4. Remove the 59 sts (53 sts) for left underarm from needle. Cast on 6 sts on RH needle (using #239 and #235 yarn), and proceed working along the front body. Work based on colour assignment, but disregard those stitches which have been removed. Work until the stitch marked for neck opening.

5. Remove the marked stitch from needle. Cast on 12 sts on RH needle using #235 and #239 yarn. (See p.33) Skip 1 st and continue working along the remaining front, up to the held sts for the right underarm.

6. Remove held sts from needle and cast on 12 sts. Continue working based on colour assignment, disregarding the sts removed from needle, until EOR.

   Cast on 6 sts at EOR.

   Extra stitches are now made for both armholes and neck opening.

   (Refer to p.25 for working with *extra stitches*.)

NOTE: The first 6 *extra stitches* will be the BOR and all subsequent colour changes will be made here.

From the next round, work decreases for neckline while working three *extra stitch* sections during the round and continue up to shoulders.

Round 131 (101): Begin by working 6 *extra stitches* by repeating [1 st in PC (#235), (#235) 1 st in BGC (#239) (#239)] 3 times. Then work until the 2 sts before neck opening, then SKPO (Sl1, K1, pass slipped st over knit st) using #235 (#239).

Work 12 *extra stitches* for neck opening by repeating [1 st in BGC (#239) (#239), 1 st in PC (#235) (#235)] 3 times and [1 st in PC (#235) (#235), 1 st in BGC (#239)(#239)] 3 times, followed by knitting the first 2 body sts together (K2tog) using #235 (#239).

Working up to *extra stitches* for the other underarm, work *extra stitches* as before.

Continue working the back and the remaining 6 *extra stitches* by repeating [1 st in BGC (#239) (#239), 1 st in PC (#235) (#235)] 3 times.

Round 132 (102) to (Round 209 [173]): Work body and *extra stitches*, and at the same time, work decreases (as done on both sides of the neck opening) 2nd rnd 20 (17) times, then 1st every 4th rnd 9 (9) times and then work 2 (2) rnds even. Break yarn leaving a 3cm tail.

Join shoulders

1. Prepare for shoulder seam by working 1 additional row for back by slipping sts onto RH needle, up to the centre of *extra stitches* for right armhole.

2. Tie a knot using #235 and #998 (#235 and #239) yarn which will be used for working the additional row. Leave a 3cm tail for #235 (#235) and about three times the shoulder length for #998 (#239). The knot will be used as a 'stopper', and will be worked from the centre of the *extra stitches* for right armhole, across back body to the centre of *extra stitches* on the other side. Leave the BGC as is and cut PC leaving a 3cm tail.

3. Turn the work inside out.

   Using the remaining #998 (#239) yarn and crochet hook, work three needle cast-off (see p.31) starting from the shoulder edge. Cast off the 6 *extra stitches* for the neckband separately using slip stitch cast-off. (Make sure that the *extra stitches* are not joined together with back neckband.)

4. Join the other shoulder as well, using needle cast-off (see p.31) with #998 (#239) yarn which was kept longer, and cast off *extra stitches* using slip stitch cast-off.

5. Unravel back neck stitches. Cut the unravelled yarn at the middle and tie at the base of both shoulders.

<<Neckband>>

- Using 2.75mm circular needle (40cm), pick up and knit into all stitches and rows. On the second round, work corrugated 2x2 ribbing while decreasing to adjust stitch count. Work a total of 11 rows (including the pick-up round).

Cut open at the centre of *extra stitches*.

Round 1: Using 2.75mm circular needle and #198 yarn, pick up all stitches and rows beginning at the right back neck.

Rounds 2 & 3: Tie #235 yarn, and work corrugated 2x2 ribbing (K2 with #235, P2 with #198). Decrease 1st (both S size and M size) for back neck, and only M size needs to decrease 2 sts when working right-front neckline. There will be 60 sts (54 sts) on back neck, left-front is 80 sts (74 sts) and right-front is 78 sts (74 sts).

Work a Centred Double Decrease (CDD or S2KPO = slip 2 sts together knitwise, knit next st and pass slipped sts over) at the bottom of the 'V' for every round. During this round, work until the 2 sts before the marked st, P1, work CDD, P1, and then K2. Make sure that the marked st is always the centre stitch of CDD. Continue when working right-front, first decrease the same as other side then work to EOR. Work 1 more round using 2 colours.

Rounds 4 to 11: Work 8 more rnds, changing #198 to #239 and decreasing at the bottom of 'V'.

Finish by casting off with #235 yarn using tapestry needle and by making CDD. (See sewn cast off on p.123.)

When decreasing every round at the bottom of 'V', the stitches on both sides of the CDD will keep changing from P1, or K2, but are always symmetrical.

TIP: An alternative is to cast off with #235 by knitting K sts and purling P sts, being careful not to cast off too tight. CDD should be worked at the bottom of the 'V' as well.

Border for Armhole

Round 1: Using #198 yarn, pick up and knit 219 sts (201 sts), by knitting into all stitches and rows.

Then mark 2 sts at each corner at the bottom of armhole for working decreases.

For the left armhole, these 2 knit sts will be 29th (29th) and 30th (30th) stitch from BOR, and 31st (27th) and 32nd (28th) stitch from the EOR for the opposite corner.

Round 2: Tie #235 to #198 and work in corrugated 2x2 ribbing (K2 with #235, P2 with #198) while decreasing 3 sts (1 st) to adjust stitch count. (Note: Decreases should not be worked within those stitches that were kept on hold for underarm.)

Work up to 1 st before the first marked st, K2tog (knit next stitch and the first marked st together) with #235, then SKPO (slip the next second marked st knitwise onto RH needle, knit the next st and pass slipped st over knit st) with #235. Working these decreases will create a mitred corner and these 2 centre sts will always be knit sts and sts on both sides will be symmetrical. This will make it easy to identify any decreases which may be missed.

NOTE: When working decreases, there will be times when 6 knit sts align. In this case, be sure that the 2 strands of yarn are twisted on the WS to avoid long floats.

Round 3: Work corrugated 2x2 ribbing in the same colours, while continuing to decrease at the corner.

Rounds 4 to 11: Switch #198 to #239 and work corrugated 2x2 ribbing, and as established up to Round 11.

Cast off using tapestry needle and decreasing, as done similarly for neck opening. (See p.123 for sewn cast off.)

Work border for right armhole in the same way as for left armhole.

Treatment for extra stitches, see p.28.

Weaving in ends and washing, see p.28.

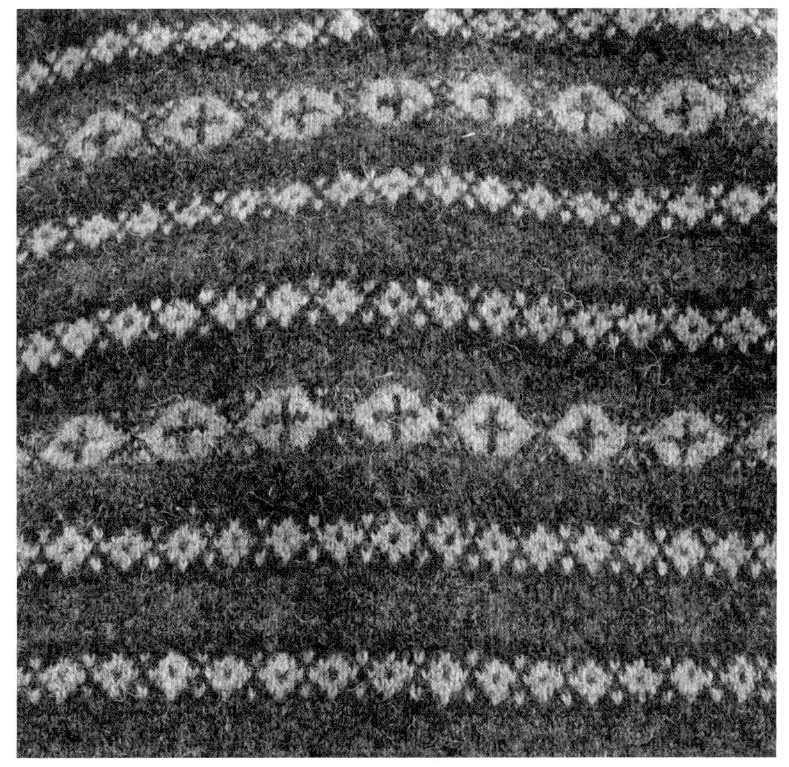

Detail of pattern

Detail of armhole

KNITTING CHART

● = Medium size

● = Small size

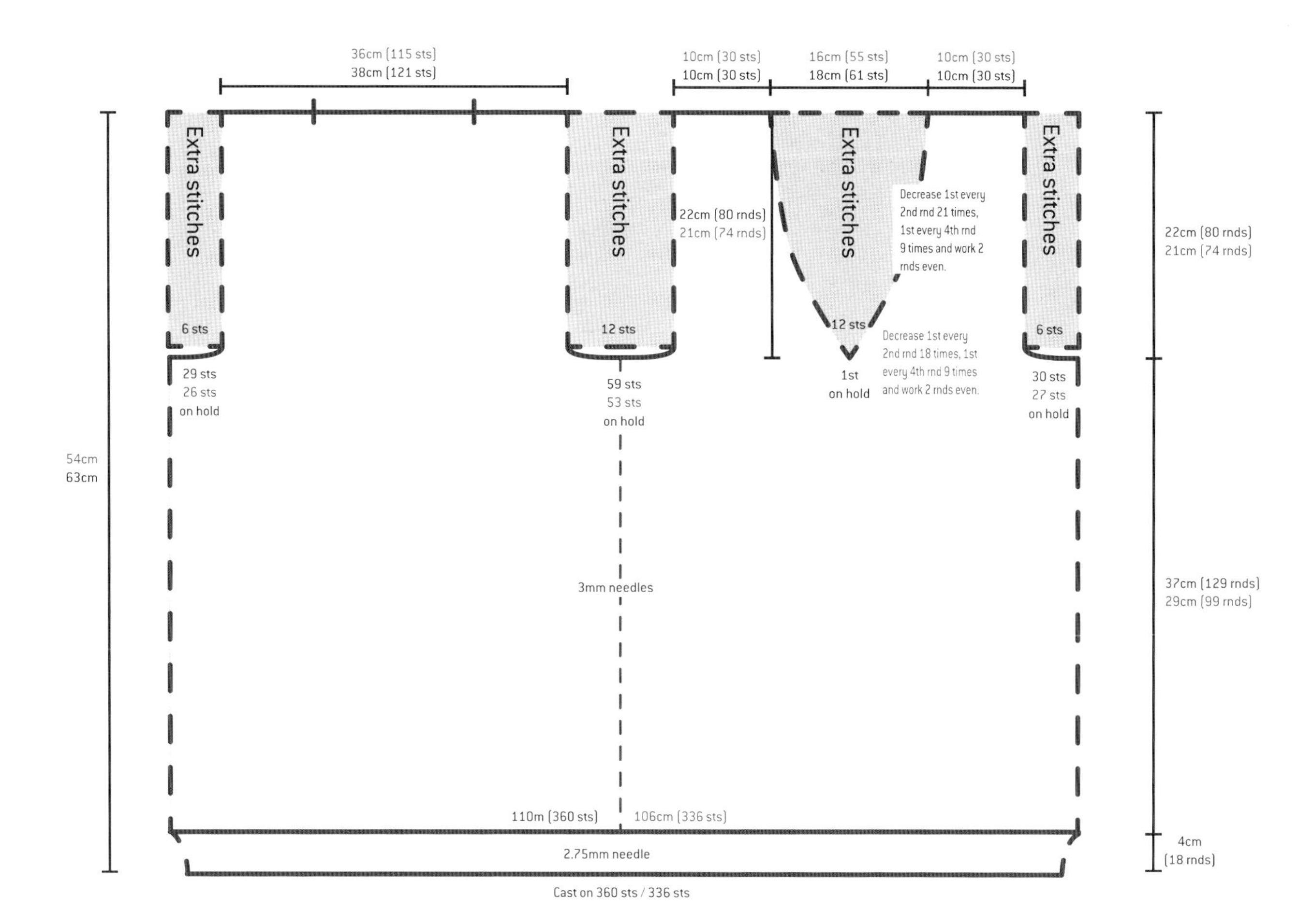

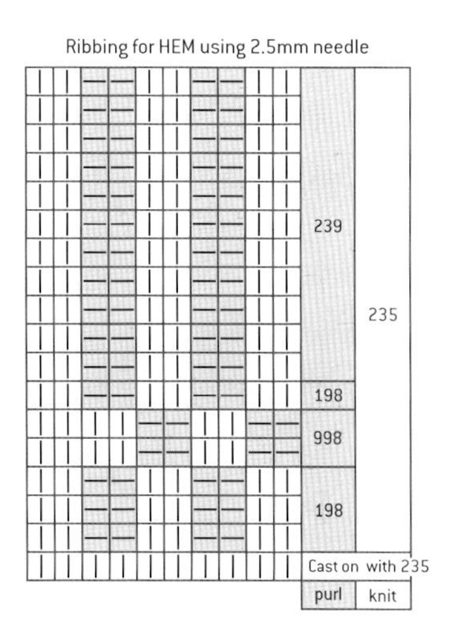

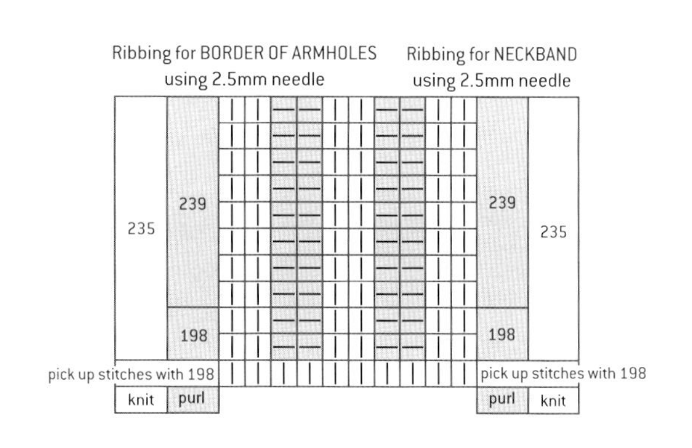

NOTE: Colour chart for ribbing is based on how it will appear on RS

S size shoulder meeting

M size under armhole & neckline

M size shoulder meeting

S size under armhole & neckline

BGC	PC
198	235
239	235
998	235
239	235
198	998
239	235
198	998
239	235
998	235
239	235
198	998
239	235
198	998

Nature shows us its great colour contrast which makes me feel the deep warmth of nature itself.

8 SEASHORE
Men's slipover

This yellow can be seen at the seashore in Shetland.
Lichen rambles over the rocks. Nature shows us its great colour contrast which makes me feel the deep warmth of nature itself.

Yarn

Total 7 colours – 14 balls

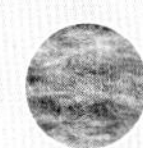 103 (Sholmit) 1 ball

 107 (Mogit) 1 ball

 109 (Shetland Black/Shaela) 2 balls

 118 (Moorit/Shaela) 3 balls

 140 (Rye) 2 balls

 183 (Sand) 3 balls

 410 (Cornfield) 2 balls

Total weight of slipover – 257g

Tools & Notions

Circular needles: 2.5mm (40cm, 60cm)
3mm (40cm, 60cm)
Crochet hook: 2.3mm
Tapestry needle: Small and medium
Waste yarn (to hold stitches)
Stitch markers

Tension

1 pattern stitch

(Medium) Flower: 12 sts x 9 rows = 3.8cm x 3cm

(Medium) Cross: 12 sts x 9 rows = 3.8cm x 3cm

(Small) Hexagon: 12 sts x 7 rows = 3.8cm x 2.2cm

(Small) Diamond: 6 sts x 7 rows = 1.9cm x 2.2cm

(Both small patterns including single colour rows underneath and on top)

Finished measurement

Bust circumference: 106cm (114cm)
Cross Back: 42cm (44cm)
Length: 54cm (60cm)

INSTRUCTIONS

Worked in the round up to shoulders by working *extra stitches* in between for armholes and neck opening.

Round 1: With 2.5mm [60cm] circular needle and with colour #109 yarn, cast on 336 [360] sts. Cast on is counted as 1 round.

Rows 2 to 16: Tie #118 onto #109 and work in corrugated 2x2 ribbing by repeating [K2 with #118, P2 with #109].

Break yarn leaving a 3cm tail.

Body

<<To work to underarm>>

Round 1: Change to 3mm needle. Tie #140, as assigned for Round 1, onto tail end of #118 remaining of hem and knit 1 round.

Rounds 2 to 98 [118]: Tie #107 onto #140 and work according to the colour assignment up to Round 98 [118].

Break yarn leaving a 3cm tail.

<<To make extra stitches for armhole and neck opening>>

1. **After working 98 [118] rounds**, with waste yarn and yarn needle, thread needle through first 27th [30th] stitch from BOR and 26th [29th] stitch from EOR so that 53 [59] sts are on waste yarn to keep on hold for underarm.

   Make sure that the stitch at the centre of the held stitches always matches the centre of the pattern.

2. Identify which stitches are to be held for the opposite underarm. This is easier by looking at larger patterns as a guide. In this case, this will be **the Cross pattern** right below the current pattern. The stitch between the 14th and 15th [15th and 16th] pattern repeat will be the 'centre stitch' for the opposite underarm. Follow this stitch together with 26 [26, 29] sts on each side all the way up to the current row, and keep on hold by threading waste yarn through using tapestry needle, while they are still on cord of the circular needle. Be careful not to sew waste yarn into these stitches.

3. Stitch for neck opening are also identified by the 'centre stitch', which is located between the 7th and 8th Cross pattern repeat [centre of 8th Cross pattern]. Follow this stitch to the current round and mark this stitch with waste yarn.

Round 99 [119]:

1. Remove the 53 [59] sts for left underarm from needle. Cast on 6 sts on RH needle using #140 [#183 and #410] yarn, and proceed

working along the front body. Work based on colour assignment, but disregard those stitches which have been removed. Work until the stitch marked for neck opening.

2. Remove the marked st from needle. Cast on 12 sts on RH needle using #140 (#183 and #410) yarn. (See p.33) Continue working along the remaining front until the held sts for the right underarm.
3. Remove held sts from needle and cast on 12 sts. Continue working, until EOR.
4. Cast on 6 sts at EOR. *Extra stitch*es are now made for both armholes and neck opening. (Refer to p.25 for working with *extra stitches*.)

NOTE: *The first 6 extra stitches will be the BOR and all subsequent color changes will be made here.*

From the next round, work decreases for neckline while working three *extra stitch* sections during the round and continue up to shoulders.

Round 100 (120): Begin by working 6 *extra stitch*es by repeating [1 st in PC (#107) (#410), 1 st in BGC (#140) (#183)] 3 times. Then work until the 2 sts before neck opening, then SKPO (Sl1, K1, pass slipped st over knit st) using #107 (#410).

Work 12 *extra stitch*es for neckline by repeating [1 st in BGC (#140) (#183), 1 st in PC (#107) (#410)] 3 times and [1 st in PC (#107) (#410), 1 st in BGC (#140) (#183)] 3 times, followed by K2tog (knitting 2 stitches together) the first 2 body sts using #107 (#410). Follow work until *extra stitch*es for the other armhole, work *extra stitch*es as before.

Continue working the back and the remaining 6 *extra stitch*es by repeating [1 st in PC (#140) (#183), 1 st in PC (#107) (#410)] 3 times.

Round 101 (101, 121) onward:

Work body and *extra stitch*es according to colour assignments, and at the same time, work decreases (as done on each side of the neck opening) 1st every 2nd rnd 11 (21) times, then decrease 1st every 4th rnd 12 (8) times and then work 2 (1) rnds even. Break yarn leaving a 3cm tail.

Join shoulders

1. Prepare for shoulder seam by working 1 additional row for back by slipping stitches onto RH needle, up to the centre of *extra stitch*es for right armhole.
2. Tie a knot using #118 and #183 (#103 and #140) yarn which will be used for working the additional row. Leave a 3cm tail for #118 (#103) and about three times the shoulder length for #183 (#140). The knot will be used as a 'stopper', and will be worked from the centre of the *extra stitch*es for right armhole, across back body to the centre of *extra stitch*es on the other side.

   Leave the BGC as is and cut PC leaving a 3cm tail.
3. Turn the work inside out.

   Using the remaining #183 (#140) yarn and crochet hook, work three needle cast-off (See p.25) starting from the shoulder edge. Cast off the 6 *extra stitch*es for the neckband separately using slip stitch cast-off. (Make sure that the *extra stitch*es are not joined together with back neckband.)
4. Join the other shoulder as well, using three needle cast-off (See p.21) with #183 (#140) yarn which was kept longer, and cast off *extra stitch*es using slip stitch cast-off.
5. Unravel back neck stitches. Cut the unravelled yarn at the middle and tie at the base of both shoulders.

<<Neckband>>

Cut open at the centre of *extra stitches* for neck opening.

Round 1: Using 2.5mm circular needle and #109 yarn, pick up all stitches and rows beginning at the right back neck.

Round 2: Tie #118 yarn, and work corrugated 2x2 ribbing (K2 with #118, P2 with #109) while decreasing 3 (0) sts for back neck so that there will be 46 (61) sts M-size, working both front neckline it will be 195 sts in round. L-size, decreasing 2 sts when working left front neckline, and decreasing 3 sts when working right front neckline. So that there will be 211 sts in a round (including centre stitch which is held).

Work a Centered Double Decrease (CDD or S2KPO = slip 2 sts tog knitwise, knit next st and pass slipped sts over) at the bottom of the 'V' for every round. During this round, work to 2 sts before the marked st, P1, work CDD, P1, and then K2. Make sure that the marked st is always the centre stitch of CDD. Then continue working right-front to EOR.

Rounds 3 to 10: Work 8 more rnds using 2 colors, work the same as Round 2.

Finish by casting off with #109 yarn and using tapestry needle and by making CDD. (See sewn cast off on p.123.) When decreasing every round at the bottom of 'V', the stitches on both sides of the CDD will keep changing from purl 1, or knit 2, but are always symmetrical.

TIP: An alternative is to cast off with #109 by knitting K sts and purling P sts, being careful not to cast off too tightly. CDD should be worked at the bottom of the 'V' as well.

Border for armhole

Round 1: Using #109 yarn, pick up and knit 201 (213) sts, by knitting into all stitches and rows.

Then mark 2 sts at each corner at the bottom of armhole for working decreases.

For the left armhole, these 2 knit sts will be 29th and 30th (29th and 30th) stitch from BOR, and 27th and 28th (31st and 32nd) stitch from EOR for the opposite corner.

Round 2: Tie #118 to #109 and work in corrugated 2x2 ribbing (K2 with #118, P2 with #109) while decreasing 1 st (2 stitches) to adjust stitch count. (Note: decreases should not be worked within those stitches that were kept on hold for underarm.) Work until 1 st before the first marked st, K2tog (knit next st and the first marked st together) with #118, then SKPO (slip the next second marked st knitwise onto RH needle, knit the next st and pass slipped st over knit st) with #118. Working these decreases will create a mitered corner and these 2 centre sts will always be knit stitches and stitches on both sides will be symmetrical. This will make it easy to identify any decreases which may be missed.

When working decreases, there will be times when 6 knit stitches align. In this case, be sure that the 2 strands of yarn are twisted on the WS to avoid long floats.

Rounds 3 to 11: Work corrugated 2x2 ribbing, as Round 2.

Cast off using tapestry needle and decreasing, as done similarly for neckline. (See p. 123 for sewn cast off.)

Work border for right armhole in the same way as for left armhole.

Treatment for extra stitches, see p.28.

Weaving in ends and washing, see p.28.

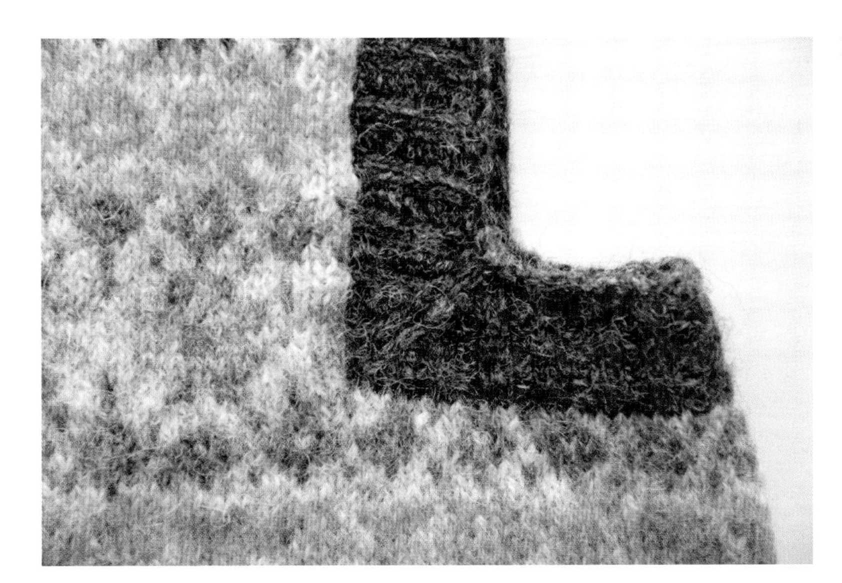

Detail of armhole's decreasing

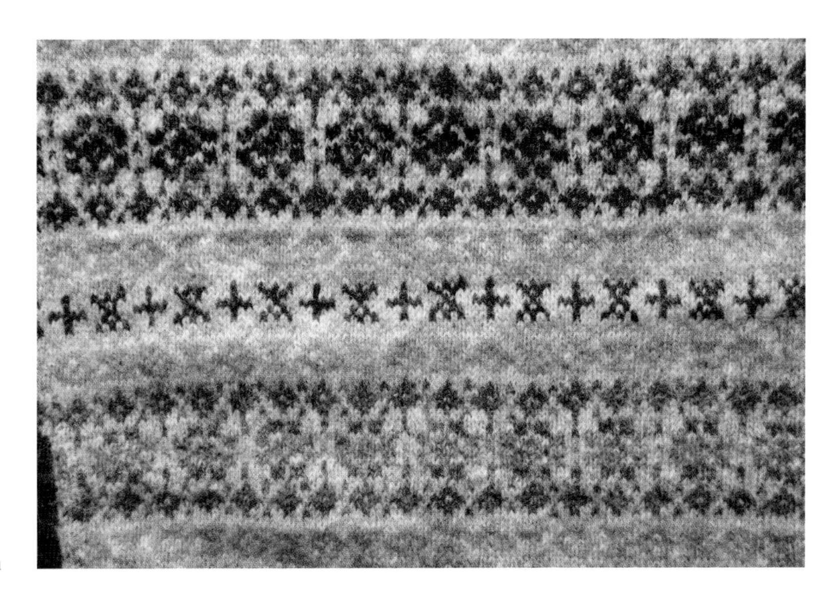

Detail of pattern

KNITTING CHART

● = Large size

● = Medium size

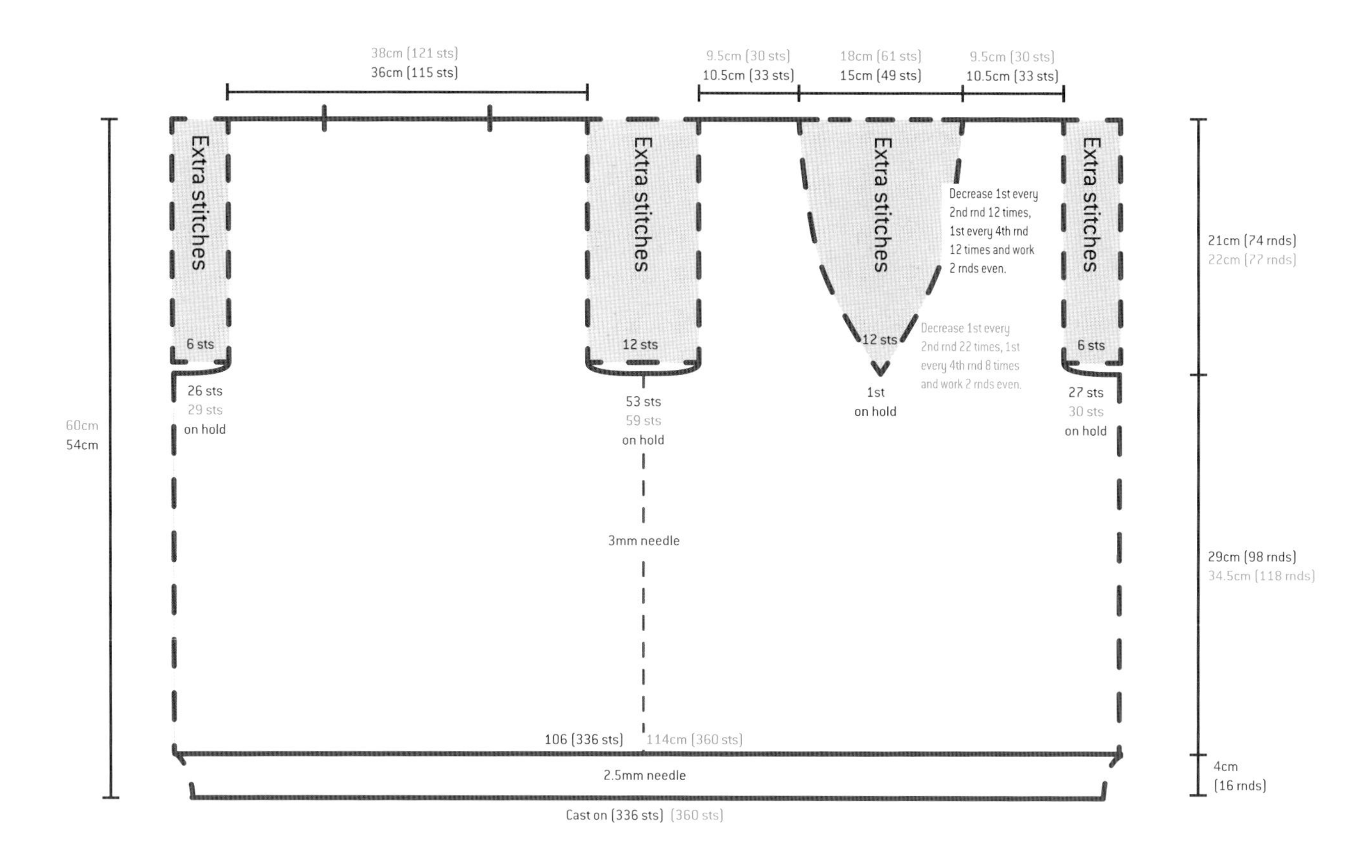

Ribbing for HEM using 2.5mm needle

109 | 118

Cast on with #109

purl | knit

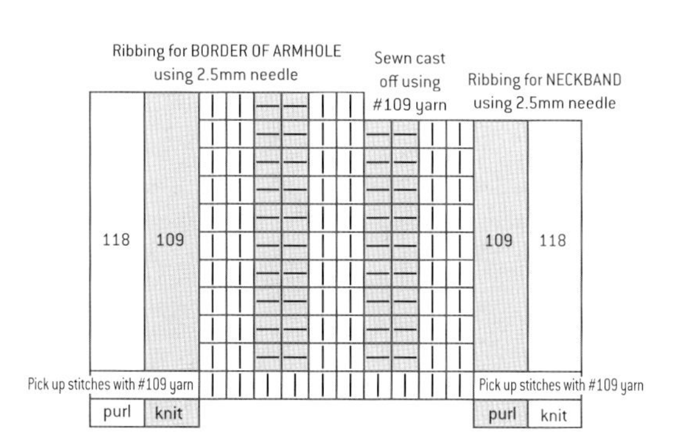

NOTE: Colour assignment for ribbing is based on how it will appear on RS

M size shoulder meeting

M size under armhole & neckline

L size shoulder meeting

M size under armhole & neckline

BGC	PC
	410
183	118
	410
	118
140	109
	118
	410
183	118
	410
	107
140	103
	107

I would love to see
young mothers knit
for their children.

9 DREAM OF BEING A PRINCESS
Girl's slipover

When I watch my granddaughters playing I sense they have extraordinary dreams. So I designed this for them, cute little ladies. I would love to see young mothers knit for their children. This is easy enough for beginners.

Yarn

Total 7 colours – 8 balls

 135 Surf 1 ball

 183 Sand 2 balls

 188 Sherbet 1 ball

 241 Tan Green 1 ball

 423 Burnt Ochre 1 ball

 580 Cherry 1 ball

 757 Splash 1 ball

Total weight of slipover – 82g

Tools & Notions

Circular needles: 2.5mm (40cm), 3mm (40cm), 3.25mm (40cm)

Crochet hook: 2.3mm

Tapestry needle: Small and medium

Waste yarn (to hold stitches)

Stitch markers

Tension

1 pattern repeat

(Large) Flower: 18 sts x 17 rows + 1 prior & subsequent rows = 5.1cm x 5.2cm

(Large) Star: 12 sts x 15 rows + 1 prior row = 3.4cm x 4.2cm

Base pattern: 30 sts x 51 rows = 10cm x 10cm

Finished measurement

Bust circumference: 62cm

Cross Back: 21cm

Length: 32cm

INSTRUCTIONS

Worked in the round up to underarm, and then the front and back, and eventually right and left fronts are worked separately up to shoulders.

Worked in pattern stitch throughout, except for the Fair Isle pattern for the hem.

Pattern stitch for hem

Round 1: With 2.5mm 40cm circular needle and with colour #183 yarn, cast on 192 sts. Cast on is counted as 1 round.

Round 2: Work in 1x1 (K1, P1) ribbing.

Round 3: K to EOR.

Rounds 4 to 14: Repeat Rounds 2 and 3. End by working Round 2. Break yarn leaving a 3cm tail leaving yarn.

Body

<<To work to underarm>>

Worked in the round.

Round 1: Change to 3mm needle. With #183, repeat (K8, YO) to EOR. (24 sts increased, 216 sts in total.)

Rounds 2 to 35: Tie PC #423 onto #183 and work according to the colour assignment. Be sure to work YO through the back loop.

Work up to Round 35 by changing colours as charted, working in Fair Isle pattern.

Round 36: Change to 2.5mm (40cm) circular needle. With #183, repeat (K7, K2tog) 24 times. (24 sts decreased, 192 sts in total.)

Round 37: Work in 1x1 ribbing to EOR.

Round 38: K to EOR.

Round 39 to 71: Repeat last 2 rnds for 33 more rnds. Last round is as in Round 37. Then break yarn leaving a 3cm tail.

<<Underarm to shoulders >>

1. **Work section [1] of knitting chart**. Slip first 16 sts onto waste yarn and leave them on hold. Attach #183 to A and starting from the 17th stitch, work in 1x1 ribbing to 32nd stitch. Decrease 1 st the row after next, and then on every 4th row 15 times along the neckline. This is done working flat, which means the decrease will be worked on the WS row, making sure to maintain the 1x1 ribbing pattern. Then work 2 rows even. Break yarn by leaving a longer tail (about three times the length of shoulder) for shoulder seaming. Leave the 16 sts on waste yarn on hold.

2. Attach yarn #183 to B on chart, and **work section (2)** of front in the same way as for (1). When finished, break yarn leaving a 3cm tail. Leave the 16 sts on waste yarn on hold.

TIP: Work tightly on the edge, so it is not too loose.

3. **Work section (3) of chart.** Continue from the bottom of section (2), slipping 31 sts onto waste yarn. Attach #183 to C on chart, and work section (3) evenly in pattern sts to shoulder. When working the 65 sts on the first row, be sure to slip the remaining 15 sts onto waste yarn.

4. **Join shoulders:** After the above steps have been worked, with WS facing, work slip stitch seam with crochet hook and remaining yarn.

Finishing armhole and neckline

1. For both armhole and neckline, pick up and knit into all stitches and rows using 3.25mm circular needle. Adjust stitch count to work 1x1 ribbing.

2. *(K1, P1), then pass knit stitch over purled stitch. Leave purled sts on needle. Repeat from * to EOR. Only purl sts will remain on needle.

3. Turn work. From the WS, slip first 2 sts onto RH needle, pass first over second. Slip next st on LH needle onto RH needle. Pass st already on RH needle over the newly slipped st. Repeat this to EOR. Break yarn. Using tail end, sew beginning and end together to smoothen the gap.

NOTE: *Take care to make good tension.*

Finishing and washing

- Weave in ends on the WS into floats, first by inserting the yarn needle into floats by rotating, and then threading tail end through needle and drawing through. Inserting the needle first makes it easy to weave in no matter how short the ends are.
- After weaving in all ends, be sure to hand wash. Wash as normal wool wash. Washing will bring out the best features of the yarn.
- Once dried, trim off all ends carefully. Make sure not to cut any other parts of the garment.

KNITTING CHART

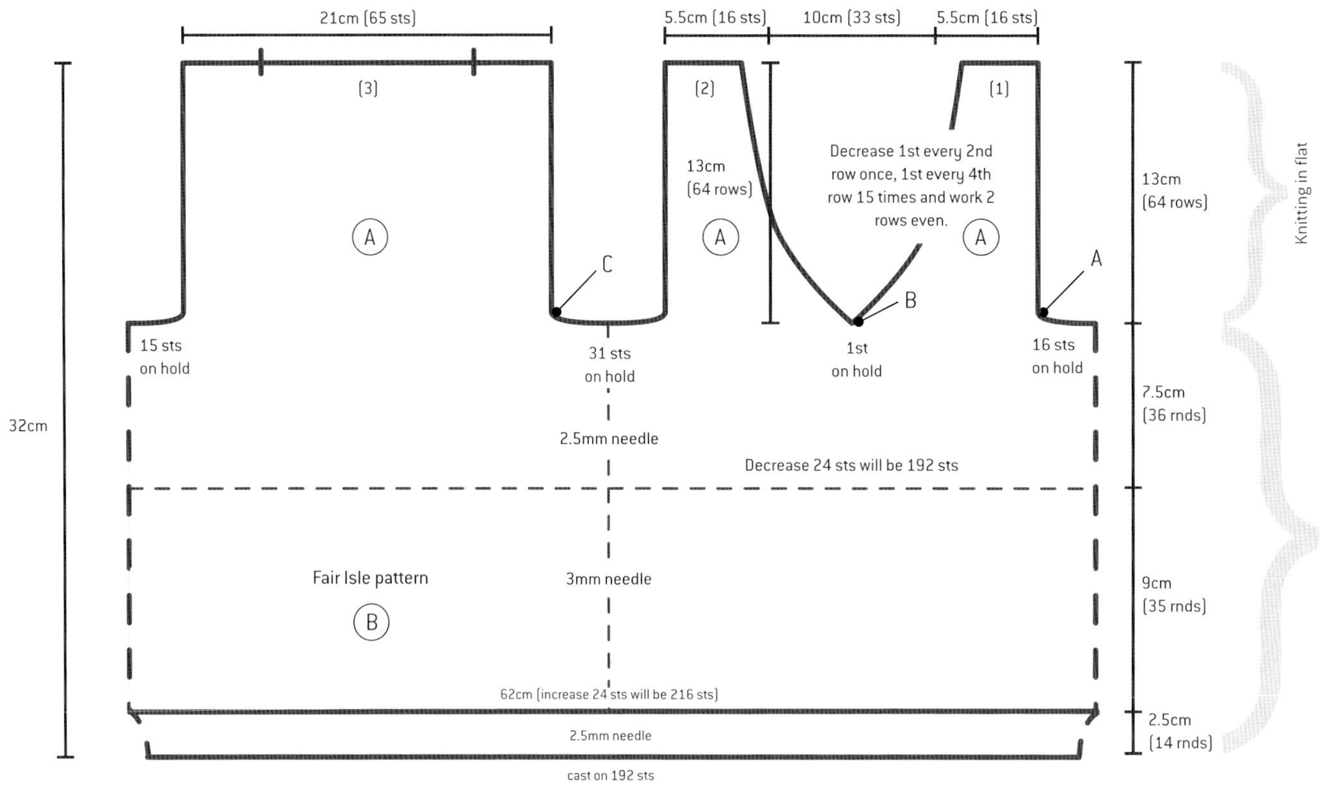

21cm (65 sts)
(3)
5.5cm (16 sts)
10cm (33 sts)
5.5cm (16 sts)
(2)
(1)
13cm
(64 rows)
Decrease 1st every 2nd row once, 1st every 4th row 15 times and work 2 rows even.
A
C
B
15 sts on hold
31 sts on hold
1st on hold
16 sts on hold
32cm
2.5mm needle
Decrease 24 sts will be 192 sts
Fair Isle pattern
B
3mm needle
62cm (increase 24 sts will be 216 sts)
2.5mm needle
cast on 192 sts
13cm
(64 rows)
7.5cm
(36 rnds)
9cm
(35 rnds)
2.5cm
(14 rnds)
Knitting in flat
Knitting in round

A

Pattern stitch

<table>
<tr><td>—</td><td>|</td><td>—</td><td>|</td><td>—</td><td>|</td><td>—</td><td>|</td></tr>
<tr><td>|</td><td>|</td><td>|</td><td>|</td><td>|</td><td>|</td><td>|</td><td>|</td></tr>
<tr><td>—</td><td>|</td><td>—</td><td>|</td><td>—</td><td>|</td><td>—</td><td>|</td></tr>
<tr><td>|</td><td>|</td><td>|</td><td>|</td><td>|</td><td>|</td><td>|</td><td>|</td></tr>
<tr><td>—</td><td>|</td><td>—</td><td>|</td><td>—</td><td>|</td><td>—</td><td>|</td></tr>
<tr><td>|</td><td>|</td><td>|</td><td>|</td><td>|</td><td>|</td><td>|</td><td>|</td></tr>
<tr><td>—</td><td>|</td><td>—</td><td>|</td><td>—</td><td>|</td><td>—</td><td>|</td></tr>
<tr><td>—</td><td>|</td><td>—</td><td>|</td><td>—</td><td>|</td><td>—</td><td>|</td></tr>
<tr><td>—</td><td>|</td><td>—</td><td>|</td><td>—</td><td>|</td><td>—</td><td>|</td></tr>
<tr><td>|</td><td>|</td><td>|</td><td>|</td><td>|</td><td>|</td><td>|</td><td>|</td></tr>
<tr><td>—</td><td>|</td><td>—</td><td>|</td><td>—</td><td>|</td><td>—</td><td>|</td></tr>
<tr><td>|</td><td>|</td><td>|</td><td>|</td><td>|</td><td>|</td><td>|</td><td>|</td></tr>
<tr><td>—</td><td>|</td><td>—</td><td>|</td><td>—</td><td>|</td><td>—</td><td>|</td></tr>
<tr><td>|</td><td>|</td><td>|</td><td>|</td><td>|</td><td>|</td><td>|</td><td>|</td></tr>
</table>

NOTE: | knit and — purl, these symbols are based on how it will appear on RS

BGC	PC
423	135
	757
	580
	757
	135
183	423
188	241
	757
	241
183	423
BGC	PC

”

Little children running around
are a very natural scene.

“

10 WARM NATURE
Boy's slipover

This has the same pattern as 'Dream of being a Princess'.
Little children running around are a very natural scene.
But nowadays, we do not see many natural scenes.
My longing for them pushed me to knit this.
This is for beginners and easily resized for adults.

Yarn

Total 6 colours – 7balls

231 (Bracken) 1 ball

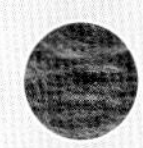

241 (Tan Green) 1 ball

253 (Seaweed) 1 ball

423 (Burnt Ochre) 1 ball

789 (Marjoram) 1 ball

825 (Olive) 2 balls

Total weight of slipover – 82g

Tools & Notions

Circular needles: 2.5mm (40cm), 3mm (40cm), 3.25mm (40cm)

Crochet hook: 2.3mm

Tapestry needle: Small and medium

Waste yarn (to hold stitches)

Stitch markers

Tension

1 pattern repeat

(Large) Flower: 18 sts x 17 rows + 1 prior & subsequent rows = 5.1cm x 5.2cm

(Large) Star: 12 sts x 15 rows + 1 prior row = 3.4cm x 4.2cm

Base pattern: 30 sts x 51 rows = 10cm x 10cm

Finished measurement

Bust circumference: 62cm

Cross Back: 21cm

Length: 32cm

INSTRUCTIONS

Worked in the round up to underarm, and then the front and back, and eventually right and left fronts are worked separately up to shoulders.

Worked in pattern stitch throughout, except for the Fair Isle pattern for the hem.

Pattern stitch for hem

Round 1: With 2.5mm 40cm circular needle and with colour #825 yarn, cast on 192 sts. Cast on is counted as 1 round.

Round 2: Work in 1x1 (K1, P1) ribbing.

Round 3: K to EOR.

Rounds 4 to 14: Repeat Rounds 2 and 3. End by working Round 2. Break yarn leaving a 3cm tail.

Body

<<To work to underarm>>

Worked in the round.

Round 1: Change to 3mm needle. With #253 repeat (K8, YO) to EOR. (24 sts increased, 216 sts in total.)

Rounds 2 to 35: Tie PC #789 onto #253 and work according to the colour assignment. Be sure to work YO through the back loop.

Work up to Round 35 by changing colours as charted, working in Fair Isle pattern.

Round 36: Change to 2.5mm (40cm) circular needle. With #825, repeat (K7, K2tog) 24 times. (24 sts decreased, 192 sts in total.)

Round 37: Work in 1x1 ribbing to EOR.

Round 38: K to EOR.

Round 39 to 71: Repeat last 2 rnds for 33 more rnds. Last round is as in Round 37. Then break yarn leaving a 3cm tail.

<<Underarm to shoulders >>

1. **Work section [1] of knitting chart**. Slip first 16 sts onto waste yarn and leave them on hold. Attach #825 to A and starting from the 17th stitch as shown in [1] on chart, work in 1x1 ribbing to 32nd stitch. Decrease 1 st the row after next, and then on every 4th row 15 times along the neckline. This is done working flat, which means the decrease will be worked on the WS row, making sure to maintain the 1x1 ribbing pattern. Then work 2 rows even. Break yarn by leaving a longer tail (about three times the length of shoulder) for shoulder seaming. Leave the 16 sts on waste yarn on hold.

2. Attach yarn #825 to B on chart, and **work section (2)** of front in the same way as for (1). When finished, break yarn leaving a 3cm tail. Leave the 16 sts on waste yarn on hold.

TIP: Work tightly on the edge, so it is not too loose.

3. **Work section (3) of chart.** Continue from the bottom of section (2), slipping 31 sts onto waste yarn. Attach #825 to C on chart, and work section (3) evenly in pattern sts to shoulder. When working the 65 sts on the first row, be sure to slip the remaining 15 sts onto waste yarn.
4. **Join shoulders:** After the above steps have been worked, with WS facing, work slip stitch seam with crochet hook and remaining yarn.

Finishing armhole and neckline

1. For both armhole and neckline, pick up and knit into all stitches and rows using 3.25mm circular needle. Adjust stitch count to work 1x1 ribbing.
2. *(K1, P1), then pass knit stitch over purled stitch. Leave purled sts on needle. Repeat from * to EOR. Only purl sts will remain on needle.
3. Turn work. From the WS, slip first 2 sts onto RH needle, pass first over second. Slip next st on LH needle onto RH needle. Pass st already on RH needle over the newly slipped st. Repeat this to EOR. Break yarn. Using tail end, sew beginning and end together to smoothen the gap.

NOTE: *Take care to make good tension.*

Finishing and washing

- Weave in ends on the WS into floats, first by inserting the yarn needle into floats by rotating, and then threading tail end through needle and drawing through. Inserting the needle first makes it easy to weave in no matter how short the ends are.
- After weaving in all ends, be sure to hand wash. Wash as normal wool wash. Washing will bring out the best features of the yarn.
- Once dried, trim off all ends carefully. Make sure not to cut any other parts of the garment.

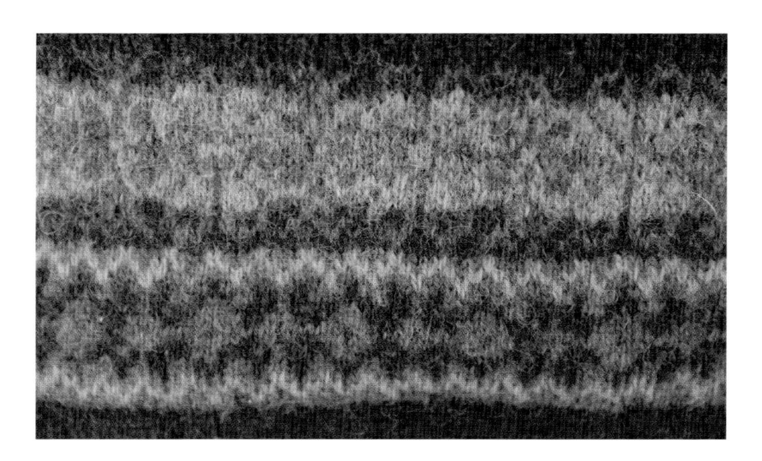

Details of pattern

KNITTING CHART

21cm (65 sts)
(3)
5.5cm (16 sts)
10cm (33 sts)
5.5cm (16 sts)
(2)
(1)
13cm
(64 rows)
Decrease 1st every 2nd row once, 1st every 4th row 15 times and work 2 rows even.
13cm
(64 rows)
Knitting in flat
A
A
A
A
C
B
15 sts
on hold
31 sts
on hold
1st
on hold
16 sts
on hold
7.5cm
(36 rnds)
32cm
2.5mm needle
Decrease 24 sts will be 192 sts
Fair Isle pattern
B
3mm needle
9cm
(35 rnds)
62cm (increase 24 sts will be 216 sts)
2.5mm needle
2.5cm
(14 rnds)
cast on 192 sts

NOTE: | knit and — purl, these symbols are based on how it will appear on RS

BGC	PC
825	241
253	423
	231
	789
	231
	423
825	241
253	789
	825
	241
	825
	789

He is a little boy but
sometimes he gives the
impression of being very old.

11 ROCKING CHAIR
Boy's cardigan

I knitted this for my grandson. He is a little boy but sometimes he gives the impression of being very old. A quiet colouration matches the image of an old man sitting on a rocking chair. Occasionally, quiet colouration brightens up little children.

Yarn

Total 9 colours – 12 balls

103 (Solmit) 1 ball

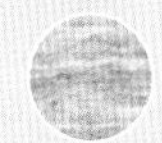
105 (Eesit) 2 balls

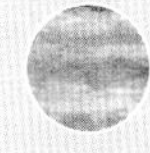
140 (Rye) 2 balls

246 (Wren) 1 ball

272 (Fog) 2 balls

274 (Green Mist) 1 ball

290 (Oyster) 1 ball

720 (Dewdrop) 1 ball

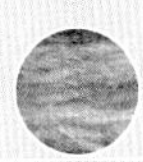
769 (Willow) 1 ball

Total weight of cardigan – 227g

Tools & Notions

Circular needles: 2.5mm (40cm and 80cm or longer), 3mm (40cm and 80cm or longer)
Crochet hook: 2.3mm crochet hook
Tapestry needle: Small and medium
Waste yarn (to hold stitches)
Stitch markers
Buttons (desired number)

Tension

1 pattern repeat

(Medium) Octagon 14 sts x 11 rows = 4cm x 3.2cm

(Narrow) Wave pattern 7 sts x 7 rows = 2cm x 1.3cm

(including single colour rows underneath and on top)

Finished measurement

Bust circumference: 70cm

Back neck to sleeve edge: 47.5cm

Length: 41cm

INSTRUCTIONS

Worked in the round up to shoulders, apart from hem, by working *extra stitches* in between for front bands, armholes and neck opening.

Ribbing for hem

Worked flat for 13 rows, including cast on.

Row 1: With 2.5mm 40cm circular needle and with color #140 yarn, cast on 224 sts.

Rows 2 to 13: Tie #105 onto #140. Begin on the WS row by P3 with #105 and continue working in corrugated 2x2 ribbing [K2with #140, P2 with #105] and end the row in P3 with #105. First and last 3 stitches should be knit on the RS and purled on the WS.

After working a total of 13 rows as established, yarn, break #140 and #105 leaving a 3cm tail.

Body

The body of this cardigan is knitted in the round throughout.

<<Work to underarm>>

Round 1: Change to 3mm needle. Cast on 6 sts on RH needle using #140 which is assigned for Round 1 according to colour assignment, and K112, M1, K112.

At the EOR, cast on 6 sts using backward loop cast-on. This together with the first 6 cast-on sts makes the set of extra stitches for front band. Proceed to work in the round. (Refer to page 19 for working with extra stitches.)

Rounds 2 to 84: Work according to the colour assignment, working *extra stitches* in between the centre of front body. Make sure to knit the YO through the back loop.

<<To make *extra stitches* for armhole>>

After working Round 84: Thread waste yarn through underarm stitches on each side using tapestry needle, by identifying the centre of the underarm stitches.

1. The centre of the right underarm will be 57th stitch from BOR; the centre of the left underarm will be 57th stitch from EOR.
2. This centre stitch can be easily identified, since there are 16. Octagon pattern repeats for this cardigan – 8 patterns for the back and 4 patterns for each of the fronts. Therefore, the centre stitch will be located in between patterns.
3. Thread waste yarn through this 'centre stitch' together with 8 sts on each side (17 sts all together). These stitches will still be on the cord of the circular needle. Do this for both underarms.

Round 85: With #105 and #246, work up to the sts held for right underarm. Remove the 17 sts with waste yarn from needle. Cast on 12 sts using #105 and #246. (See p. 33)

Proceed by working along the back body up to the sts held for left underarm. Remove sts from needle and cast on 12 sts as done for right underarm, and work to EOR.

Extra stitches are now made for both armholes.

Be sure to decrease at both sides of armhole every 2nd rnd 3 times.

Continue working for 35 rnds.

<<To make extra stitches for neckline>>

Round 120: Cast off 6 *extra stitches* using two colours before proceeding to body and then cast off 6 *extra stitches* in the same way at the EOR. Break yarn.

After working Round 120

Slip 11 sts for left and right neck onto waste yarn.

Round 121: Cast on 6 sts using #105 and #246, decrease (K2tog) at the beginning of body, and proceed working along right front, 12 *extra stitches*, along back, 12 *extra stitches*, left front, decrease SKPO (Sl1, K1, pass slipped st over knit st) at the end of body and cast on 6 sts again.

These 12 newly cast-on stitches will become the *extra stitches* for neck opening and the centre of these *extra stitches* will become the BOR and all subsequent colour changes will be done here.

Round 122 to 138: Decreases for neckline will be worked on both sides of the *extra stitches* as follows:

(Note that no increases or decreases will be made within the 12 *extra stitches*.)

Decrease 1 st every 4 rnd, then 1 st every 2nd rnd 6 times, and work even for 1 rnd to shoulder. Break yarn leaving a 3cm tail.

Join shoulders

1. Prepare for shoulder seam by working 1 additional row for back by slipping stitches onto RH needle, up to the centre of *extra stitches* for right sleeve.
2. Tie a knot using #290 and #274 yarn which will be used for working the additional row. Leave a 3cm tail for #290 and about three times the shoulder length for #274. The knot will be used as a 'stopper', and will be worked from the centre of the *extra stitches* for right sleeve, across back body to the centre of *extra stitches* on the other side. Leave the BGC as is and cut PC leaving a 3cm tail.
3. Turn the work inside out.

   Using the remaining #274 yarn and crochet hook, work three needle cast-off starting from the shoulder edge. Cast off the 6 *extra stitches* for the neckband separately using slip stitch cast-off. (Be careful not to join *extra stitches* together with back neckband.) (See p.21)
4. Join the other shoulder as well, using slip stitch seam with #274 yarn which was kept longer, and cast off *extra stitches* using slip stitch cast-off.
5. Unravel back neck stitches. Cut the unravelled yarn at the middle and tie at the base of both shoulders.

Sleeves

1. Cut open *extra stitches* and pick up and knit into all stitches and rows, beginning at the centre of the held stitches, using #140 yarn. Pick up and knit stitches from between *extra stitches* and body. (See p.22.)

   Adjust stitch count to 108 sts on the second round.

NOTE: *This cardigan uses a pattern with top and bottom halves that are not symmetrical, therefore the rows for the colour assignment for the sleeve will need to be worked in the reverse order.*

2. Decrease at inside sleeve 1st every 4th rnd 18 times, and then every 6th rnd 6 times. Decrease by knitting to the last st of the previous round (the round before the decrease), slip the last st onto RH needle unworked, and then work a double decrease (SK2PO = Sl1, K2tog, pass slipped st over knit st) between the last st of the previous round and the first 2 sts of the decrease round. This way, the decrease for inside sleeves will not be missed.

   Then work 7 rnds even.
3. After working 115 rnds.

   <<Cuff>>

   Change to 2.5mm circular needle. Cuff will be 60 sts.

   Rounds 1 to 11: Work in corrugated 2x2 ribbing (K2 with #105, P2 with #140) for 11 rnds.

   Break #105 leaving a 3cm tail.

   Round 12: Purl with #140. Finish by casting off with #140 and yarn needle. (See sewn cast off on p.123.)
4. Work other sleeve in the same way and cast off using tapestry needle.

Neckband and front bands

<<Neckband>>

Worked flat, by cutting open at the centre of *extra stitches* along neckline.

Row 1: Using 2.5mm circular needle (40cm) and #140, pick up and knit a total of 99 sts from every stitch and every row, beginning with the 11 sts held for right front, from between *extra stitches* and right front of body, from sts held for back body, from between *extra stitches* and left front of body, and sts held for left front of body (see p.22).

Row 2 (WS): Tie #105 onto #140, and work in corrugated 2x2 ribbing (K2 with #140, P2 with #105), beginning and ending in P3 with #105 so that they will appear (K2 with #105, P2 with #140) and beginning and end 3 sts as knit stitches on RS (odd row), and decreasing 3 sts at the centre back. (Total 96 sts.)

Rows 3 to 11: Work 9 rows in corrugated 2x2 ribbing, break #105.

Row 12 (WS): Knit with #140 to EOR.

Finish by casting off with #140 and tapestry needle. (See sewn cast off on p.123)

<<Front bands>>

Worked flat, by cutting open at the centre of *extra stitches*.

Row 1: Using 2.5mm (40cm) circular needle and #140 yarn, pick up and knit from all rows. Begin at the bottom of hem ribbing for right front and from the neck edge for left front. Be sure to leave a selvedge stitch when picking up and knitting stitches from the ribbing section of hem and neckline, and between body and *extra stitches* for body. There will be a need to shift by one-half of a stitch when working between ribbing section to body section with *extra stitches*, to work tightly to avoid any gaps.

Rows 2 to 12: Tie #105 onto #140 and work in corrugated 2x2 ribbing on WS (even row) [P2 with #105 K2 with #140] on RS (odd row) [K2 with #105, P2 with #140]. Beginning and end 2 sts should be knit sts from RS while decreasing, ending up with 114.

Continue working 11 rows with the same colour.

Row 13: Break #105, cast off with #140, knitting K sts and purling P sts.

Work the same for the other front band.

Treatment for extra stitches, see p.28.

Weaving in ends and washing, see p.28.

Make button holes, see p.31.

After washing –

Make button holes in between stitches and work whip stitch around the hole.

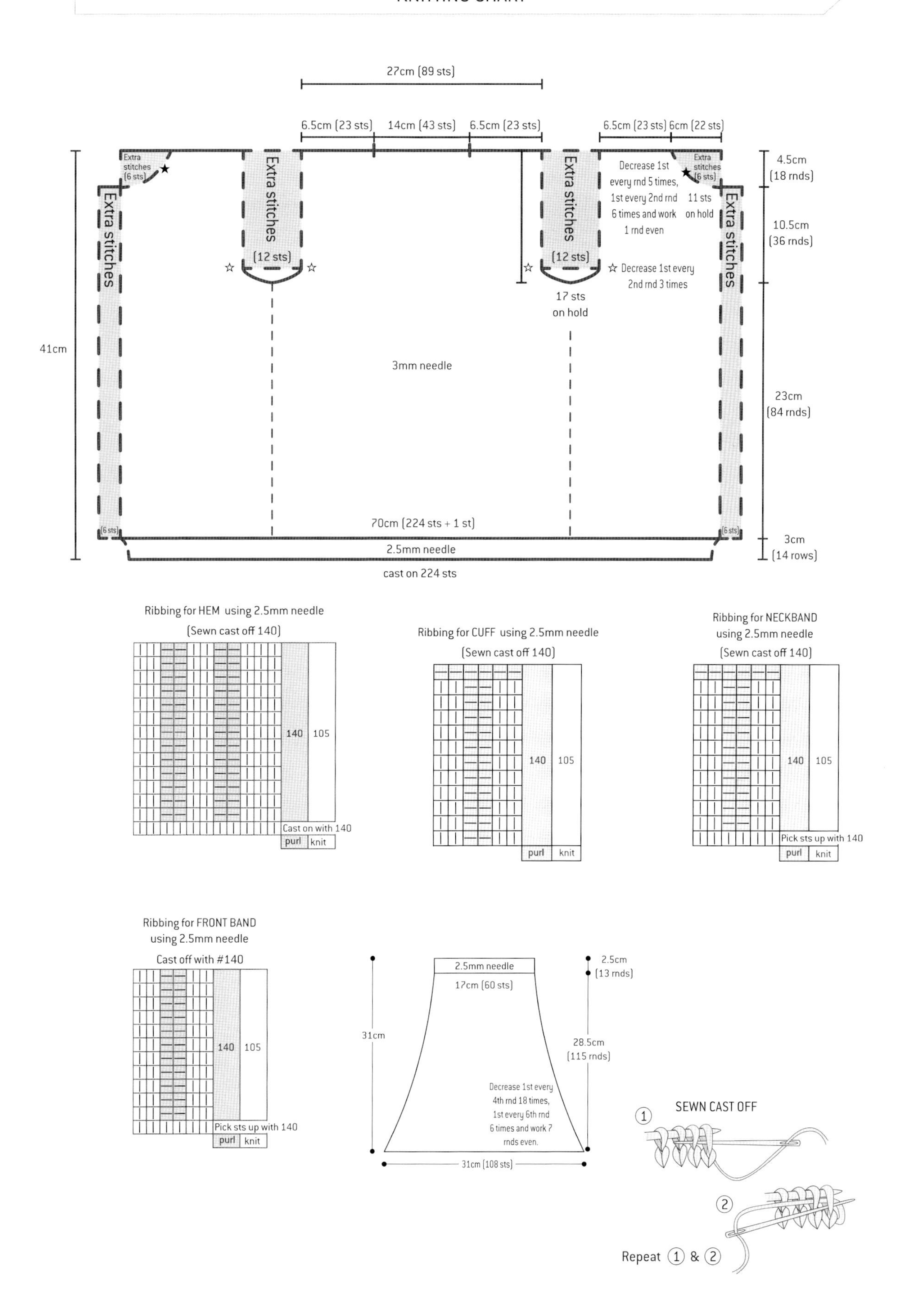

NOTE: Colour assignment for ribbing is based on how it will appear on RS

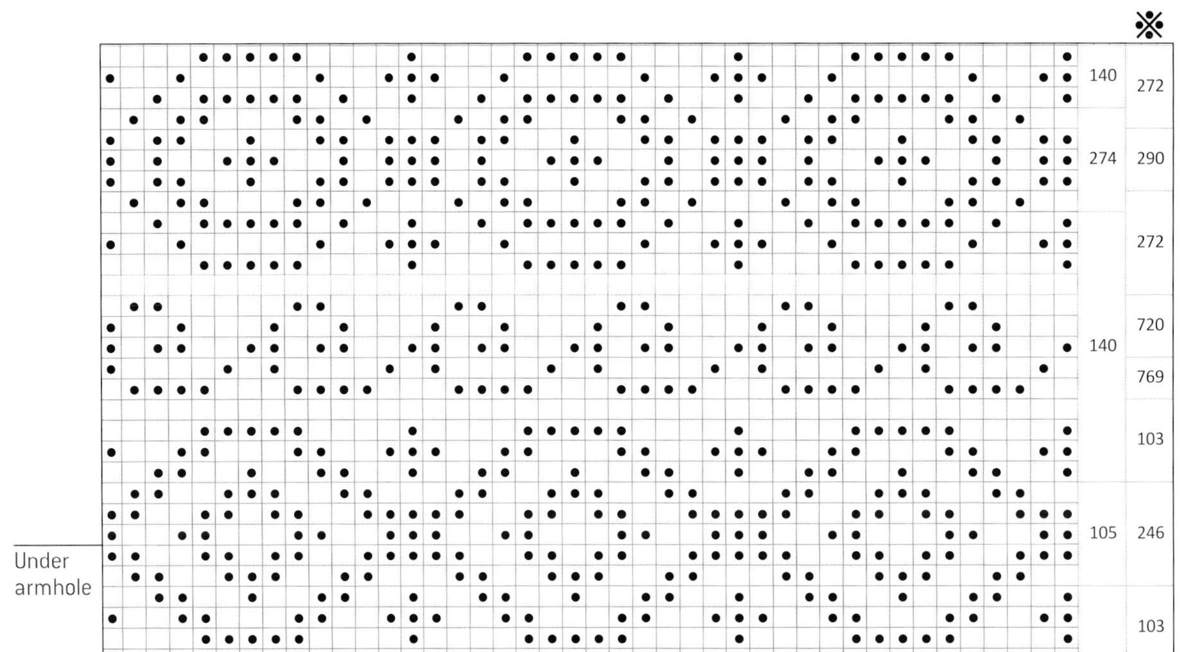

140
272
274
290
272
720
140
769
103
105
246
103
Under armhole

Shoulder meeting

Neckline

Sleeve start

BGC	PC
140	720
	769
	290
274	272
	290
	720
140	
	769
	246
105	103
	246
	720
140	
	769
	272
274	290
	272
	720
140	
	769
	103
105	246
	103
140	720
	769

※

She started to realize the
difference between girls and
boys. This is my girly colouration

12 GOOD OLD MEMORY
Girl's cardigan

This is for my granddaughter with the same pattern as 'The Rocking Chair'.
She started to realize the difference between girls and boys. This is my girly colouration.

Yarn

Total 8 colours – 12 balls

 130 (Sky) 1 ball

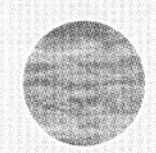 134 (Blue Danube) 2 ball

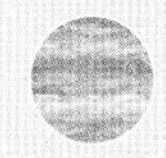 135 (Surf) 1 ball

 140 (Rye) 2 balls

 268 (Dog Rose) 1 ball

 272 (Fog) 1 ball

 274 (Green mist) 2 balls

 768 (Egg Shell) 2 balls

Total weight of cardigan – 227g

Tools & Notions

Circular needles: 2.5mm (40cm and 80cm or longer), 3mm (40cm and 80cm or longer)

Crochet hook: 2.3mm crochet hook

Tapestry needle: Small and medium

Waste yarn (to hold stitches)

Stitch markers

Buttons (desired number)

Tension

1 pattern repeat

(Medium) Octagon 14 sts x 11 rows = 4cm x 3.2cm

(Narrow) Wave pattern 7 sts x 7 rows = 2cm x 1.3cm

(including single colour rows underneath and on top)

Finished measurement

Bust circumference: 70cm

Back neck to sleeve edge: 47.5cm

Length: 41cm

INSTRUCTIONS

Worked in the round up to shoulders, apart from hem, by working *extra stitches* in between for front bands, armholes and neck opening.

Ribbing for hem

Worked flat for 13 rows, including cast on.

Row 1: With 2.5mm 40cm circular needle and with colour #768 yarn, cast on 224 sts.

Rows 2 to 13: Tie #140 onto #768. Begin on the WS row by P3 with #140 and continue working in corrugated 2x2 ribbing [K2 with #768, P2 with #140] and end the row in P3 with #140. First and last 3 stitches (for hem) should be knit from the RS and purled on the WS.

After working a total of 13 rows as established, break #768, #140 yarn leaving a 3cm tail.

Body

The body of this cardigan is knitted in the round throughout.

<<Work to underarm>>

Round 1: Change to 3mm needle. Cast on 6 sts on RH needle using #768 which is assigned for Round 1 according to colour assignment, and K112, M1, K112.

At the EOR, cast on 6 sts using backward loop cast-on. This together with the first 6 cast-on sts makes the set of extra stitches for front band. Proceed to work in the round. (Refer to p.25 for working with extra stitches).

Rounds 2 to 84: Work according to the colour assignment and work *extra stitches* in between the centre of front body. Make sure to knit the 'yarn overs' (YO) through the back loop.

<<To make *extra stitches* for armhole>>

After working Round 84: Thread waste yarn through underarm stitches on each side using tapestry needle, by identifying the centre of the underarm stitches.

1. The centre of the right underarm will be 57th stitch from BOR; the centre of the left underarm will be 57th stitch from EOR.

2. This centre stitch can be easily identified, since there are 16. Octagon pattern repeats for this cardigan – 8 patterns for the back and 4 patterns for each of the fronts. Therefore, the centre stitch will be located in between patterns.

3. Thread waste yarn through this 'centre stitch' together with 8 sts on side (17 sts all together). These stitches will still be on the cord of the circular needle. Do this for both underarms.

   Round 85: With #140 and #272, work up to the sts held for right underarm. Remove the 17 sts with waste yarn from needle. Cast on 12 stitches using #140 and #272. (See p.33)

   Proceed working along the back body up to the sts held for left underarm. Remove sts from needle and cast on 12 sts as done for right underarm, and work to EOR.

   Extra stitches are now made for both armholes.

   Be sure to decrease at both sides of armhole every 2nd rnd 3 times.

   Continue working for 35 rounds.

   <<To make *extra stitches* for neckline>>

   Round 120: Cast off 6 *extra stitches* using two colours before proceeding to body and then cast off 6 *extra stitches* in the same way at the EOR. Break yarn.

   After working Round 120

   Slip 11 sts for left and right neck onto waste yarn.

   Round 121: Cast on 6 sts using #140 and #272, decrease (K2tog) at the beginning of body, and proceed working along right front, 12 *extra stitches*, along back, 12 *extra stitches*, left front, decrease SKPO (Sl1, K1, pass slipped st over knit st) at the end of body and cast on 6 sts again.

   These 12 newly cast-on stitches will become the *extra stitches* for neck opening, and the centre of these *extra stitches* will become the BOR and all subsequent colour changes will be done here.

   Round 122 to 138: Decreases for neckline will be worked on both sides of the *extra stitches* as follows.

   (Note that no increases or decreases will be made within the 12 *extra stitches*.)

   Decrease 1 st every 4 rnd, then 1 st every 2 rnd 6 times, and work even for 1 rnd to shoulder. Break yarn leaving a 3cm tail.

   Join shoulders

1. Prepare for shoulder seam by working 1 additional row for back by slipping stitches onto RH needle, up to the centre of *extra stitches* for right sleeve.
2. Tie a knot using #140 and #272 yarn which will be used for working the additional row.

   Leave a 3cm tail for #140 and about three times the shoulder length for #272. The knot will be used as a 'stopper', and will be worked from the centre of the *extra stitches* for right sleeve, across back body to the centre of *extra stitches* on the other side. Leave #272 as is and cut #140 leaving a 3cm tail.
3. Turn the work inside out.

   Using the remaining #272 yarn and crochet hook, work three needle cast-off starting from the shoulder edge. Cast off the 6 extra sts for the neckband separately using slip stitch cast-off. (Be careful not to join *extra stitches* together with back neckband.) (See p.21)
4. Join the other shoulder as well, using three needle cast-off with #272 yarn which was kept longer, and cast off *extra stitches* using slip stitch cast-off.
5. Unravel back neck stitches. Cut the unravelled yarn in the middle and tie at the base of both shoulders.

   Sleeves

1. Cut open *extra stitches* and pick up and knit into all stitches and rows beginning at the centre of the held stitches using #768 yarn. Pick up and knit stitches from between *extra stitches* and body. (See p.22.) Adjust stitch count to 108 sts on the second round.

NOTE: *This cardigan uses a pattern with top and bottom halves that are not symmetrical, therefore the rows for the colour assignment for the sleeve will need to be worked in reverse order.*

2. Decrease at inside sleeve 1st every 4th rnd 18 times and then 1st every 6th rnd 6 times. Decrease by knitting to the last st of the previous round (the round before the decrease), slip the last st onto RH needle unworked, and then work a double decrease (SK2PO = Sl1, K2tog, pass slipped st over knit st) between the last st of the previous round and the first 2 sts of the decrease round. This way, the decrease for inside sleeves will not be missed.

   Then work 7 rnds even.
3. After working 115 rounds

   <<Cuff>>

   Change to 2.5mm circular needle. Cuff will be 60 sts.

   Rounds 1 to 11: Work in corrugated 2x2 ribbing (K2 with #140, P2 with #768) for 11 rnds.

   Break #140 leaving a 3cm tail.

   Round 12: Purl with #768. Finish by casting off with #768 and tapestry needle. (See sewn cast off on p. 131.)

4. Work other sleeve in the same way and cast off using tapestry needle.

Neckband and front bands

<<Neckband>>

Worked flat, cut open at the centre of *extra stitches* along neckline.

Row 1: Using 2.5mm circular needle (40cm) and #768, pick up and knit a total of 99 sts from every stitch and every row beginning with the 11 sts held for right front, from between *extra stitches* and right front of body, the sts held for back body, from between *extra stitches* and left front of body, and the sts held for left front. (See p.22)

Row 2 (WS): Tie #140 onto #768 and work in corrugated 2x2 ribbing (K2 with #768, P2 with #140), beginning and ending in P3 with #140 so that they will appear (K2 with #140, P2 with #768) and beginning and end 3 sts as knit stitches on RS. (odd row), and decreasing 3 sts at the centre back. (Total 96 sts.)

Rows 3 to 11: Work 9 rows in corrugated 2x2 ribbing. Break #140.

Row 12 (WS): Knit with #768 to EOR.

Finish by casting off with #768 and tapestry needle. (See sewn cast off on p.131.)

<<Front bands>>

Worked flat, by cutting open at the centre of *extra stitches*.

Row 1: Using 2.5mm (40cm) circular needle and #768 yarn, pick up and knit from all rows. Begin from the bottom of hem ribbing for right front and from the neck edge for left front. Be sure to leave a selvedge stitch when picking up and knitting stitches from the ribbing section of hem and neckline, and between body and *extra stitches* for body. There will be a need to shift by one-half of a stitch when working between ribbing section to body section with *extra stitches*, to work tightly to avoid any gaps.

Rows 2 to 12: Tie #140 onto #768 and work in corrugated 2x2 ribbing on WS (even row) [P2 with #140, K2 with #768], on RS (add row) [K2 with #140, P2 with #768] Beginning and end 2 sts should be knit sts from RS while decreasing, ending up with 116 sts. Continue working 11 rows with the same colour.

Row 13: Break #140, cast off with #768, knitting K sts and purling P sts.

Work the same for the other front band.

Treatment for extra stitches, see p.28.

Weaving in ends and washing, see p.28.

Make button holes, see p.31.

After washing –

Make button holes in between stitches and work whip stitch around the hole.

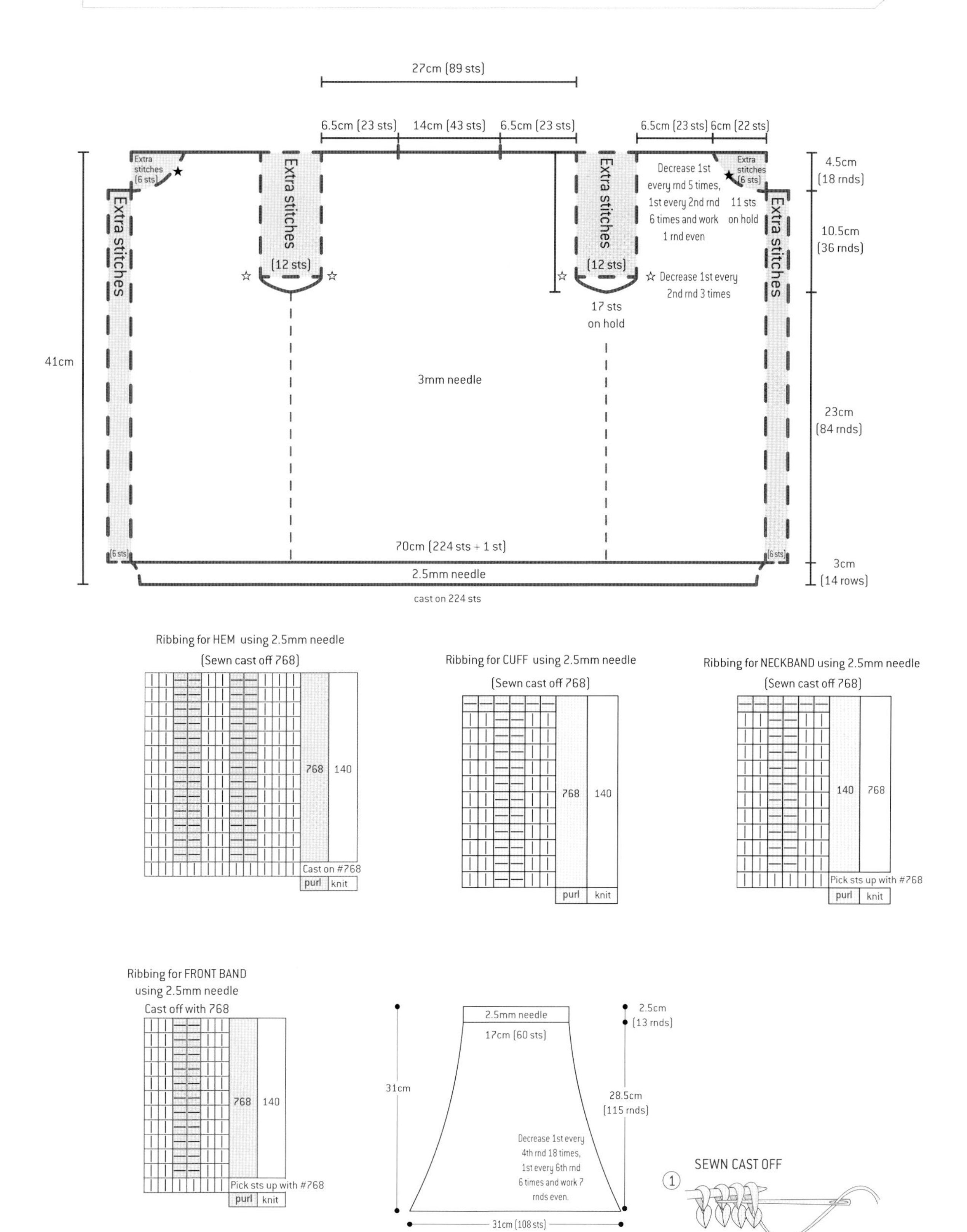

NOTE: Colour assignment for ribbing is based on how it will appear on RS

768
135
268
140 272
268
135
768
134 274
768
130
268
140 272
268
130
768

BGC	PC
134	274
140	768
	268
135	272
140	268
	768
134	274
140	768
	268
130	272
140	268
	768
134	274
135	768
	268
140	272
135	268
	768
134	274
130	768
	268
140	272
130	268
	768
134	274
	768

Whenever I see peat turf banks,
I imagine cosmic space.

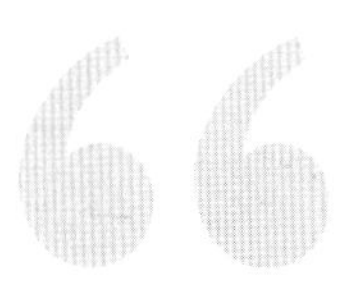

13 COSMIC SPACE
Men's cardigan

Pattern 4 'Sakura' is used for this work. Whenever I see peat turf banks, I imagine cosmic space. After cutting, the peat turfs are dried in neat layers. Some Shetlanders say "these are dead heath". I feel a big rotation in it. I used very simple repetition of colouration for this work.

Yarn

Total 5 colours – 25 balls

102 (Shaela) 4 balls

103 (Solmit) 5 balls

113 (Sholmit/Nat. White) 3 balls

121 (Mogit/Eesit) 6 balls

1340 (Cosmos) 7balls

Total weight of cardigan – 588g

Tools & Notions

Circular needles: 2.5mm (40cm and 80cm or longer), 3mm (40cm and 80cm or longer)

Crochet hook: 2.3mm crochet hook

Tapestry needle: Small and medium

Waste yarn (to hold stitches)

Stitch markers

Buttons (desired number)

Tension

1 pattern stitch

(Medium) Flowers 12 sts x 15 rows = 3.7cm x 5cm

(Medium + Zigzag) Wave and Cross Pattern

12 sts x 19 rows = 3.7cm x 6cm

Finished measurement

Bust circumference: 130cm

Back neck to sleeve edge: 86.5cm

Length: 70cm

INSTRUCTIONS

Worked in the round up to shoulders, apart from hem, by working *extra stitches* in between for front bands, armholes and neck opening.

Ribbing for hem

Worked flat for 28 rows, including cast on.

Row 1: With 2.5mm 60cm circular needle and with colour #103 yarn, cast on 408 sts.

Row 2: Tie #121 onto #103. Begin on the WS row by P3 with #121 and continue working in corrugated 2x2 ribbing [K2 with #103, P2 with #121] and end the row in P3 with #121. First and last 3 sts should appear as knit sts from the RS. After working a total of 28 rows as established, break both yarns leaving a 3cm tail.

Body

The body of this cardigan is knitted in the round throughout.

<<Work to underarm>>:

Round 1: Change to 3mm needle. Cast on 6 sts on RH needle using #103 which is assigned for Round 1 according to colour chart, and K204, M1, K204.

At EOR cast on 6 sts using backward loop cast-on. This together with the first 6 cast-on sts makes the set of *extra stitches* for front band. Proceed to work in the round. (Refer to p.25 for working with *extra stitches*.)

Rounds 2 to 105: Work according to the colour assignment and work *extra stitches* in between the centre of front body. Make sure to knit yarn over (YO) through the back loop.

Be careful which hand and finger holds which yarn, as the BGC becomes the PC and the PC becomes the BGC for this cardigan.

After working up to Round 105, begin decreasing for neckline as follows:

Round 106 (Decrease round): Knit 6 *extra stitches* then knit the first 2 right front sts together.

Work with #121 only until the 2 sts before *extra stitches*, SKPO (Sl1, K1, pass slipped st over knit st), and then work the remaining 6 *extra stitches*.

Work a decrease round every 4th rnd 20 times and then every 6th rnd 6 times. Then work 5 rnds even.

<<Make extra stitches for armhole>>

After working Round 133: thread waste yarn through underarm sts to be kept on

hold. These underarm sts can be easily and accurately identified by looking at the number of pattern repeats.

Since 1 pattern stitch has 12 sts, there are 34 pattern repeats all together, which means there are 8.5 patterns repeats each for left and right fronts. Look for a pattern in an area where neckline decreases have not started yet, and identify the 12-sts pattern repeat. The centre st of the 9th pattern will be the centre of the underarm.

Follow this stitch up to the current level (which will be 103rd stitch from BOR) together with 10 sts on both sides (making a total of 21 sts). These shall be kept on hold by threading waste yarn through using a tapestry needle. Be sure that these sts are still on the needle as well.

In the same way, identify underarm sts for left armhole, and thread waste yarn through (103rd sts from EOR) together with 10 sts on both sides.

NOTE: *When identifying this stitch, mark sts on both sides with pins and make sure that the number of pattern repeats on both sides is the same.*

Round 134: With #102, work up to the held sts for right underarm, remove the held sts from needle and continue casting on 12 sts using back loop cast-on method.

Continue working back up to left underarm and again remove held sts from needle and cast on 12 sts, and proceed to EOR. *extra stitch*es are now complete for both armholes.

Round 135: Begin working 6 *extra stitch*es by repeating [1 st in PC (#102), 1 st in BGC (#103)] 3 times. Then work right front until the 2 sts before *extra stitch*es for right armhole, then SKPO (Sl1, K1, pass slipped st over knit st).

Work the armhole *extra stitch*es as follows:

[1 st in BGC (#103), 1 st in PC (#102)] 3 times, [1 st in PC (#102), 1 st in BGC (#103)] 3 times, and then knit the first 2 back sts together. Continue to work along the back until the 2 sts before *extra stitch*es for the opposite armhole, then SKPO (Sl1, K1, pass slipped st over knit st).

[1 st in BGC (#103), 1 st in PC (#102)] 3 times, [1 st in PC (#102), 1 st in BGC (#103)] 3 times, and then knit the first 2 left front sts together.

NOTE: *Work body and extra stitches according to colour assignments up to shoulder, while decreasing on both sides of armhole every 2nd rnd 4 times, and decreasing for neck opening at the same time.*

Join shoulders

1. Prepare for shoulder seam by working 1 additional row for back by slipping stitches onto RH needle, up to the centre of *extra stitch*es for right sleeve.
2. Tie a knot using #113 and #1340 yarn which will be used for working the additional row. Leave a 3cm tail for #1340 and about three times the shoulder length for #113. The knot will be used as a 'stopper', and will be worked from the centre of the *extra stitch*es for right sleeve, across back body to the centre of *extra stitch*es on the other side. Leave the BGC #113 as is and cut PC #1340 leaving a 3cm tail.
3. Turn the work inside out.

   Using the remaining #113 yarn and crochet hook, work three needle cast-off (see p.21) starting from the shoulder edge. Cast off the 6 *extra stitch*es for the neckband separately using slip stitch cast-off. (Be careful not to join *extra stitch*es together with back neckband.)
4. Join the other shoulder as well, using three needle cast-off with #113 yarn which was kept longer, and cast off *extra stitch*es using slip stitch cast-off.
5. Unravel back neck stitches. Cut the unravelled yarn in the middle and tie at the base of both shoulders.

Sleeves

1. Cut open *extra stitch*es and pick up and knit into all stitches and rows beginning at the centre of the held stitches using #103 yarn. Pick up and knit stitches from between *extra stitch*es and body. (See p.22.) Adjust stitch count to 180 sts on the second round.

NOTE: *This cardigan uses a pattern with top and bottom halves that are not symmetrical, therefore the rows for the colour assignment for the sleeve will need to be worked in reverse order.*

2. Decrease at inside sleeve every 2nd rnd 12 times, and then every 4th rnd 36 times. Decrease by knitting to the last st of the previous rnd (the rnd before the decrease), slip the last st onto RH needle unworked, and then work a double decrease (SK2PO = Sl1, K2tog, pass slipped st over knit st) between the last st of the previous rnd and the first 2 sts of the decrease rnd. This way, the decrease for inside sleeves will not be missed. Then work 15 rnds even.

3. After working 183 rnds:

   <<Cuffs>>

   Rounds 1 to 19: Change to 2.5mm circular needle and work in corrugated 2x2 ribbing [K2 with #121, P2 with #103] for 19 rnds. Break #121 leaving a 3cm tail.

   Round 20: Purl with #103 to end of row.

   Finish by casting off with #103 and tapestry needle. [See sewn cast off on p.131]

4. Work other sleeve in the same way and cast off using tapestry needle.

Neckband and front bands

Worked flat, along the neckline and front bands.

Using 2.5mm circular needle [80cm or longer] pick up and knit every stitch and every row and then work in corrugated 2x2 ribbing.

Row 1: With #103, pick up and knit a total of 563 sts from every stitch and every row, beginning at the bottom edge of the right front band, over and down to the bottom of left front band.

Row 2 (WS): Tie #121 and work in corrugated 2x2 ribbing repeating [P2 with #121, K2 with #103], while decreasing 1 st at the centre back neck and ending in P2 with #121. [Total 562 sts.]

Rows 3 to 18: All even numbered rows: Work as Row 2.

All odd numbered rows: Repeat [K2 with #121, P2 with #103] and end in K2 with #121.

After working 18 rnds, break #121 and cast off in 2x2 ribbing as established with #103.

Make sure that the cast-off does not loosen.

Treatment for extra stitches, see p.28.

Weaving in ends and washing, see p.28.

Make button holes, see p.31.

After washing –

Make button holes in between stitches and work whip stitch around the hole.

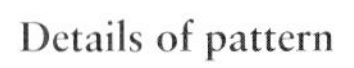

Details of pattern

KNITTING CHART

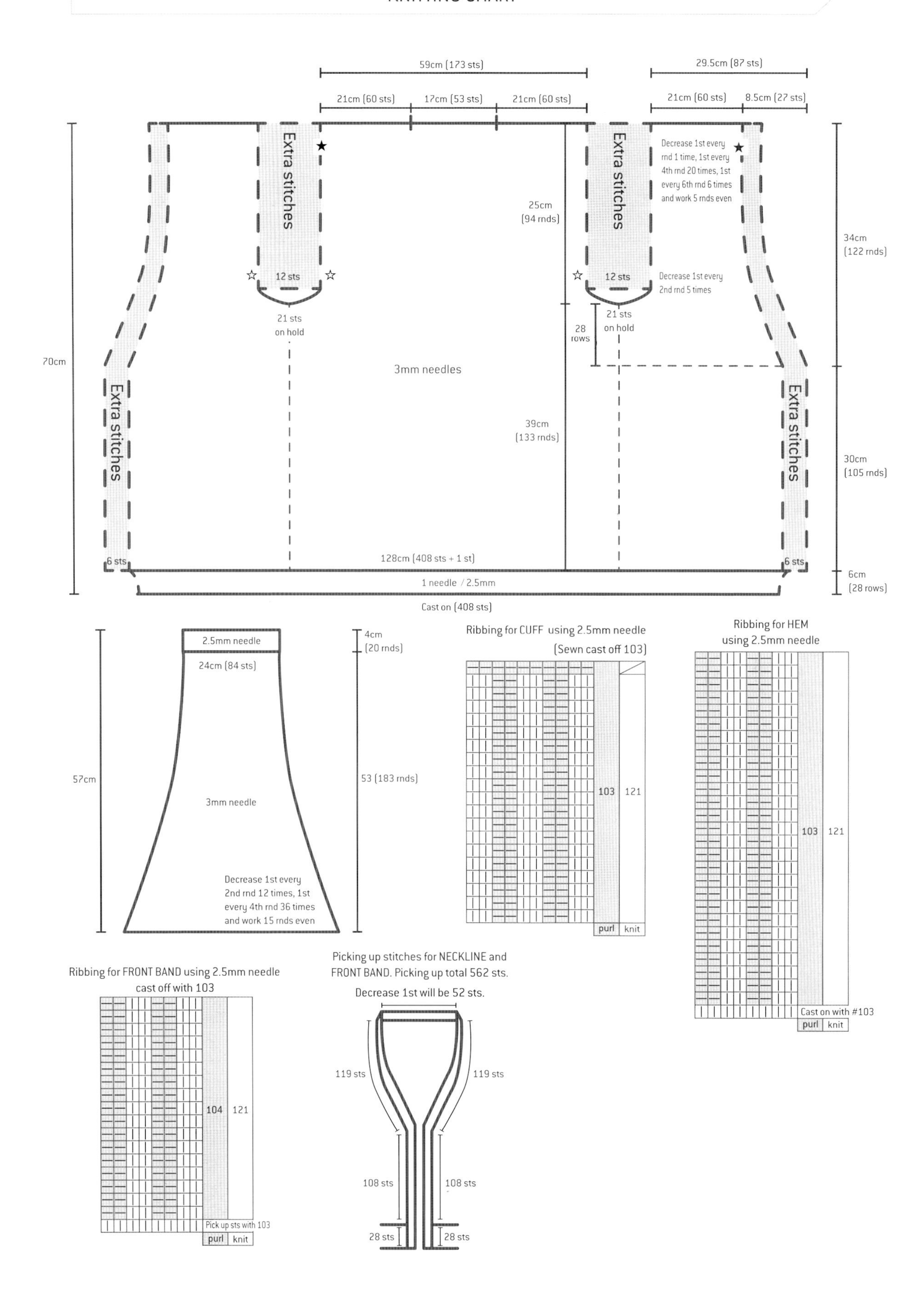

NOTE: Colour assignment for ribbing is based on how it will appear on RS

BGC	PC
103	102
102	1340
113	1340
102	1340
103	102
121	103
121	1340
121	103
103	102
102	1340
113	1340
102	1340
103	102
121	103
121	1340
121	103

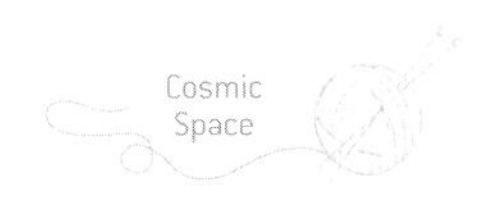

Ancient Japan was called
HI-IZURU-KUNI

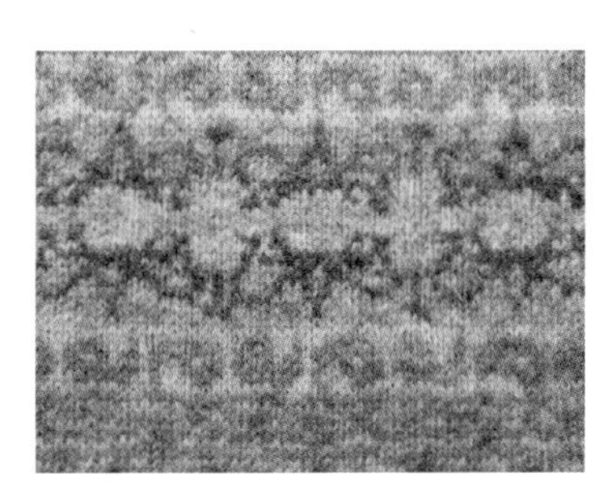

14 HI-IZURU-KUNI
Women's jumper

Ancient Japan was called Hi-Izuru-Kuni. I had a chance to see a very fine watch named Hi-Izuru-Kuni. This is my original pattern. Motifs are magatama (ancient comma-shaped beads) a stream and old crest.

Yarn

Total 6 colours – 19 balls

 130 (Sky) 4 balls

 135 (Surf) 3 balls

 140 (Rye) 3 balls

 170 (Fjord) 3 balls

 620 (Lilac) 4 balls

 768 (Egg shell) 2 balls

Total weight of jumper – 383g

Tools & Notions

Circular needles: 2.5mm (40cm, 60cm and 80cm or longer), 3mm (60cm and 80cm or longer)

Crochet hook: 2.3mm

Tapestry needle: Small and medium

Waste yarn (to hold stitches)

Stitch markers

Tension

1 pattern stitch

(Large) David's Star
20 sts x 23 rows = 6.3cm x 6.2cm

(Small) Magatama pattern
16 sts x 7 rows = 5cm x 2cm

(Small) the Stream pattern
16 sts x 7 rows = 5cm x 2cm

Finished measurement

Bust circumference: 100cm

Back neck to sleeve edge: 72cm

Length: 51cm

INSTRUCTIONS

Worked in the round up to shoulders by working *extra stitches* in between for armholes and neck opening.

Ribbing for hem

Round 1: With 2.5mm 60cm circular needle and with colour #140 yarn, cast on 320 sts. Cast on is counted as 1 round.

Rounds 2 & 3: Tie #130 onto #140 and work in corrugated 2x2 ribbing by repeating [K2 with #130, P2 with #140]. Work 2 rnds.

Rounds 4 to 15: Switch from #140 to #135 and work in corrugated 2x2 ribbing by repeating [K2 with #130, P2 with #135]. Work 12 rnds. Break yarn leaving a 3cm tail.

Body

<<Work to underarm>>

Round 1: Change to 3mm needle. Work 1 round with #768 according to colour assignment chart by tying #768 onto either one of the remaining tail ends from the hem.

Rounds 2 to 99: Tie #620 onto #768 and work up to Round 99. Then break yarn leaving a 3cm tail.

NOTE: *Floats tend to get longer when a pattern repeat has a bigger stitch count, so make sure to twist the yarn on the WS when a float extends over 6 sts or more.*

<<Make *extra stitches* for armhole>>

1. **After working Round 99**, slip 21 sts onto waste yarn and leave them on hold for underarm, using yarn threaded through tapestry needle. Mark the centre stitch (11 sts from BOR and 10 sts from EOR).

NOTE: *Make sure that the stitch at the centre of the held sts always matches the centre of the pattern.*

2. Then identify which sts are to be held for the opposite underarm. These underarm sts can be easily and accurately identified by looking at the number of pattern repeats. The David's Star pattern st has 20 sts, there are 16 pattern repeats all together, which means there are 8 patterns repeat for front and back. BOR is centre of the David's Star pattern. Count 7 full patterns and the centre stitch of the next pattern will be the centre of the underarm sts (161st stitch from BOR). This, together with 10 sts on each side (total of 21 sts), shall be kept on hold by threading waste yarn through using tapestry needle. Be sure that these sts are still on the needle as well. Be careful not to sew waste yarn into these sts.

*When identifying this st, mark sts on both sides with pins and make sure that the number of pattern repeats on both sides are the same.

Round 100: Remove the 21 sts for left underarm from needle. Cast on 6 sts on RH needle using #135 and #140 yarn (See p.33), and proceed working along the front body. Work based on colour assignment, but disregard those sts which have been removed.

Work up to the held sts for the right underarm. Remove held sts from needle. Cast on 12 sts on RH needle using #135 and #140 yarn.

Continue working to EOR. Cast on 6 sts at EOR. *Extra sts* are now made for both armholes. (Refer to p.25 for working with extra stitches.)

From the next round, be sure to decrease at both sides of armholes every 2nd rnd 3 times.

The next round, Round 101 will be worked as follows:

Round 101: Begin working 6 *extra stitches* by repeating [1 st in PC (#135), 1 st in BGC (#140)] 3 times, then **knit the first 2 front sts together**. Continue working along the remaining front, until **2 sts before** *extra stitches* for right armhole, then SKPO (Sl1, K1, pass slipped st over knit st).

Work the armhole *extra stitches* [1 st in BGC (#140), 1 st in PC (#135)] 3 times, [1 st in PC (#135), 1 st in BGC (#140)] 3 times, and then knit the first 2 back sts together.

Continue to work along the back until the 2 sts before *extra stitches* for the opposite armhole then work SKPO (Sl1, K1, pass slipped st over knit st). Work the remaining 6 *extra stitches* by repeating [1 st in BGC (#140), 1 st in PC (#135)] 3 times.

Then work according to colour assignment until before neck line.

<<Make *extra stitches* for neck opening>>

After working 56 Rounds (from armhole) slip 31 sts for neck opening onto waste yarn to be kept on hold. (The centre stitch will be 67th stitch from BOR together with 15 sts on each side.)

Rounds 57: Work with #620 until 2 sts before the held sts and then decrease by SKPO.

Remove held sts from needle and cast on 12 sts on RH needle. Knit the first 2 sts of right front together, skip the pattern for the removed sts. And work to the EOR.

While working according to colour assignment, decrease at both sides of the neck opening every rnd 11 times, then every 2nd rnd 3 times. Break yarn leaving a 3cm tail.

Join shoulders

1. Prepare for shoulder seam by working 1 additional row for back by slipping sts onto RH needle, up to the centre of *extra stitches* for right sleeve.
2. Tie a knot using #135 and #140 yarn which will be used for working the additional row. Leave a 3cm tail for #135 and about three times the shoulder length for #140. The knot will be used as a 'stopper', and will be worked from the centre of the *extra stitches* for right sleeve, across back body to the centre of *extra stitches* on the other side.

   Leave the BGC as is and cut PC leaving a 3cm tail.
3. Turn the work inside out.

   Using the remaining #140 yarn and crochet hook, work three needle cast-off starting from the shoulder edge. Cast off the 6 *extra stitches* for the neck opening separately using slip stitch cast-off. (Make sure that the *extra stitches* are not joined together with back neckband.) (See p.21)
4. Join the other shoulder as well, using three needle cast-off with #140 yarn which was kept longer, and cast off *extra stitches* using slip stitch cast-off.
5. Unravel back neck sts. Cut the unravelled yarn at the middle and tie at the base of both shoulders.

Sleeves

1. Cut open at the centre of *extra stitches* and pick up and knit into all sts and rows beginning at the centre of the held sts, using #620 yarn. Pick up and knit sts from between *extra stitches* and body. (See p.22.) Adjust stitch count to 160 sts on the second round.

TIP: As it is difficult to adjust stitch count and decrease to shape inside sleeve based on colour assignment at the same time, placing markers in advance on the 2 sts to be worked together to adjust st count will help, as this will allow you to focus on matching the pattern st without forgetting about the decrease.

NOTE: *This jumper uses a pattern with top and bottom halves that are not symmetrical, therefore the rows for the colour assignment for the sleeve will need to be worked in reverse order.*

2. Decrease at inside sleeve every 2nd rnd 6 times, every 4th rnd 15 times, every 6th rnd 13 times and then work 12 rnds even. Decrease by knitting to the last st of the previous round (the round before the decrease), slip the last st onto RH needle unworked, and then work a double decrease (SK2PO = Sl1, K2tog, pass slipped st over knit st) between the last st of the previous round and the first 2 sts of the decrease round. This way, the decrease for inside sleeves will not be missed.
3. **After working 162 rounds:** Break PC #620 BGC #768 leaving a 3cm tail each.

   <<Cuffs>>

   Rounds 1 to 13: Change to 2.5mm circular needle and work with #130 and #135 yarn. Work in corrugated 2x2 (K2 with #130, P2 with #135) for 13 rnds.

   Rounds 14 & 15: Switch from #135 to #140 and work in corrugated 2x2 (K2 with #130, P2 with #140) for 2 rnds. Break #130 leaving a 3cm tail.

   Round 16: Purl with #140 to EOR. Finish by casting off with #140 using tapestry needle. (See sewn cast off on p.131.)
4. Work other sleeve in the same way.

Neckband

Cut open at the centre of *extra stitches* along neckline.

Round 1: Using 2.75mm circular needle (40cm)and #135 yarn, pick up and knit into all sts and rows beginning at the right back neck. (Total 128 sts.)

(Including the pick-up round)

Rounds 2 to 8: Tie #130 yarn, and work in corrugated 2x2 (K2 with #130, P2 with #135), for 7 rnds.

Rounds 9 & 10: Switch from #135 to #140 and work in corrugated 2x2 (K2 with #130, P2 with #140) for 2 rnds. Break #130 leaving a 3cm tail.

Round 11: Purl with #140 to EOR. Finish by casting off with #140 and tapestry needle. (See sewn cast off on p.131.)

Treatment for extra stitches, see p.28.

Weaving in ends and washing, see p.28.

Details of pattern

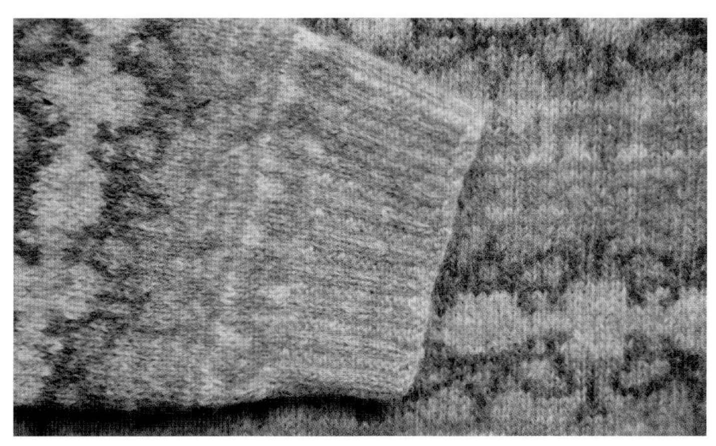

Details of cuff

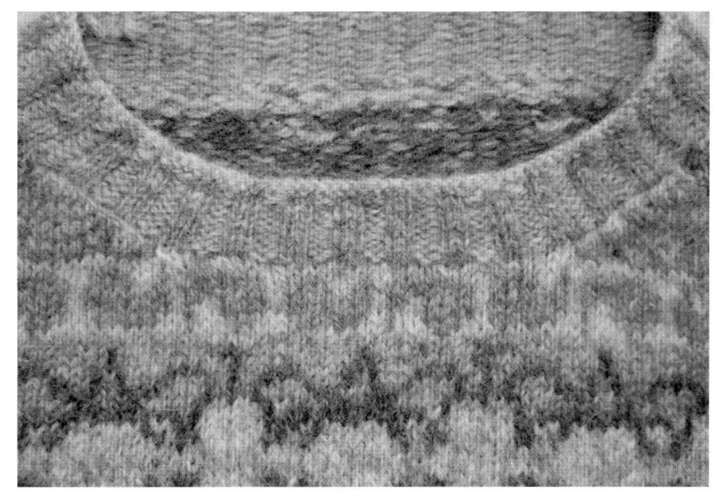

Details of neck

KNITTING CHART

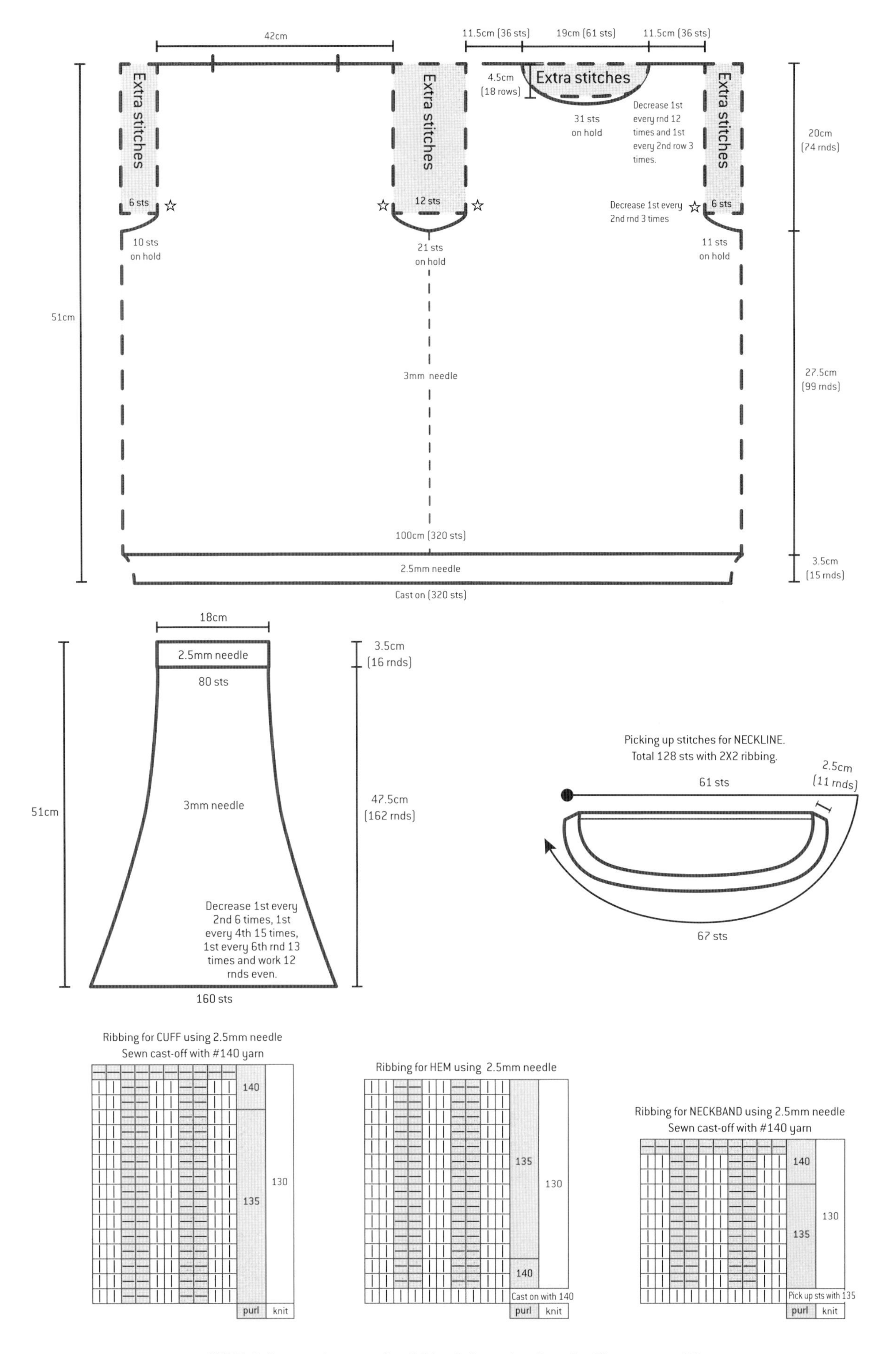

NOTE: Colour assignment for ribbing is based on how it will appear on RS

Sleeve start

Under armhole & shoulder meeting

Neckline

BGC	PC
130	170
140	135
130	170
768	620
620	135
130	170
140	135
130	170
620	135
768	620

Motifs are big waves, a bamboo grove and a Fair Isle pattern...

15 NEXT GENERATION
Women's jumper

This is another original pattern and emphasized with very simple colouration. I used only 3 colours. Motifs are big waves, a bamboo grove and a Fair Isle pattern which is very similar to Japanese keyhole pattern. This work is complicated and requires good knitting tension.

Yarn

Total 3 colours – 19 balls

140 (Rye) 9 balls

162 (Neptune) 6 balls

628 (Parma) 4 balls

Total weight of jumper – 455g

Tools & Notions

Circular needles: 2.5mm (40cm, 60cm and 80cm or longer), 3mm (60cm and 80cm or longer)

Crochet hook: 2.3mm

Tapestry needle: Small and medium

Waste yarn (to hold stitches)

Stitch markers

Tension

1 pattern stitch

(Large) Wave 42 sts x 32 rows = 12.6cm x 8.8cm

(Medium) Bamboo 24 sts x 23 rows = 7.5cm x 6.8cm

(Small) Keyhole 14 sts x 13 rows = 4.3cm x 3.7cm (including single colour rows underneath and on top)

Finished measurement

Bust circumference: 100cm

Back neck to sleeve edge: 76cm

Length: 59.5cm

INSTRUCTIONS

Worked in the round up to shoulders by working *extra stitches* in between for armholes and neck opening.

Ribbing for hem

Round 1: With 2.75mm 60cm circular needle and with colour #162 yarn, cast on 336 sts. Cast on is counted as 1 rnd.

Rounds 2 & 3: Tie #140 onto #162 and work in corrugated 2x2 ribbing by repeating [K2 with #140, P2 with #162].

Rounds 4 to 6: Switch #162 to #628 and work in corrugated 2x2 ribbing by knitting P sts and purling K sts – [P2 with #628, K2 with #140].

Rounds 7 to 16: Switch #628 to #162 and work in corrugated 2x2 ribbing as in Row 2, by repeating [K2 with #140, P2 with #162].

Rounds 17 & 18: Switch #162 to #628, and work in corrugated 2x2 ribbing, by repeating [K2 with #140, P2 with #628]. Break 140 yarn leaving a 3cm tail, leaving #628 yarn.

Body

<<Work to underarm>>

Round 1: Change to 3mm needle. Work 1 rnd with #628 which is the remaining tail from the hem.

Rounds 2 to 127: Tie #140 onto #162 and work up to Round 127, by changing colours according to colour assignment. Only change background colour. Then break yarn leaving a 3cm tail.

NOTE: *Floats tend to get longer when a pattern repeat has a bigger stitch count, so make sure to twist the yarn on the WS when a float extends over 6 sts or more.*

<<Make *extra stitches* for armhole>>

After working Round 127: Slip 21 sts onto waste yarn and leave them on hold for underarm.

Thread waste yarn through the first 11 sts and last 10 sts of the round. The centre of the held stitches should always match the centre of a pattern stitch. Make sure to check that this is the case.

To identify the sts to be held for the opposite underarm, use the Keyhole pattern as a guide: The small Keyhole pattern is a repeat of 14 sts, therefore there are 24 repeats in total 12 repeats for each front and back. The BOR starts with half a pattern followed by 11 complete patterns. The centre of the 12th pattern becomes the centre stitch of the opposite underarm. (This is 168th stitch from BOR.) Thread waste yarn through this st as the centre st together with 10 sts on each side, with these sts still on the cord of the circular needle.

Be sure to thread through the stitch.

Round 128: Remove the 21 sts for left underarm from needle. Cast on 6 sts on RH needle using #140 and #628 yarn (See p.33), and proceed working along the front body. Work based on colour assignment, but disregard those sts which have been removed.

Work up to the held sts for the right underarm. Remove held stitches from needle.

Cast on 12 sts on RH needle using #140 and #162 yarn.

Continue working based on colour assignment, until EOR. Cast on 6 sts at EOR.

*Extra stitch*es are now made for both underarms. (Refer to p.25 for working with extra stitches.)

From the next round, be sure to decrease at both sides of armholes every 2nd rnd 4 times.

Round 129: Begin working 6 *extra stitch*es by repeating [1 st in PC (#140), 1 st in BGC (#628)] 3 times, then knit the first 2 front sts together. Continue working along the remaining front, until the 2 sts before *extra stitch*es for right armhole, then SKPO (Sl1, K1, pass slipped st over knit st).

Work the armhole *extra stitch*es [1 st in BGC (#162), 1 st in PC (#140)] 3 times, [1 st in PC (#140), 1 st in BGC (#628)] 3 times, and then knit the first 2 back sts together.

Continue to work along the back until the 2 sts before *extra stitch*es for the opposite armhole then work SKPO (Sl1, K1, pass slipped st over knit st). Work the remaining 6 *extra stitch*es by repeating [1 st in BGC (#628), 1 st in PC (#140)] 3 times.

Then work according to colour assignment until before neck line.

<<Make *extra stitches* for neck opening>>

After working Round 51: Slip 55 sts for neck opening onto waste yarn to be kept on hold. (The centre stitch will be 74th stitch from BOR together with 27 sts on each side.)

Round 52: Work with #140 and #162 until the 2 sts before the held sts and then decrease by SKPO.

Remove held sts from needle and cast on 12 sts on RH needle.

Knit the first 2 sts of right front together, skip the pattern for the removed sts and work to EOR.

Decrease at both sides of the neck opening **every rnd 7 times**, then **every 2nd rnd 7 times and work 1 rnd even**. Break yarn leaving a 3cm tail.

Join shoulders

1. Prepare for shoulder seam by working 1 additional row for back by slipping sts onto RH needle, up to the centre of *extra stitch*es for right sleeve.
2. Tie a knot using #140 and #162 yarn which will be used for working the additional row. Leave a 3cm tail for #140 and about three times the shoulder length for #162. The knot will be used as a 'stopper', and will be worked from the centre of the *extra stitch*es for right sleeve, across back body based on colour assignment, to the centre of *extra stitch*es on the other side.

   Leave #162 as is and cut #140 leaving a 3cm tail.
3. Turn the work inside out.

   Using the remaining #162 yarn and crochet hook, work three needle cast-off starting from the shoulder edge. Cast off the 6 *extra stitch*es for the neckband separately using slip stitch cast-off. (See p.21)
4. Join the other shoulder as well, using three needle cast-off with #162 yarn which was kept longer, and cast off *extra stitch*es using slip stitch cast-off.
5. Unravel back neck sts. Cut unravelled yarn in the middle and tie to the base of each shoulder.

Sleeves

1. Cut open at the centre of *extra stitch*es and pick up and knit into all stitches and rows beginning at the centre of the held sts using #162 yarn. Pick up and knit sts from between *extra stitch*es and body. (See p.22.) Adjust st count to 160 sts on the second round.

TIP: As it is difficult to adjust stitch count and decrease to shape inside sleeve based on colour assignment at the same time, placing markers in advance on the 2 sts to be worked together to adjust st count will help, as this will allow you to focus on matching the pattern st without forgetting about the decrease.

NOTE: *This jumper uses a pattern with top and bottom halves that are not symmetrical, therefore the rows for the colour assignment for the sleeve will need to be worked in reverse order. However, this will result in the wave pattern being asymmetrical. For a perfect finish, to make the waves on both sides symmetrical, work one sleeve in reverse order and the other following the order of colour assignment but following the wave pattern from top to bottom. (Normally, the pattern will be worked from bottom to top, but this should be reversed.)*

2. Decrease at inside sleeve every 2nd rnd 12 times, every 4th rnd 18 times, every 6th rnd 10 times and then work 24 rnds even. Decrease by knitting to the last st of the previous round (the round before the decrease), slip the last st onto RH needle unworked, and then work a double decrease (SK2PO = Sl1, K2tog, pass slipped st over knit st) between the last st of the previous round and the first 2 sts of the decrease round. This way, the decrease for inside sleeves will not be missed.
3. **After working 180 rnds** change to 2.5mm circular needle.

   <<Cuff>>

   Rounds 1 to 3: Work in corrugated 2x2 (K2 with #140, P2 with #628).

   Rounds 4 to 15: Switch from #628 to #162 and work in corrugated 2x2 (K2 with #140, P2 with #162). Break #140 leaving a 3cm tail.

   Round 16: Purl with #162 to EOR. Finish by casting off with #162 and tapestry needle. (See sewn cast off on p.125.)

Work other sleeve in the same way.

Neckband

Cut open at the centre of *extra stitches* along neckline.

Round 1: Using 2.5mm circular needle (40cm) and #162, begin to pick up and knit sts from the right shoulder side of back neck. Pick up and knit all sts and rows.

Rounds 2 to 9: Tie #140 and work in corrugated 2x2 ribbing (K2 with #140, P2 with #162). At the same time decrease 2 sts along back neck, adjusting the total st count to 184 sts. Continue working in corrugated 2x2 ribbing.

Rounds 10 & 11: Switch from #162 to #628 and work in corrugated 2x2 ribbing. Break #628 leaving a 3cm tail, and cast off by knitting K sts and purling P sts with #140, and break yarn.

Treatment for extra stitches, see p.28.

Weaving in ends and washing, see p.28.

Details of pattern

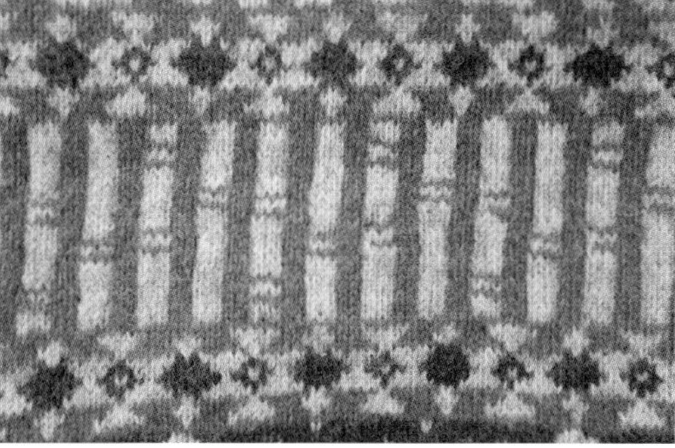

KNITTING CHART

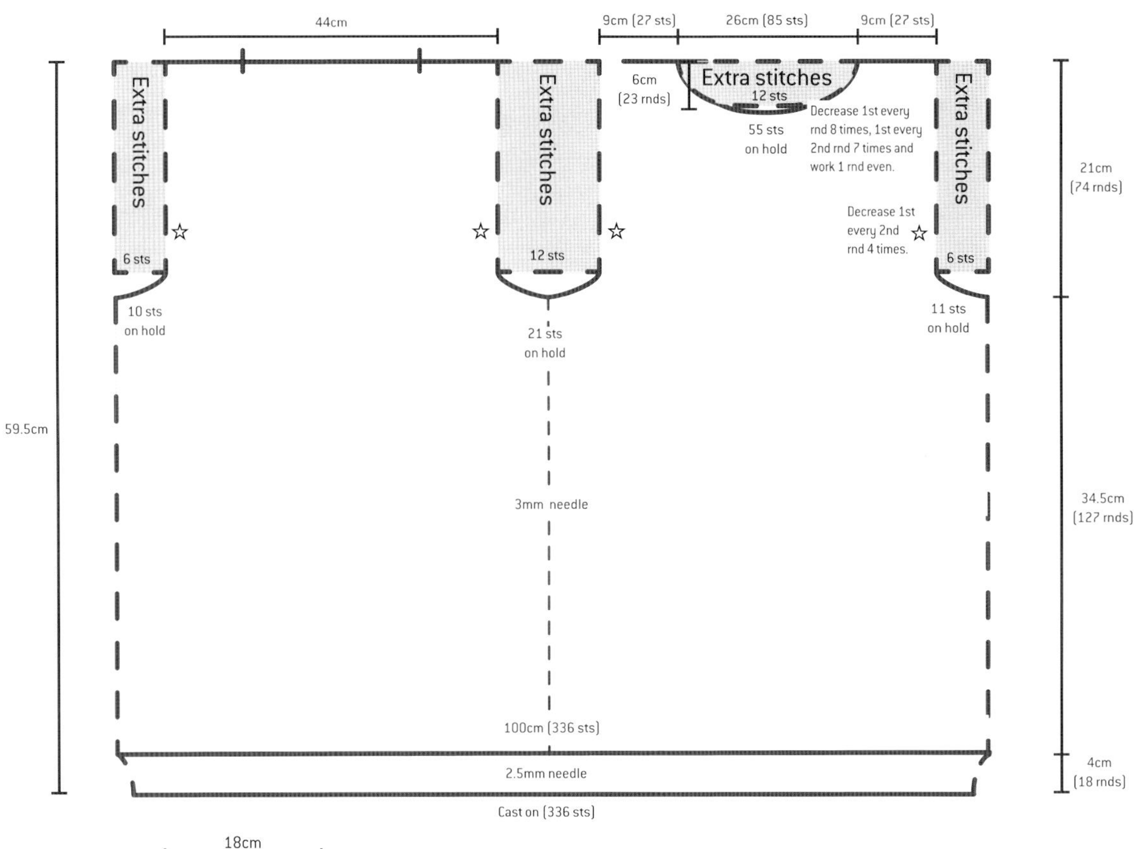

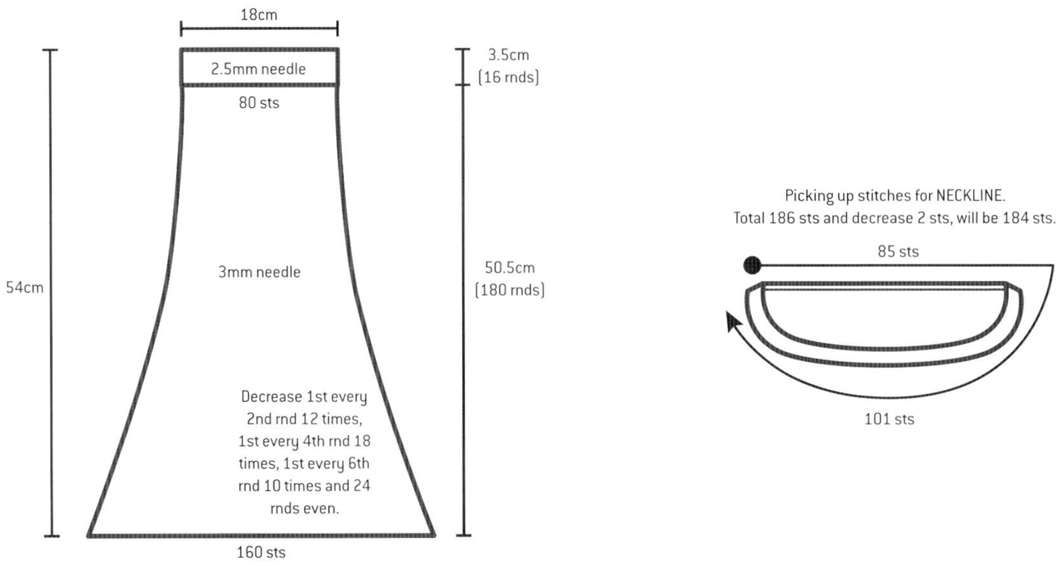

Ribbing for CUFFS using 2.5mm needle
Sewn cast-off with #162 yarn

162
162
140
628
purl knit

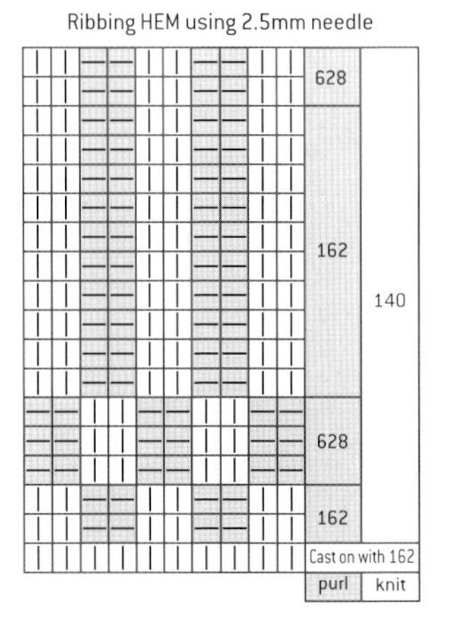

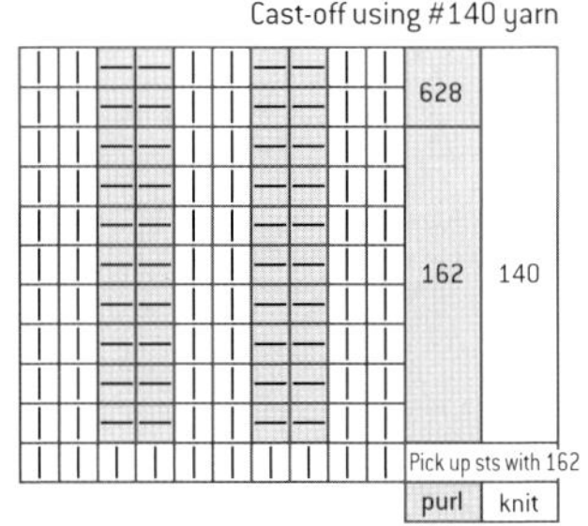

NOTE: Colour assignment for ribbing is based on how it will appear on RS

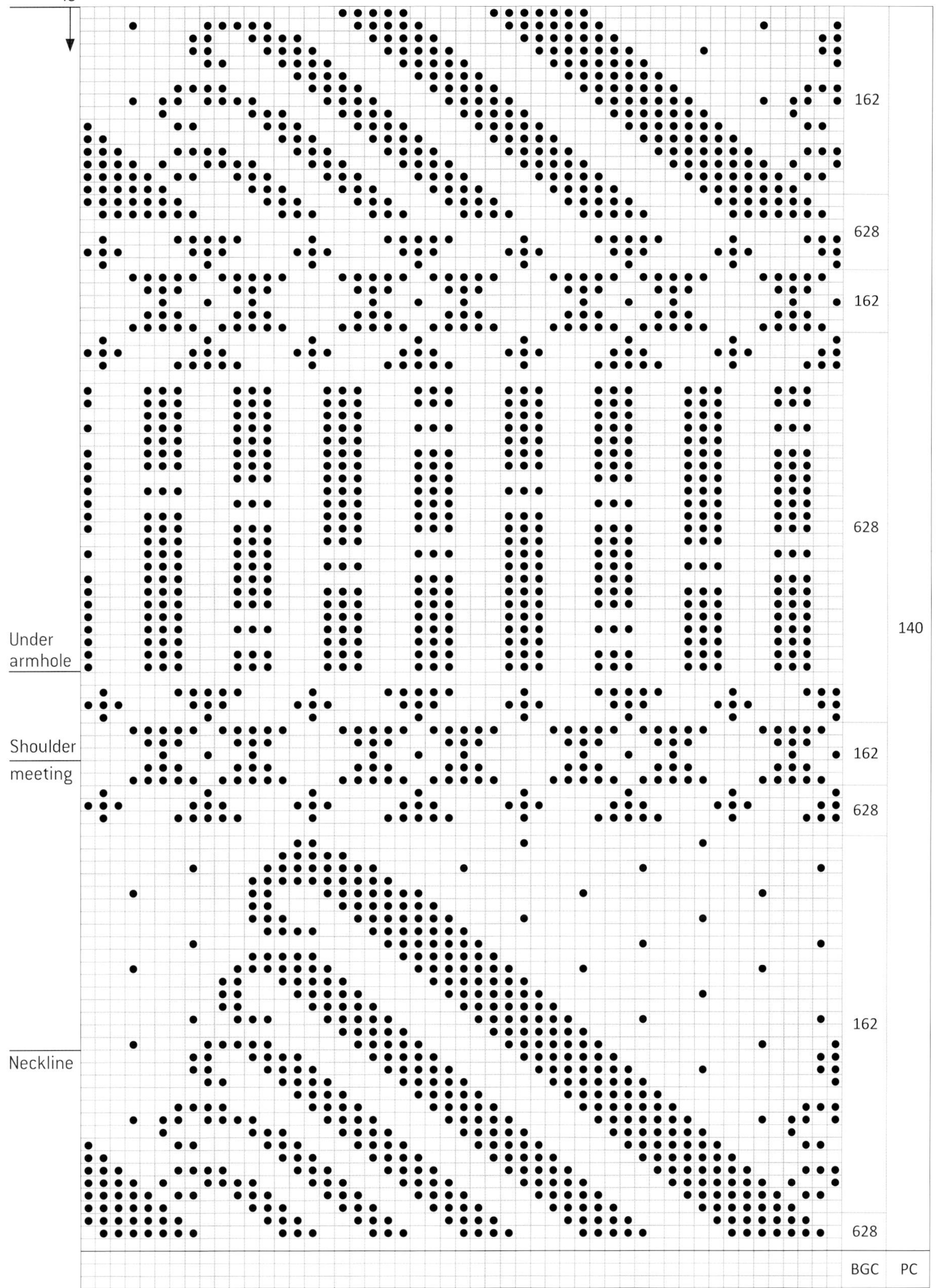
Sleeve start
162
628
162
628
Under armhole
140
Shoulder
meeting
162
628
162
Neckline
628
BGC
PC

Next
Generation

”

Can you imagine that
I could hear them walking?

“

16 & 17 SUMBURGH HEAD
Caps

These caps are for both adults and children. The children's have two variations of finishing. In summer 2015, I had a splendid experience at Sumburgh Head which is a famous place for puffin watching. I had never seen so many of them before. Can you imagine that I could hear them walking?

Yarn

Total for adults (inc. child's) 11 colours – 11 balls

One ball of each of the following colors:

 127 (Pebble)

 150 (Atlantic)

 182 (Buttercup)

 183 (Sand)

 227 (Earth)

 268 (Dog Rose)

 290 (Oyster)

 410 (Cornfield)

 462 (Ginger)

 688 (Mermaid)

 1130 (Lichen)

Total weight of cap – 56g adult/37g child

Tools & Notions

Circular needles: 2.5mm (40cm) and 3mm (40cm)
Short DPN: 3mm
Crochet hook: 2.3mm
Tapestry needle: Small and medium
Stitch markers

Tension

1 pattern stitch

(Large) Flowers with waves on both sides

12 sts x 29 rows = 3.5cm x 8.5cm

Finished measurement

Adult: Head circumference of 52cm
Child's: Head circumference of 44cm
Comfortably stretch: Adult to 58cm
Child to 52cm

INSTRUCTIONS

This cap is worked in the round throughout.

ADULT

Ribbing

Round 1: With 2.5mm 40cm circular needle and with #688 yarn, cast on 180 sts. Cast on is counted as 1 round.

Rounds 2 to 4: Tie #227 onto #688, and work 3 rnds corrugated 2x2 ribbing by [K2 with #227, P2 with #688].

Round 5: Switch #688 to #127, and work in 2x2 ribbing. This time work in corrugated 2x2 ribbing by knitting P sts and purling K sts [P2 with #127, K2 with #227].

Rounds 6 to 10: Switch #127 to #290 and #227 to #150, and work in corrugated 2x2 ribbing as in Round 2 [K2 with #150, P2 with #290].

Round 11: Switch #290 to #183 and work as established

Body of cap

Round 1: Change to 3mm needle, and knit 1 rnd with #183.

Rounds 2 to 49: Tie #227 onto #183. Work according to colour assignment chart then decrease when working the following rnds.

Round 50: With #688 and #1130, work as charted, at the same time repeat [K13, K2tog] until EOR. (12 sts decreased. 168 sts in total.)

Continue working as charted, while decreasing when working the following rnds:

Round 57: Repeat [K12, K2tog] until EOR. (12 sts decreased. 156 sts in total.)

Round 61: Repeat [K11, K2tog] until EOR. (12 sts decreased. 144 sts in tota.l)

Round 66: Repeat [K4, K2tog] until EOR. (24 sts decreased. 120 sts in total.)

Round 70: Repeat [K3, K2tog] until EOR. (24 sts decreased. 96 sts in total.)

Round 77: K2tog until EOR. (48 sts decreased. 48 sts in total.)

Round 80: K2tog until EOR. (24 sts decreased. 24 sts remain.)

Decoration on top

With the remaining 24 sts, make 1 increase (total 25 sts). Then dividing them into five groups of 5 sts, work i-cord for 25 rows each, changing colours in the following order: #688, #410, #462, #182, #227.

Leave a long tail for #227.

Fold each cord in half and sew them securely onto the top.

With the remaining tail (#227) sew all the cords together and close the top of cap.

CHILD

Ribbing

Round 1: With 2.5mm 40cm circular needle with #688 yarn, cast on 144 sts. This is counted as rnd 1.

Rounds 2 to 8: Tie #1130 onto #688, and work 7 rnds in 2x2 ribbing by [K2 with #668, P2 with #1130].

Body of cap

Round 1: Change to 3mm needle, and knit 1 rnd with #1130.

Rounds 2 to 56: Tie #227 onto #1130. Work according to colour assignment chart.

With WS facing slip stitch cast off using #688 yarn and crochet hook.

Shape as desired either by sewing on the WS, as shown by dotted line on chart, or tie with yarn into a shape of cat's ears with the RS facing.

Washing

- After weaving in all ends, be sure to hand wash. Wash as normal wool wash. Washing will bring out the best features of the yarn.

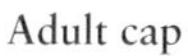

Adult cap

Child's cap

KNITTING CHART

ADULTS

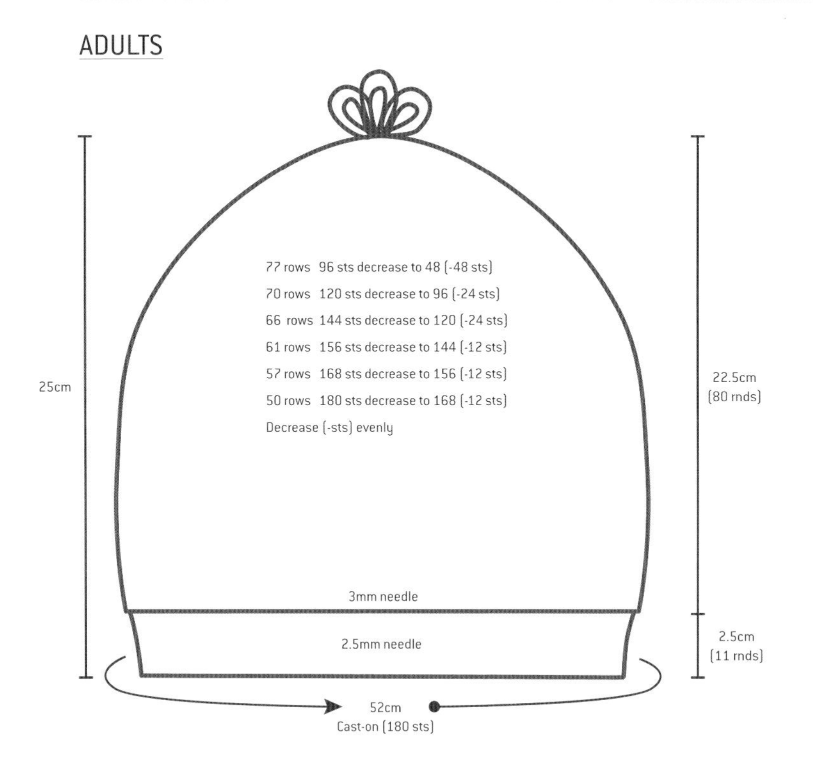

Work i-cord (5 cords) use 5 sts, 25 rows (6.5cm) knitting with #688, #410, #462, #182, #227 yarn.

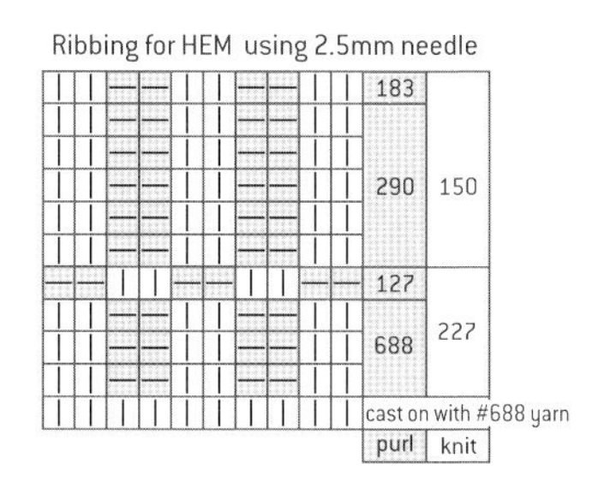

CHILDS

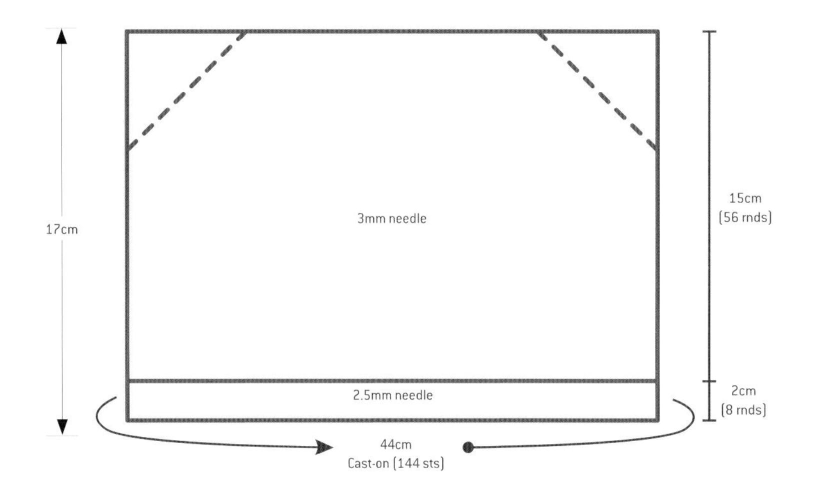

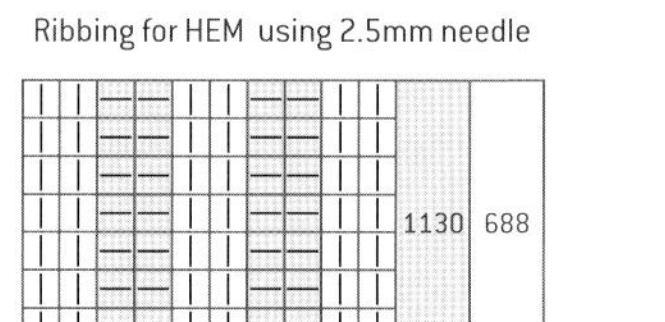

NOTE: Colour assignment for ribbing is based on how it will appear on RS

Childs

PC	BGC
1130	688
290	
1130	
268	
183	
127	150
1130	688
290	
1130	
227	1130
462	
410	127
182	
410	
462	
227	1130

Adults

BGC	PC
150	127
688	1130
	290
	1130
	268
	183
150	127
688	1130
	290
	1130
	268
	183
150	127
688	1130
	290
	1130
1130	227
	462
127	410
	182
	410
	462
183	227

Chihiro, I taught you not to use
close colours in one work.

18 SWING CAP

I often use these colours together though my teacher said,
'Chihiro, I taught you not to use close colours in one work.'
I hope you enjoy making the tassels which which would
be good practice for various techniques.

Yarn

Total 6 colours – 6 balls

One ball each of:

 102 (Shaela)

 119 (Mooskit/Sholmit)

 140 (Rye)

 183 (Sand)

 575 (Lipstick)

 768 (Egg Shell)

Total weight of cap – 75g

Tools & Notions

Circular needles: 2.5mm (40cm) and 3mm (40cm)

Short DPN: 2.5mm

Tapestry needle: Small and medium

Stitch markers

Tension

1 pattern stitch

(Large) Flowers with waves on both sides

12 sts x 29 rows = 3.5cm x 8.5cm

Finished measurement

Head circumference: 52cm

Comfortably stretch to 58cm

INSTRUCTIONS

This cap is worked in the round throughout.

Ribbing

Round 1: With 2.5mm 40cm circular needle with #102 yarn, cast on 180 sts. Cast on is counted as 1 round.

Round 2: Tie #119 onto #102, and work a round of corrugated 2x2 ribbing [K2 with #119, P2 with #102].

Rounds 3 & 4: Switch #102 to #768, and work 2 rnds in corrugated 2x2 ribbing as established.

Rounds 5 & 6: Switch #768 to #183, and this time work in corrugated 2x2 ribbing by knitting P sts and purling K sts corrugated 2x2 ribbing. [P2 with #183, K2 with #119].

Rounds 7 to 14: Switch #183 to #768 and work corrugated 2x2 ribbing as in Round 3 [K2 with #119, P2 with #768].

Body of cap

Round 1: Change to 3mm needle, and knit 1 rnd with #768.

Rounds 2 to 45: Tie #183 onto #768. Work according to colour assignment chart up to Round 45.

Round 46: K6, SK2PO (Sl1 knitwise, K2tog, pass slipped st over knit st), (K12, SK2PO) 11 times, and K6. (24 sts decreased. 156 sts in total.)

Rounds 47 to 49: Work evenly following colour assignment.

Round 50: K5, SK2PO, (K10, SK2PO) 11 times, and K5. (24 sts decreased. 132 sts in total.)

Rounds 51 & 52: Work evenly. (Note to work with single colour from Round 51.)

Round 53: K4, SK2PO, (K8, SK2PO) 11 times, and K4. (24 sts decreased. 108 sts in total.)

Round 54: Work evenly.

Round 55: K3, SK2PO, (K6, SK2PO) 11 times, and K3. (24 sts decreased. 84 sts in total.)

Fringes on top of cap

Work 15 fringes using three types of techniques: stockinette st, i-cord, and knitting in the bias.

Fringe 1: Switch to DPN 2.5mm needle and using #119 yarn, work 6 sts back and forth in stockinette st (knit on RS, purl on WS) for 88 rows, starting with K6. Break yarn and, with tapestry needle, draw yarn through remaining 6 sts and tighten closed. Weave in remaining

end carefully along the side of fringe so that it doesn't show.

Fringe 2: With #575 yarn, work an i-cord with the next 4 sts as follows:

K4, without turning work, slip these sts back onto LH needle, carry working yarn along the WS of work, K4 again. Make sure to knit tightly. Work i-cord for 48 rows. Break yarn and finish in the same way as for Fringe 1 (using tapestry needle, draw yarn through remaining 4 sts and tighten closed). Weave end into fringe.

TIP: After working several rows of i-cord, pull the cord to neaten the sts.

Fringe 3: With #768, pick up and knit 2 sts from the back side of fringe 2 and continue knitting the next 4 sts. With 6 sts all together, work flat for 90 rows in stockinette stitch. Break yarn and, with tapestry needle, draw yarn through remaining 6 sts and tighten closed. Weave in remaining end carefully along the side.

Fringe 4: With #183, pick up and knit 2 sts from the back side of fringe 3 and continue knitting the next 4 sts. With 6 sts all together, work flat for 98 rows in stockinette stitch. Break yarn and, with tapestry needle, draw yarn through remaining 6 sts and tighten closed. Weave in remaining end carefully along the side.

Fringe 5: With #140, pick up and knit 2 sts from the back side of fringe 4 and continue knitting the next 12 sts.

Row 2: P14

Work in bias as follows:

Rows 3 to 26:

All odd numbered rows: K1, M1 (make 1 st by using needle to pick up the strand running between the next st and knitting it through the back loop), K10, K2tog, K1.

All even numbered rows: P to EOR.

Row 27: Increase 3 sts [K1, M1, K2, M1, (K3, M1) twice, K2, K2tog, K1]. (17 sts in total.)

Rows 28 to 78: P even numbered rows, K odd numbered rows.

Rows 29 to 54: All odd numbered rows: K1, M1, K13, K2tog, K1.

All even numbered rows: P to EOR.

Row 55: Increase 3 sts [K1, (M1, K2) 6 times, M1, K1, K2tog, K1]. (23 sts in total.)

Rows 56 to 78: All odd numbered rows: K1, M1, K19, K2tog, K1.

All even numbered rows: P to EOR.

After working Row 78, break yarn leaving a long tail and cast off using the sewn cast-off. Weave in remaining end carefully along the side.

Fringe 6: With #119, pick up and knit 2 sts from the back side of Fringe 5 and continue knitting the next 4 sts. With 6 sts all together, work flat for 102 rows in stockinette st. Break yarn and, with tapestry needle, draw yarn through remaining 6 sts and tighten closed. Weave in remaining end carefully along the side.

Fringe 7: With #102 yarn, work an i-cord with the next 4 sts. (Note that stitches will not be picked up from the preceding fringe.) With the 4 sts, work in the same way as for Fringe 2 for 48 rows. Break yarn and finish in the same way as for Fringe 2 using tapestry needle, draw yarn through remaining 4 sts and tighten closed. Weave in end into fringe.

Fringe 8: With #183, pick up and knit 2 sts from the back side of fringe 7 and continue knitting the next 4 sts. With 6 sts all together, work flat for 98 rows in stockinette st. Break yarn and, with tapestry needle, draw yarn through remaining 6 sts and tighten closed. Weave in remaining end carefully along the side.

Fringe 9: With #119, pick up and knit 2 sts from the back side of fringe 8 and continue knitting the next 4 sts. With 6 sts all together, work flat for 88 rows in stockinette stitch. Break yarn and, with tapestry needle, draw yarn through remaining 6 sts and tighten closed. Weave in remaining end carefully along the side.

Fringe 10: With #768, pick up and knit 2 sts from the back side of Fringe 9 and continue knitting the next 6 sts. With 8 sts all together, work flat for 88 rows in stockinette st. Break yarn and, with tapestry needle, draw yarn through remaining 8 sts and tighten closed. Weave in remaining end carefully along the side.

Fringe 11: With #140, work in the bias, but slanting in the opposite direction from Fringe 5. Pick up and knit 2 sts from the back side of Fringe 10 and continue knitting the next 12 sts.

Row 2: P14.

Work in bias as follows:

Rows 3 to 50: All odd numbered rows: K1, K2tog, K9, M1 (make 1 st by using needle to pick up the strand running between the next st and knitting it through the back loop), K2.

All even numbered rows: P to EOR.

Row 51: Increase 4 sts [K1, K2tog, K1, (M1, K2) 5 times]. (18 sts in total.)

Rows 52 to 76: All even numbered rows: P to EOR.

All odd numbered rows: K1, K2tog, K13, M1, K2.

After working Row 76, break yarn leaving a long tail and cast off using the sewn cast-off. Weave in remaining end carefully along the side.

Fringe 12: With #575 yarn, work an i-cord with the next 5 sts. (Note that sts will not be picked up from the preceding fringe.) With the 5 sts, work in the same way as for Fringe 2 for 48 rows. Break yarn and finish in the same way as for fringe 1, using tapestry needle draw yarn through remaining 5 sts and tighten closed. Weave in end into fringe.

Fringe 13: With #183, pick up and knit 2 sts from the back side of fringe 12 and continue knitting the next 4 sts. With 6 sts all together, work flat for 88 rows in stockinette st. Break yarn and, with tapestry needle, draw yarn through remaining 6 sts and tighten closed. Weave in remaining end carefully along the side.

Fringe 14: With #102 yarn, work an i-cord with the next 4 sts. (Note that stitches will not be picked up from the preceding fringe). With the 4 sts, work in the same way as for fringe 2 for 48 rows. Break yarn and finish in the same way as for fringe 1, using tapestry needle draw yarn through remaining 4 sts and tighten closed. Weave in end into fringe.

Fringe 15: With #768, work in the bias, slanting in the same direction as Fringe 11. Pick up and knit 2 sts from the back side of fringe 14 and continue knitting the next 7 sts.

Row 2: P9

Work in bias as follows:

Rows 3 to 48:

All odd numbered rows: K1, K2tog, K4, M1 (make 1 st by using needle to pick up the strand running between the next st and knitting it through the back loop), K2.

All even numbered rows: P to EOR.

Row 49: Increase 3 sts [K1, K2tog, (M1, K1) 5 times]. (12 sts in total.)

Rows 50 to 68:

All even numbered rows: P to EOR.

All odd numbered rows: K1, K2tog, K7, M1, K2.

After working Row 68, break yarn leaving a long tail and cast off using the sewn cast-off method. Weave in remaining end carefully along the side.

Washing

- After weaving in all ends, be sure to hand wash. Wash as normal wool wash. Washing will bring out the best features of yarn.
- Once dried, trim off all ends carefully. Make sure not to cut any other parts of the garment.

KNITTING CHART

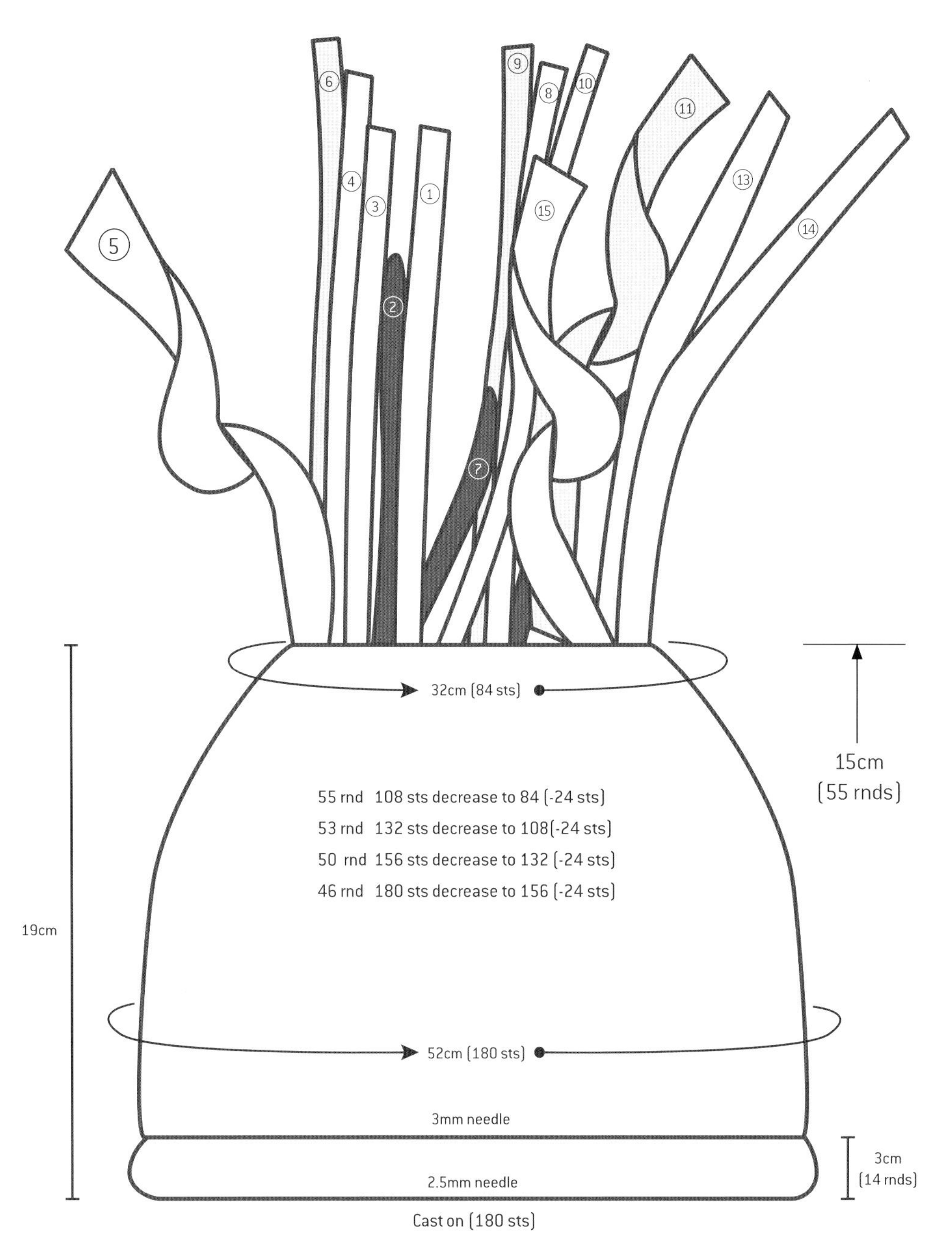

HOW TO KNIT

1. 119 / 88 rows / Stockinette stitch – 6 sts
2. 575 / 88 rows / i-cord stitch – 4 sts
3. 768 / 90 rows / Stockinette stitch – 6 sts
4. 183 / 98 rows / Stockinette stitch – 6 sts
5. 140 / 78 rows / right leaning bias – 14 sts to 23 sts
6. 119 / 102 rows / Stockinette stitch – 6 sts
7. 102 / 48 rows / i-cord stitch – 4 sts
8. 183 / 98 rows / Stockinette stitch – 6 sts
9. 119 / 88 rows / Stockinette stitch – 6 sts
10. 768 / 88 rows / Stockinette stitch – 8 sts
11. 140 / 76 rows / Knit left-leaning bias – 18 sts
12. 575 / 48 rows / i-cord stitch – 5 sts
13. 183 / 88 rows / Stockinette stitch – 6 sts
14. 102 / 48 rows / i-cord stitch – 4 sts
15. 768 / 68 rows / Knit left-leaning bias – 12 sts

Ribbing for HEM using 2.5mm needle

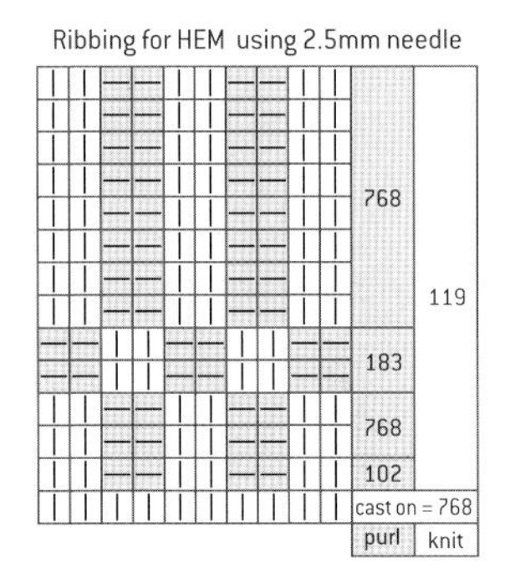

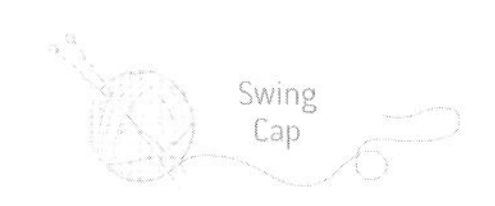

Plain colour knit

BGC	PC
119	
768	
768	140
768	119
183	140
119	768
119	140
119	575
119	140
768	183
140	102
183	102
140	102
768	183

Start decrease

I like to play with colours
of Fair Isle patterns.

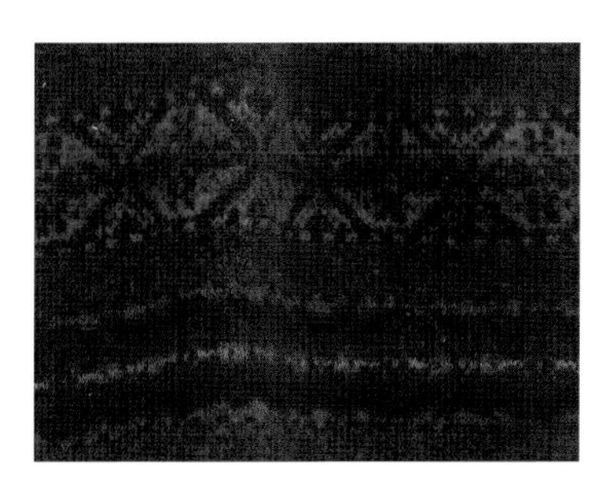

19 OPEN-MINDED
Women's jumper

Work 1, 'The Beginning' was made in 2003 and in 2016 I finished this collection with 'Open-minded Ai (Love)', using more complicated colouration and obscured contrast between ground colours and pattern colours. I like to play with colours of Fair Isle patterns. And I really enjoy knitting sleeves in a unique way, using extra stitches technique. By the phrase 'open-minded' I wanted to express that true love is not rigid or restricted but accepts everything as it is.

Yarn

Total 10 colours – 22balls

188 (Sherbet) 1 ball

323 (Cardinal) 3 balls

462 (Ginger) 2 balls

517 (Mantilla) 3 balls

525 (Crimson) 3 balls

530 (Fuchsia) 1 ball

580 (Cherry) 1 ball

585 (Plum) 2 balls

587 (Madder) 3 balls

595 (Maroon) 3 balls

Total weight of jumper – 443g

Tools & Notions

Circular needles: 2.5mm (40cm, 60cm and 80cm or longer), 3mm (60cm and 80cm or longer)

Crochet hook: 2.3mm

Tapestry needle: Small and medium

Waste yarn (to hold stitches)

Stitch markers

Tension

1 pattern stitch

(Large) Octagon: 24 sts x 19 rows = 7cm x 5.4cm

(Including single colour rows underneath and on top)

(Small+ Zigzag) 2 pattern types: 12 sts x 11 rows = 3.5cm x 3.3cm

(Small+ Zigzag) 2 pattern types: 6 sts/8 sts x 11 rows

= 1.8cm/2.4cm x 3.3cm

Finished measurement

Bust circumference: 98cm (84cm, 112cm)

Back neck to sleeve edge: 79cm (74.5cm, 81.5cm)

Length: 59cm (52.5cm, 59cm)

INSTRUCTIONS

Worked in the round up to shoulders by working *extra stitches* in between for armholes and neck opening.

Ribbing for hem

Round 1: With 2.5mm 60cm circular needle with #595 yarn, cast on 336 (288, 384) sts. Cast on is counted as 1 round.

Rounds 2 to 4: Tie #323 onto #595 and work in corrugated 2x2 ribbing by repeating [K2 with #595, P2 with #323]. Work 3 rnds.

Rounds 5 & 6: Switch yarn from #323 to #525 and work in corrugated 2x2 ribbing by knitting P sts and purling K sts [P2 with #525, K2 with #595].

Rounds 7 to 9: Switch yarn from #525 to #587 and work in corrugated 2x2 ribbing as in Round 2, by repeating [K2 with #595, P2 with #587].

Rounds 10 & 11: Switch yarn from #587 to #517and work in corrugated 2x2 ribbing by knitting P sts and purling K sts as in Round 5 [P2 with #517, K2 with #595].

Rounds 12 to 14: Switch yarn from #595 to #587 and work in corrugated 2x2 ribbing as in Round 7, by repeating [K2 with #587, P2 with #517]. Work 3 rnds.

Rounds 15 & 16: Switch yarn from #587 to 323 and #517 to #525 and work in corrugated 2x2 ribbing by repeating [K2 with #323, P2 with #525]. Break yarn #323 leaving a 3cm tail, leaving #525 yarn.

Body

To underarm

Round 1: Change to 3mm needle. Work 1 round with #525 which is the remaining tail from the hem.

Rounds 2 to 123 (99, 123): Tie #517 onto #525 and work up to Round 123 (99, 123) by changing colours according to colour assignment. Then break yarn leaving a 3cm tail.

NOTE: *Floats tend to get longer when a pattern repeat has a bigger stitch count, so make sure to twist the yarn on the WS when a float extends over 6 sts or more.*

<<Make *extra stitches* for armhole>>

1. **After working Round 123 (99, 123):** Thread yarn needle through first 11 (10, 11) sts from BOR and 10 (9, 10) sts from EOR. So that 19 (19, 21) sts are on waste yarn to keep on hold for underarm.

NOTE: *Make sure that the sts at the centre of the held sts always matches the centre of the pattern.*

2. Identify which sts are to be held for the opposite underarm. These underarm sts can be easily and accurately identified by looking at the number of pattern repeats.

   The Octagon pattern st has 24 sts, there are 14 (12, 16) pattern repeats all together, which means there are 7 (6, 8) pattern repeats for front and back. The st at BOR is centre of Octagon pattern.

   Count 6 (5, 7) full patterns and centre st of the next pattern will be the centre of the opposite underarm sts. (169th (145th, 193rd) stitch from BOR) together with 10 (9, 10) sts on both sides (a total of 21 (19, 21) sts), shall be kept on hold by threading waste yarn through using tapestry needle. Be sure that these sts are still on the needle as well. Be careful not to sew waste yarn into these sts.

NOTE: *When identifying this st, mark sts on both sides with pins and make sure that the number of pattern repeats on both sides is the same.*

Round 124 (100, 124): Remove the 21 (19, 21) sts for left underarm from needle. Cast on 6 sts on RH needle using #517 and #525 (#530, #517 and #525) yarn, and proceed working along the front body. (See p.33)

Work based on colour assignment, but disregard those sts which have been removed.

Work up to the held sts for the right underarm. Remove the marked st from needle.

Cast on 12 sts on RH needle using #517and #525 (#530, #517 and #525) yarn.

Continue working to EOR. Cast on 6 sts at EOR. *Extra stitches* are now made for both armholes. (Refer to p.25 for working with extra stitches.)

From the next round, be sure to decrease at both sides of armholes every 2nd rnd 2 times. (All sizes are the same.)

Round 125 (101, 125): Begin working 6 *extra stitches* by repeating [1 st in PC (#517) (#530, #517) 1 st in BGC (#525) (#323, #525)] 3 times, then knit the first 2 front sts together. Continue working along the remaining front until the 2 sts before *extra stitches* for right armhole, then SKPO (Sl1, K1, pass slipped st over knit st). Work the armhole *extra stitches* [1 st in BGC (#525) (#323, #525), 1 st in PC (#517) (#530, #517)] 3 times, [1 st in PC (#517) (#530, #517), 1 st in MC (#525) (#323, #525)] 3 times, and then knit the first 2 back sts together. Continue to work along the back until the 2 sts before *extra stitches* for the opposite armhole, then work SKPO (Sl1, K1, pass slipped st over knit st).

Work the remaining 6 *extra stitches* by repeating [1 st in BGC (#525) (#323, #525), 1 st in PC (#517) (#530, #517)] 3 times. Then work according to colour assignment until before neck line.

<<Make *extra stitches* for neck opening>>

All sizes are the same.

1. **After working 45 (39, 45) rounds** (from under armhole): Slip 35 sts for neck opening onto waste yarn to be kept on hold. (The centre stitch will be 78th (67th, 90th) stitch from BOR together with 17 sts on each side.)

2. **Round 46 (40, 46):** Work with #462 and #580 (#323 and #188, #462 and #580) until the 2 sts before the held stitches and then decrease by SKPO. Remove held sts from needle and cast on 12 sts on RH needle. Knit the first 2 sts of right front together, skip the pattern for the removed sts and work to EOR.

   While working, decrease at both sides of the neck opening every round 29 times.

   Break yarn leaving a 3cm tail.

Join shoulders

1. Prepare for shoulder seam by working 1 additional row for back by slipping sts onto RH needle, up to the centre of *extra stitches* for right sleeve.

2. Tie a knot using #188 and #323 (#462 and #580, #188 and #323) yarn which will be used for working the additional row. Leave a 3cm tail for #188 (#580, #188) and about three times the shoulder length for #323 (#462, #323). The knot will be used as a 'stopper', and will be worked from the centre of the *extra stitches* for right sleeve, across back body to the centre of *extra stitches* on the other side.

   Leave the BGC as is and cut PC leaving a 3cm tail.

3. Turn the work inside out.

   Using the remaining #323 (#462, #323) yarn and crochet hook, work three needle cast-off (see p.21) starting from the shoulder edge. Cast off the 6 *extra stitches* for the neckb opening separately using slip stitch cast-off.

   (Make sure that the *extra stitches* are not joined together with back neckband.)

4. Join the other shoulder as well, using three needle cast-off (see p.21) with #323 (#462, #323) yarn which was kept longer, and cast off *extra stitches* using slip stitch cast-off.

5. Unravel back neck sts. Cut the unravelled yarn in the middle and tie at the base of both shoulders.

Sleeves (All sizes are the same.)

1. Cut open at the centre of *extra stitches* and pick up and knit into all sts and rows beginning at the centre of the held sts using #525 yarn. Pick up and knit sts from between *extra stitches* and body. (See p.22.) Adjust stcount to 156 sts on the second round.

TIP: As it would be difficult to adjust st count and decrease to shape inside sleeve based on colour assignment at the same time, placing markers in advance on the 2 sts to be worked together to adjust stitch count will help, as this will allow you to focus on matching the pattern st without forgetting about the decrease.

NOTE: *This jumper uses a pattern with top and bottom halves that are not symmetrical, therefore the rows for the colour assignment for the sleeve will need to be worked in reverse order.*

Attention: For left sleeve, work up to Round 76 according to colour assignment, following the same steps for working *extra stitches* in stripes, and start Fair Isle pattern from Round 77. For right sleeve, work in Fair Isle pattern up to Round 94, and then work in stripes from Round 95 to cuffs.

Follow colour assignment entirely, if desired.

Make sure that the work does not get too tight when working in stripes.

2. Decrease at inside sleeve every 2nd rnd 12 times, every 4th rnd 8 times, every 6th rnd 18 times and then work 23 rnds even. Decrease by knitting to the last st of the previous round (the round before the decrease), slip the last st onto RH needle unworked, and then work a double decrease (SK2PO = Sl1, K2tog, pass slipped st over knit st) between the last st of the previous round and the first 2 sts of the decrease round. This way, the decrease for inside sleeves will not be missed.

3. After working 187 rnds

<<Cuffs>>

Rounds 1 to 3: Change to 2.5mm circular needle and work in corrugated 2x2 (K2 with #587, P2 with #517).

Rounds 4 & 5: Switch from #587 to #595 and work in corrugated 2x2 ribbing by knitting P sts and purling K sts [P2 with #517, K2 with #595].

Rounds 6 to 8: Switch from #517 to #587 and work in corrugated 2x2 ribbing as in Row 2, by repeating [K2 with #595, P2 with #587].

Rounds 9 & 10: Switch from #587 to #525 and work in corrugated 2x2 ribbing by knitting P sts and purling K sts [P2 with #525, K2 with #595].

Rounds 11 to 13: Switch from #525 to #323 and work in corrugated 2x2 ribbing as in Row 8, by repeating [K2 with #595, P2 with #323]. Break #323 leaving a 3cm tail.

Finish by casting off with #595 and tapestry needle. (See sewn cast off on p.125.)

4. Work other sleeve in the same way, but working stripes differently.

Neckband

Cut open at the centre of *extra stitches* along neckline.

Round 1: Using 2.5mm circular needle (40cm long) and #323 yarn, pick up and knit into all sts and rows beginning at the right back neck.

Rounds 2 to 4: Tie #595 yarn, and work in corrugated 2x2 (K2 with #595, P2 with #323).

Rounds 5 & 6: Switch from #323 to #525 and work in corrugated 2x2 ribbing by knitting P sts and purling K sts [P2 with #525, K2 with #595].

Rounds 7 to 9: Switch from #525 to #587 and work in corrugated 2x2 as in Round 2 [K2 with #595, P2 with #587].

Rounds 10 & 11: Switch from #587 to 517 and work in corrugated 2x2 ribbing by knitting P sts and purling K sts as in Round 5 [P2 with #517, K2 with #595].

Rounds 12 & 13: Switch from #595 to #587 and work in corrugated 2x2 as in Round 7 [K2 with #587, P2 with #517].

Break #517 leaving a 3cm tail.

Round 14: Knit with #587 to EOR. Finish by casting off with #587 and tapestry needle. (See sewn cast off on p.125.)

Treatment for extra stitches, see p.28.

Weaving in ends and washing, see p.28.

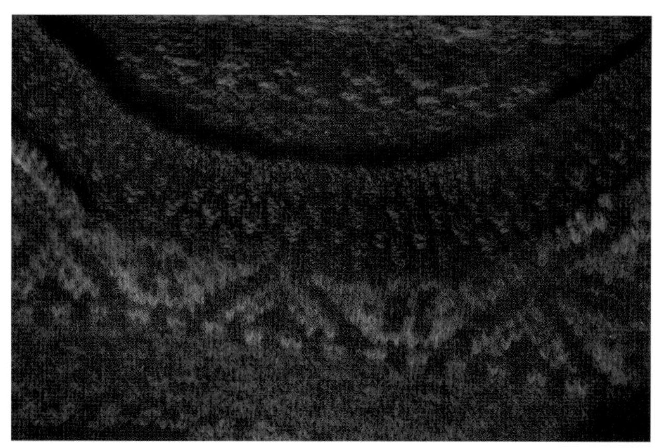

Detail of neckband

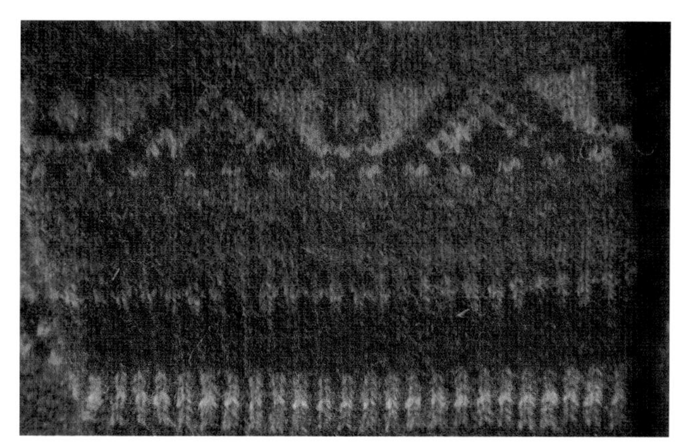

Detail of sleeve's pattern

KNITTING CHART

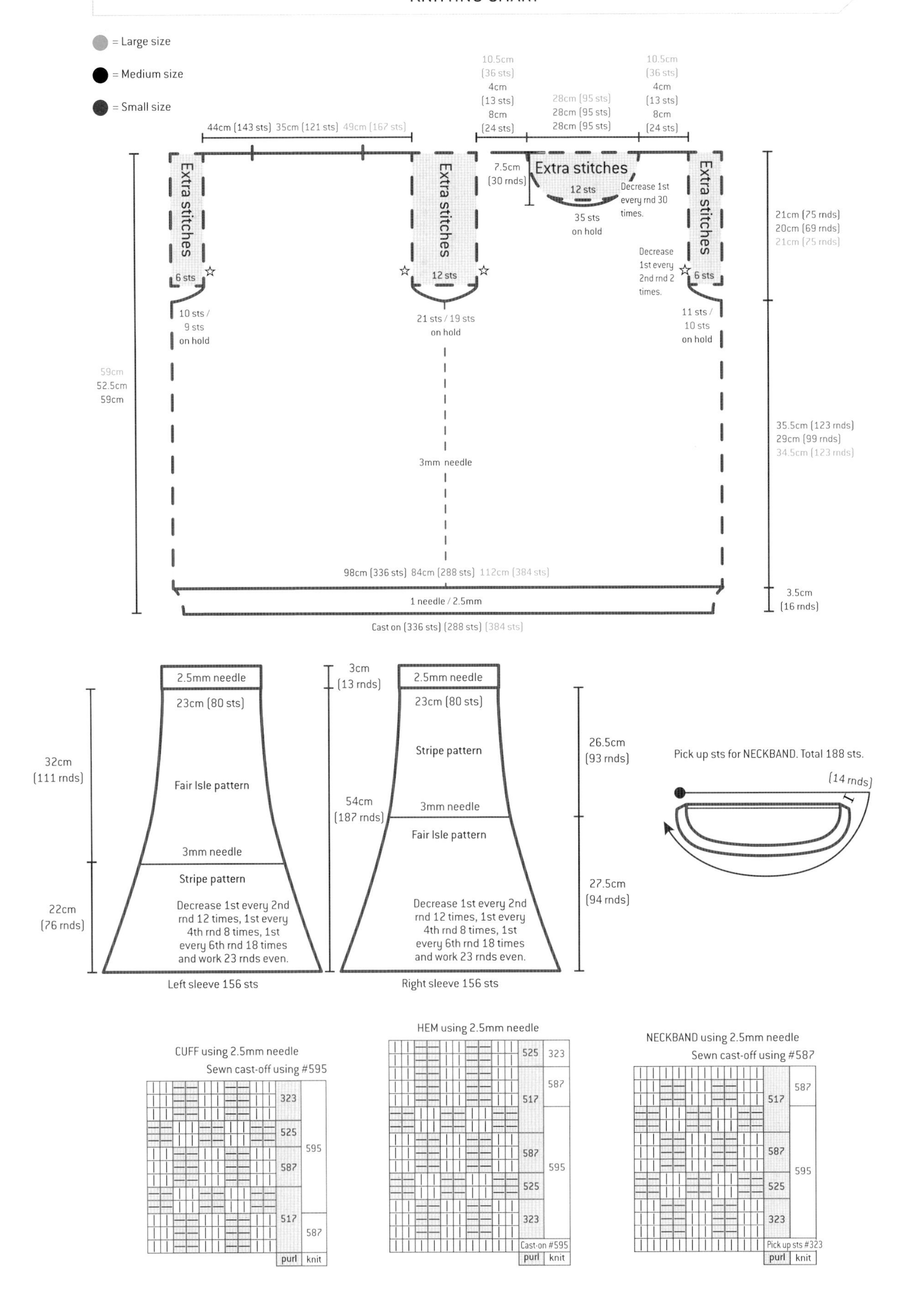

NOTE: Colour assignment for ribbing is based on how it will appear on RS

RIGHT SLEEVE

BGC	PC
517	525
595	462
	587
580	323
585	
188	
585	
580	
595	587
	462
517	525
530	323
585	
	587
580	462
	587
585	323
530	
517	525
595	462
	587
585	323
188	
585	
595	587
	462
517	525

LEFT SLEEVE

BGC	PC
323	585
	530
525	517
462	595
587	
323	580
	585
	188
	585
	580
587	595
462	
525	517
323	530
	585
587	580
462	
587	
323	585
	530
525	517

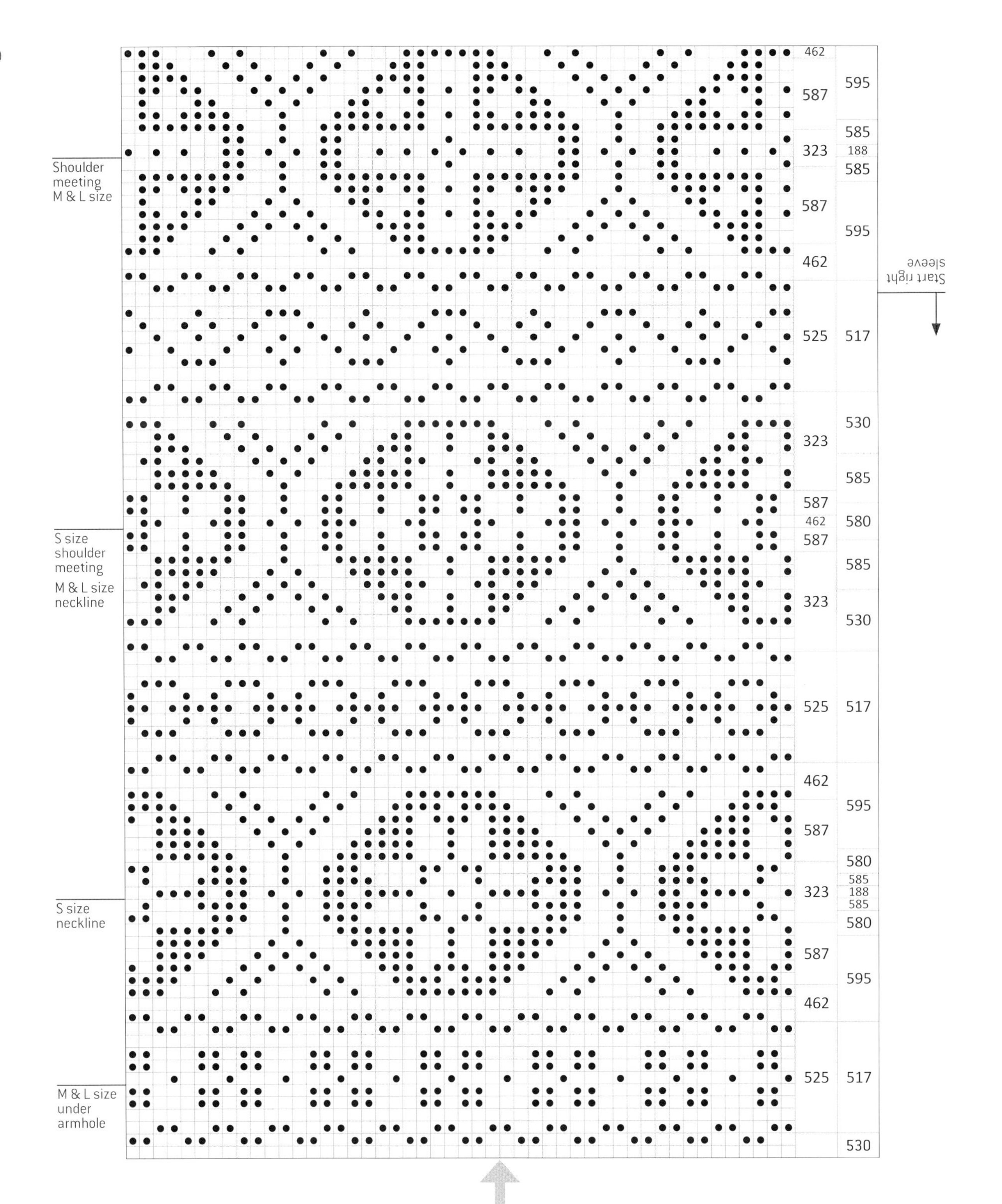
Shoulder meeting M & L size
S size shoulder meeting
M & L size neckline
S size neckline
M & L size under armhole
Start right sleeve
462
595
587
585
323
188
585
587
595
462
525
517
530
323
585
587
462
580
587
585
323
530
525
517
462
595
587
580
585
323
188
585
580
587
595
462
525
517
530

S size under armhole

Left sleeve from p.173

Go to p.173 right sleeve

BGC	PC
323	530
323	585
587	580
462	580
587	580
323	585
323	530
525	517
462	595
587	595
323	585
323	188
323	585
587	595
462	595
525	517
323	530
323	585
587	580
462	580
587	580
323	585
323	530
525	517
462	595
587	595
323	580
323	585
323	188
323	585
323	580
587	595
462	595
525	517
BGC	PC

SHADE CARDS

[1]

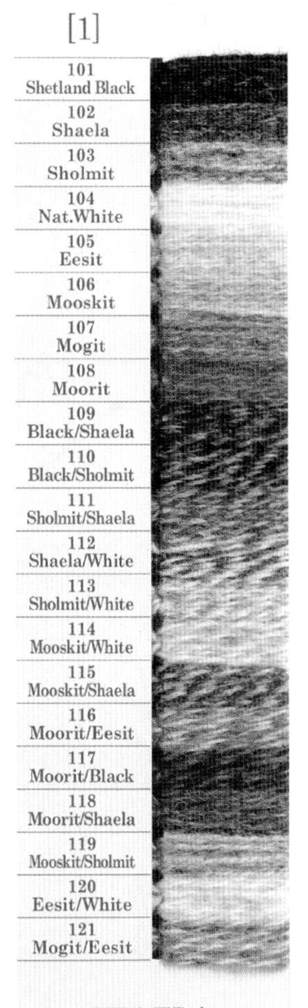

[2]

768
Eggshell
764
Cloud
655
China Blue
130
Sky
660
Lagoon
134
Blue Danube
665
Bluebell
136
Teviot Blue
168
Clyde Blue
195
Moorland
684
Cobalt
700
Royal
730
Dark Navy
198
Peat
727
Admiral Navy
160
Midnight
238
Osprey
726
Prussian Blue
710
Gentian
162
Neptune

SHAELA

[3]

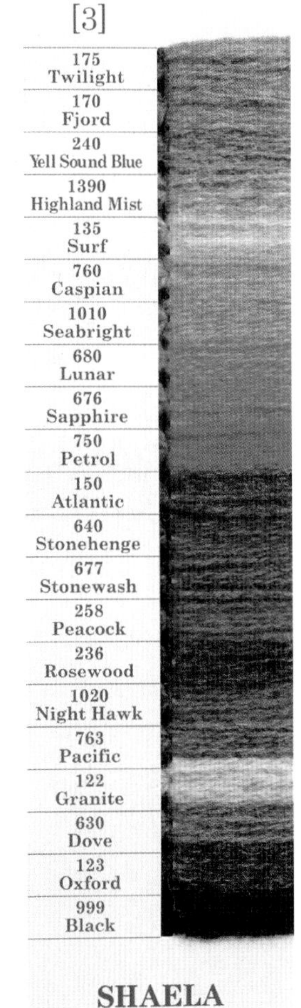

[4]

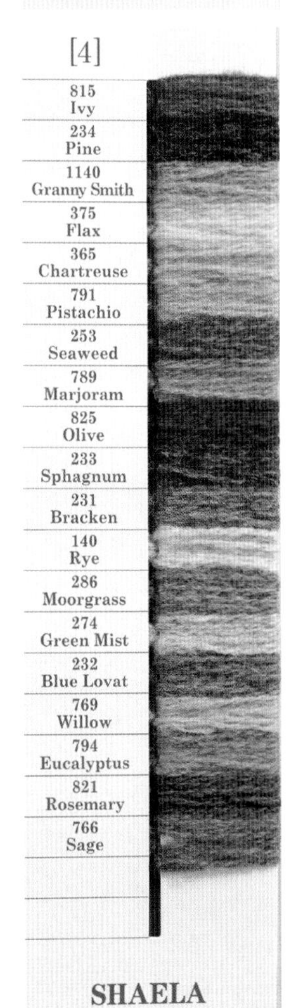

[5]

772
Verdigris
318
Wood Green
770
Mint
787
Jade
805
Spruce
785
Apple
792
Emerald
790
Celtic
780
Lime
259
Leprechaun
788
Leaf
147
Moss
800
Tartan
820
Bottle
144
Turf
292
Pine Forest
272
Fog
462
Ginger
525
Crimson
500
Scarlet
524
Poppy

SHAELA

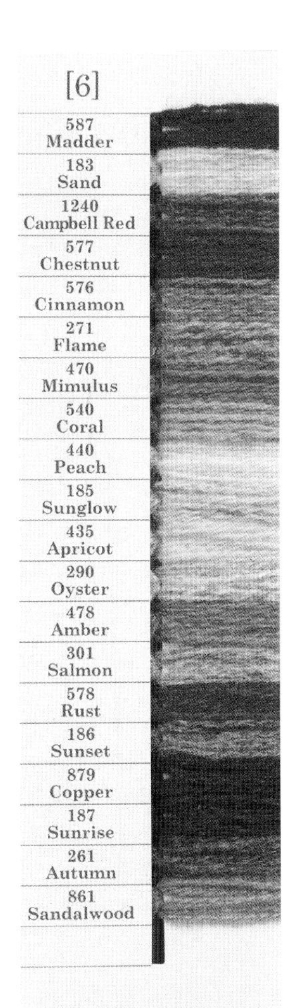

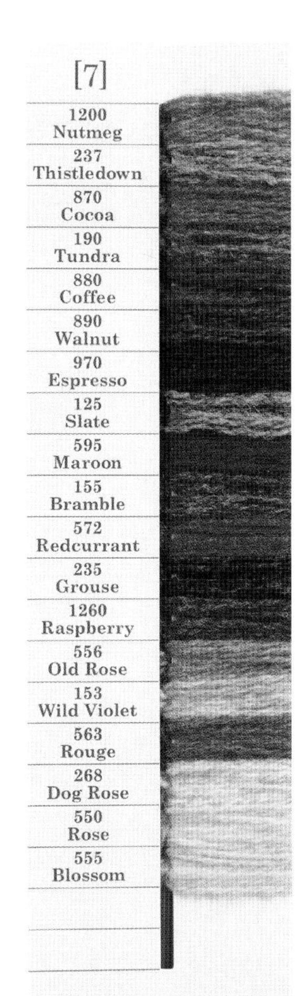

[8]

570 Sorbet
575 Lipstick
580 Cherry
585 Plum
530 Fuchsia
1190 Burnt Umber
230 Yellow Ochre
289 Gold
429 Old Gold
425 Mustard
1160 Scotch Broom
182 Buttercup
400 Mimosa
410 Cornfield
390 Daffodil
350 Lemon
304 White
547 Orchid
603 Pot-Pourri
562 Cyclamen
596 Clover

SHAELA

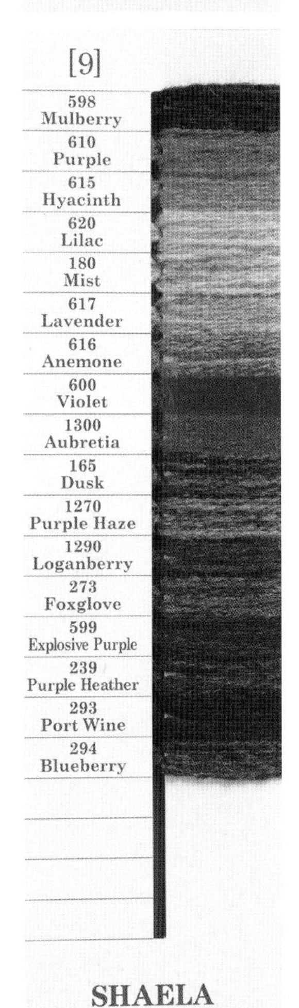

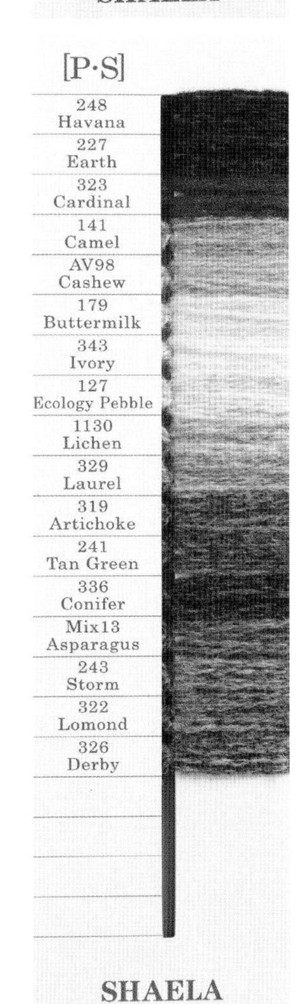

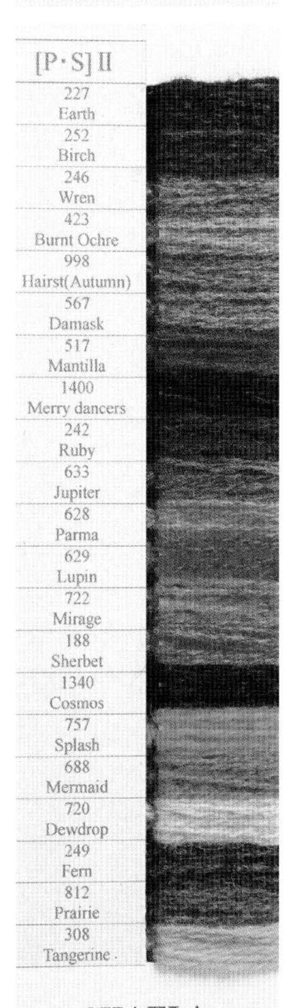